COLUMBIA UNIVERSITY STUDIES IN ENGLISH
AND COMPARATIVE LITERATURE

ENGLISH
IN THE LAW COURTS

ENGLISH IN THE LAW COURTS

THE PART THAT ARTICLES, PREPOSITIONS AND CONJUNCTIONS PLAY IN LEGAL DECISIONS

BY
MARGARET M. BRYANT
Instructor in English, Hunter College of the City of New York

NEW YORK
COLUMBIA UNIVERSITY PRESS
1930

Published November, 1930

Printed in the United States of America
WAVERLY PRESS, INC., Baltimore, Md.

TO
MY TEACHER, COLLEAGUE, AND FRIEND
MINNIE CLARE YARBOROUGH
WHO HAS ALWAYS ENCOURAGED
AND INSPIRED ME

ACKNOWLEDGMENTS

I wish to express my sincere thanks to those who have aided me in this study. Let me acknowledge first my indebtedness to the editor, Mr. Alexander N. Sloan, for his kindness in reading the work in manuscript with a view to testing its lucidity and consistency of expression. A similar acknowledgment is due to Professor Minnie C. Yarborough of Hunter College, to whom this book is dedicated. I also wish to thank Mr. Albert C. Uthe and Mr. William M. Todd for criticizing my legal phraseology. To Professor George P. Krapp of Columbia University who helped me in the preparation of this dissertation, the subject of which was suggested by one of his lectures, I am unable to express my obligation. He has shown his kindly interest in multitudinous ways, putting his valuable time and his thorough scholarship at my disposal with a generosity that only I can appreciate.

M. M. B.

Columbia University
July, 1930

CONTENTS

Abbreviations x

I. Introduction 1

II. Form-words 4

III. Articles 26

IV. Prepositions 44

V. Conjunctions 202

Conclusion 295

Bibliography of Books on Language 296

Notes 298

Index 313

ABBREVIATIONS

Abb. N. C. Abbot's New Cases
Adm'r. Administrator
Ala. Alabama
Ark. Arkansas
Ass'n. Association
Atk. Atkyns' English Chancery Reports
Atl. Atlantic Reporter
Ave. Avenue
Barn. and Adol. Barnewall and Adolphus' English King's Bench Reports
Baxt. Baxter
Bldg. Building
Cal. California
Co. Company
Com'rs. Commissioners
Conn. Connecticut
Const. Construction
D. C. Ga. District Court of Georgia
D. C. N. Y. District Court of New York
Dem. Sur. Demarest's Surrogate
Dist. District
Dud. Dudley
East. East's English King's Bench Reports
Exch. English Exchequer Reports
Ex. rel. *Ex relatione*
Ex'rs. Executors
Fed. Federal Reporter
Fed. Cas. Federal Cases
Ga. Georgia
Grat. Grattan
Heisk. Heiskell
How. Howard
Humph. Humphrey
Ill. Illinois
Ind. Indiana
Ins. Insurance
Johns. Johnson
Ky. Kentucky
Law. J. Ch. Law Journal, New Series, Chancery
Law J. Q. B. Law Journal, New Series, Queen's Bench
Man. and G. Manning and Granger's English Common Pleas Reports
Mass. Massachusetts
Me. Maine
Mfg. Manufacturing
Mo. Missouri
Mo. App. Missouri Appeal Reports
Mont. Montana
Nat. National
N. C. North Carolina
N. E. Northeastern Reporter
Nev. Nevada
N. H. New Hampshire
N. J. New Jersey
N. J. Eq. New Jersey Equity
N. J. Law New Jersey Law
N. W. Northwestern Reporter
N. Y. New York
N. Y. Supp. New York Supplement
Okl. Oklahoma
Pa. Pennsylvania
Pac. Pacific
Pick. Pickering
R. I. Rhode Island
Ry. Railway
Sandf. Sandford
Sax. Saxon
S. C. South Carolina
S. E. Southeastern Reporter
South. Southern Reporter
Super. Ct. Superior Court
S. W. Southwestern Reporter
Tenn. Tennessee
Term R. Term Reports, English King's Bench (Durnford and East's Reports)
Tex. Texas
Va. Virginia
Vt. Vermont
U. S. United States
Wall. Wallace
Wheat. Wheaton
Wis. Wisconsin
W. Va. West Virginia

CHAPTER I

INTRODUCTION

MY PURPOSE in this study is not to solve all the problems of the lawyer, but to deal with the difficulties which center around what Henry Sweet, one of the world's greatest scholars in the science of language, calls form-words. Briefly, form-words are not definite content words which present a specific idea to the mind, but are words which show relationship. In a following chapter on form-words, I try not only to define them in detail, but also to show the number that we have and where we find them, illustrating each of my statements by a specific example.

After the discussion of form-words in general, I turn my attention entirely to those that are most frequently employed: namely, articles, prepositions, and conjunctions. At least one of these three groups is used in almost every sentence that is spoken or read; occasionally, all three groups are present. Of course, there are many elliptical sentences, especially in speaking, where a great part of the sentence is omitted in actual words, but is understood, for the words are supplied in the mind of both speaker and listener. Since these words are so generally used, even by the most illiterate, it seems that they should present little difficulty. On the other hand, these are the words that cause most of the trouble, for they are used freely and indiscriminately. The person who uses the word does not realize that he must not only select the correct word of relationship, but must also use it in the right place. If either necessity is violated, the whole meaning is changed. It is then that semasiology, the science which traces the development of the meaning of words; etymology; the dictionary; and the history of the language must be called in.

Collectively speaking, in the law courts have appeared many more cases which turn on the definition of content words than on the definition of form-words. The reason for this is that there are many more content words in our vocabulary than form-words. If all the form-words were considered together, I dare say the number would not reach five hundred. On the other hand, content words are almost innumerable. Each year, as occasion demands, more are added to the list. Considering their number, one would naturally expect to find more cases in the law courts hinging on the definition of content words than on the definition of form-words. This is actually the situation with regard to the sum total of all words in the respective groups, but when the words are examined individually, we find many more cases involving specific form-words than involving specific content words. For example, centering on the meaning of the one word *about*, I have found on record more than one hundred and fifty cases at law, whereas I have come across no instance of a content word's appearing in so great a number of cases. After making this observation, I sought an explanation.

In many sentences emphasis determines whether a word is a form-word or a content word, as will be made clear in the chapter entitled "Form-words." Therefore, I have limited myself to the parts of speech which are most often used and which are always form-words—the definite article, *the*, the indefinite articles, *a* and *an*, the single prepositions, the single conjunctions, and the correlative conjunctions. I omit the phrasal prepositions and conjunctions, which are ordinarily considered in the same light as a single preposition or conjunction, for in the law courts stress is usually put upon one word of the phrase, without considering the phrase as a whole. Such treatment of a phrase changes its whole meaning and the outcome of the case.

Limiting my subject in this manner, I then turn my attention to the hundreds of cases turning upon these words of relationship. In each particular instance it is the problem of the court to find out the meaning of the disputed word. After that is determined, as best it can be, the judgment is given.

Since the courts use different methods of ascertaining the meaning of the particular word or phrase under discussion, I have tried to find out how the decision in each case was reached. I have endeavored to find out the psychology back of each judge's decision. I have attempted to discover what facts a particular judge had in mind and what methods of reasoning he used when he wrestled with the meaning of the article, preposition, or conjunction around which a specific case revolved.

In my investigation I have discovered thirteen methods used by the law courts in arriving at decisions, each of which is explained at the beginning of the chapter entitled "Articles." After the definitions are given, cases are cited under each article, preposition, and conjunction representative of these thirteen methods used in the law courts.

In addition to the psychological classification, I have included a linguistic classification after the representative cases which turn on each particular word, thereby attempting to show to what extent and in what manner the law courts must consider the ordinary speech of everyday life among common people.

In selecting the illustrative cases I have restricted myself to the use of the volumes of citations of law cases, entitled *Words and Phrases*, a monumental work of nineteen volumes, in three series, by the editorial staff of the National Reporter System. The *First Series* appeared in 1904; the *Second Series* in 1914; and the *Third Series* in 1928. In these volumes one can find citations of all reported American cases of the higher courts of record and a comparatively small number of contemporary English cases, along with the judicial interpretation of each case, alphabetically arranged so that the material is easily accessible. The cases used are found in the state reports, those of the National Reporter System, those of the Federal Reporter, those of the Federal Cases, and those of the United States Supreme Court. After each illustrative case a note is given stating first the series of the *Words and Phrases* from which the citation comes and then the place in which the case read is reported. If it is not stated that the second or the third series of *Words and Phrases* is used, it is to be understood that the title *Words and Phrases* alone refers to the first series.

Chapter II

FORM-WORDS

EVERY word has a definite external form, which is different from that of every other word, for each one is composed of a certain number of letters arranged in a definite order, according to rules of spelling. *Rat*, for instance, consists of the three letters, *r*, *a*, and *t*. Those letters must always be placed so that the *r* comes first, the *a* next, and the *t* last, if the person who sees or hears the word is to get the concept of a rat. If the order be reversed, the concept is an entirely different one, for instead of the word *rat*, the word *tar* is formed. The two words are made up of the same letters, but an entirely different effect is produced by the rearrangement. As far as *tar* and *rats* are concerned as objects in themselves, there is nothing in common. In the sense of having a definite combination of letters standing in a certain relationship to one another all words are form-words. One may consider, however, more than the outward appearance of the word. One may go beneath the surface and seek for meaning. If in the search nothing is found except the form of a word, then one may call that word a form-word, for it is a word in form only. It is, therefore, the logical side of language, which is based on psychology, the science of the mind, with which I am concerned and not the formal side, which is based on phonetics, the science of speech-sounds.

This search for meaning cannot be an isolated one; the word must have definite surroundings. No isolated word has meaning in itself. Many will say that when one sees or hears the word *dog* one has a definite picture of a dog. That statement is true, but that concept has been built up by past experience. A person hears many statements about dogs and observation of many dogs verifies these statements. Even then the picture the person calls to mind depends upon the dog with which he has had most experience. If a person hears or sees the name of an animal which he has not heard before, does the word mean anything to him? It is only after definite statements are made about the animal that the concept is built up. The left-over ideas about an animal of which one knows have been built up by complete statements regarding that animal, either expressed or understood. Then one must look for meaning in complete statements; in other words, in sentences. The meaning of a word depends upon its use in the sentence. Consider the word *by*. The meaning of the word *by* in the sentence *He went by the window* is entirely different from the meaning of the same word in the sentence *The word "by" is a short word.*

There are sentence-words in which a sentence is expressed by a single word, such as *Go!* The meaning of the word *go* does not depend upon the accompanying words, but expresses a complete thought in itself. So it is with interjections, such as *Lo! Alas!*, which express various emotions. These words are not words in form only, but are words with a great deal of significance.

Although each word depends upon a person's experience for the impression it conveys, around words that are not form-words certain ideas gather. Several of these words grouped together in a logical way, according to the rules of grammar, express a definite independent thought; for example, *Dogs eat meat.* Around each one of these words in that sentence can be built by experience a concept—that is, each word has meaning of its own. To make a picture the three words must be used in the right order. The placing of the words is similar to the arranging of the parts of a picture-puzzle. After the picture is complete there is what we may call a unit-of-meaning, for we have a picture which conveys a definite impression. For the sake of convenience, we may call the whole sentence the major unit-of-meaning, which may be divided into minor units-of-meaning. Then each sound-group around which a concept can be built may be called a unit-of-meaning. Thus in the major unit-of-meaning, *Dogs eat meat*, the smallest unit-of-meaning into which it can be divided is *dog*. *Dogs* is the plural of *dog*—only an inflection, not a different word.

If a word is a unit-of-meaning in a sentence, it is not a form-word. In the sentence *A horse is an animal*, it is easy to select *horse* and *animal* as units-of-meaning, for each one of these words brings to mind a definite picture. In the case of *a*, *is*, and *an*, the words, though independent in form, are not independent in meaning. They do not convey ideas as do *horse* and *animal*. They merely give a sense of a certain relationship which leads the mind onward to look for the word to which that sense of relationship attaches itself. Then *a*, *is*, and *an* are lacking in meaning and are thus form-words. The word *is*, although at times a word of meaning, when used in the sense of existense, as *God is*, serves to join subject and predicate and, as a result, forms a sentence. No one is concerned with *is*, but with *horse* and *animal*. The fact that it connects the important words in the sentence gives it, however, a grammatical function in the sentence. As for *a*, it serves only to show that any horse, and not some other animal, is to be considered. The same statement may be made of *an*, which shows that a horse belongs to a general class, namely, *animal*.

Determining whether a word is a unit-of-meaning or not is the chief way of deciding whether a word is a form-word or not. There are two practical methods that help one to reach this decision. One is a matter of stress. The important words are always stressed more than the form-words, for there is a natural tendency to subordinate the latter. Even in sentences in Anglo-Saxon, form-words and words of subordinate meaning generally had weak stress. Conjunctions, such as *and*, prepositions, such as *of* and *on* and the definite article *sē*, "the," were among the words that received weak stress. In present English, as in Anglo-Saxon, the most general principle of stress is that subordinate words, especially form-words, have weak stress. In *A horse is an animal*, the words that are given strong stress are *horse* and *animal*, while the others receive weak stress. In *God is* we are asserting the fact that God is in existence and *is* receives as much stress as *God*. This matter of stress cannot be laid down as a hard and fast rule, for even prepositions which have a definite meaning, especially in emphatic or antithetic passages, may have full stress, as in *Look behind the table, not on it*, where *behind* receives as much stress as *table*. Of course, those that have not a definite meaning are usually subordinate, such as *at*, *of*, *on*. Whether they are also stressed or not depends on the combination of words. In the sentence *What of it?* the *of*, since there is no verb in the sentence, receives more stress than any other word in the group.

Form-words, also can often be omitted by changing the phrasing slightly. For instance, *a ball of rubber* may be changed into *a rubber ball* without altering the sense. Although the *of* is left out, the meaning is identical and the phrase is just as clear.

So far as the origin or ultimate etymology of form-words is concerned, nothing need be added to what is given in the etymologies of the New English Dictionary. Form-words, according to John Horne Tooke in his fantastic but entertaining philological treatise, *The Diversions of Purley*, are nothing more than abbreviations of the two parts of speech, the noun and the verb. Dr. M. C. Yarborough, in her thorough exposition of Tooke's work, says: "With the exception of nouns and verbs, which are the only kinds of words essential to the communication of thoughts, all the so-called parts of speech are, according to Tooke's theory of language, merely abbreviations. In other words, verbs and nouns are the immediate signs of ideas or objects, and all other words are the signs of signs."[1] William Hazlitt, a disciple of Horne Tooke, in *The Spirit of the Age* published an essay on "The Late Mr. Horne Tooke," in which he says: "The whole of his reasoning turns upon showing that the Conjunction *That* is the pronoun *That* which is itself the participle of a verb, and in like manner that all the other mystical and hitherto unintelligible parts of speech are derived from the only two intelligible ones, the Verb and Noun." Tooke explains that such prepositions as *before, behind, below, beside* are "merely the imperative *be* compounded with the nouns *fore, hind, low, side*."[2] He accounts for other words in the same way, but his conclusions are far more speculative than scientific.

When we try to decide which words are form-words and which are content words, we are inclined to believe that perhaps Tooke was essentially right, though we cannot prove or accept his historical etymologies. It is not always an easy matter to distinguish between form-words and content words despite the fact that we have more than one method of determining the difference. There is no line of demarcation which divides form-words from other words. For example, in the sentence *He must go, must* may or may not be a form-word. If *must* is stressed, as it often is, it is not a form-word. If, however, *He must go* is a simple assertion, *must* is a form-word. I shall, however, take up each part of speech and discuss it in relation to form-words.

Form-words are not definitely restricted to particular parts of speech. It is true that all articles, prepositions, and pure conjunctions are form-words, but we have already seen how the verb *to be* may or may not be a form-word. So it is with most of the other parts of speech. Nouns, pronouns, and interjections are not often considered as form-words, for they have too much significance. They are, so to speak, always in the limelight or near it. Each part of speech, however, has special form-words associated with it, such as *a bird*, *the bird*, *to fly*, *is flying*.

First, I shall consider nouns as form-words. As I have said before, usually they are content words, for it is about a noun, or some word that stands in the place of a noun, that some assertion is made. The subject of the sentence is a pure noun, or a word, phrase, or clause that is used in the place of a noun. If the verb is transitive there is always an object, for which the same principle holds true. If the verb is intransitive there may or may not be a noun, or its equivalent, to complete the statement. There may be the sentence, *He is a doctor*, where *doctor* is a noun connected to *he* by the verb *is*. Instead of *He is a doctor*, the sentence may be *He is sad*, where the completing word is an adjective instead of a noun, or its equivalent. If there are modifying clauses, the same principle must be applied to each clause. The same principle, however, does not apply to modifying phrases, for phrases are usually formed by joining a preposition—the more common ones being *of*, *to*, and *with*—to a noun, or its equivalent; for example, *of metal*. It is only a matter of stress, or rather a lack of stress, that would make one class a noun as a form-word. In the sentence, *Give him a drink of water, for water is necessary for life*, it is not the word *drink* that is stressed, but the word *water*. In this instance the word *drink* almost falls into insignificance. Whether it should be called a form-word or not is questionable. There is, however, no question about the word *water*; although joined with the preposition *of* it becomes a phrase modifying the word *drink*. In that sense it is secondary to the word *drink*, but logically the word *drink* is secondary to the word *water*. Nouns are usually not form-words themselves, but are almost always used in connection with form-words. For instance, the articles *a*, *an*, and *the* are always used with nouns, never with any other part of speech, as *the bird*, *a house*, *an owl*. Then again, phrases always contain nouns, or their equivalents, which are usually linked with form-words, especially prepositions, such as *by the sea*, *in the house*, etc. To place a preposition before a noun is grammatically equivalent to adding an inflection. The statement *the tail of a horse* means exactly the same as *the horse's tail*; thus the phrase *of a horse* is equivalent to an inflection of the word *horse*.

After considering nouns, one logically turns to pronouns. Most of the statements made about nouns hold true for pronouns, for they are usually used in the place of nouns. There are several kinds of pronouns: (1) the personal, (2) the possessive, (3) the emphatic, (4) the reflexive, (5) the reciprocal, (6) the demonstrative, (7) the interrogative, (8) the relative, (9) the conjunctive.

The personal pronouns include the first, second, and third person pronouns. The first person, in turn, includes *I* in the singular and *we* in the plural, *we* meaning *I* + *you*, or *I* + *he*, *she*, *it*, or *they* (*I* cannot be made plural in any other way); the second person includes *you* in both singular and plural; and the third person includes *he* (masculine), *she* (feminine), and *it* (neuter) in the singular and *they* for all genders in the plural. None of these personal pronouns may be classified as form-words, except the neuter pronoun in such a sentence as *It snows*, where *it* does not refer to a definite thing. *It* is thrown in to complete the statement and is entirely without meaning, for the logical subject of the sentence is contained in *snows*. The word *snow* in itself contains the elements of a sentence, though it is not put in the form of a statement. It means *white crystals falling from the sky*. In Latin there are no grammatical subjects, for the personal pronoun is contained in the verb. For instance, *ningit* means *it snows*. In English there must always be an expressed subject. Usually the subject is an actor, for an actor performing an action has become the universal form for the sentence. This construction, however, is not always true, for the object affected is sometimes used as the subject, shown in what is known as the "passive voice," as in *The man was killed.* If there is no actor at all, we use in English the purely formal word *it*, which has no meaning and which is used as the grammatical subject only, as in *It is raining.* The word *raining* contains in itself the logical subject, and *it* only fulfills a custom.

The possessive pronouns (*my*, *your*, *his*, etc.) are never form-words, for they denote possession and are in most cases emphasized. Nor do we find form-words among the emphatic pronouns (*I cut it myself*, *myself* being the emphatic pronoun). The name, *emphatic*, in itself shows that the pronouns have meaning. In this same group falls the reflexive pronoun, also formed by adding *self* to the personal pronoun, but used as the object of a verb or of a preposition, and at the same time repeating the logical subject of the verb, such as *I told him to allow himself much freedom*, and *She thinks too little of herself.* Moreover, the reciprocal pronouns, *each other* and *one another*, as well as the demonstratives, *this*, *that*, *these*, and *those*, and the interrogative pronouns, *who*, *what*, and *which*—used in asking such questions as, *Who is she?*, *What is that?*, *Which did you do?*—are never form-words, for they are always stressed.

It is when we consider relative and conjunctive pronouns that the question of form-words may arise. In the sentence *The man whom I saw yesterday is your brother*, *whom* is the relative pronoun. It cannot stand alone. It depends entirely for its meaning upon its antecedent *man* with which it has to be closely connected. It may be left out without altering the meaning and often is in conversation. Thus relative pronouns have weak stress and should be considered form-words. On the other hand, in conjunctive pronouns the meaning is included in itself. The sentence *I know what it is* illustrates this fact. *What* is the conjunctive pronoun used as the subject of the verb *is* in the clause *What it is* and at the same time as a connective joining the subordinate clause to the verb *know* of the principal clause. *What* is also a stressed word.

In addition to these nine classes of pronouns, there are a number of words, such as *some*, *many*, *any*, *much*, *less*, *more*, *few*, *several*, which Sweet calls quantitative pronouns, but which, to my mind, should be called indefinite quantitative adjectives, especially in the sense in which he uses them—that is, as modifying words. Sweet, however, includes the articles *a*, *an*, and *the* under the classification of definite and indefinite pronouns. At times the indefinite quantitative words may be regarded as pronouns. For instance, if a bowl of apple sauce were in front of John, he might say, *I want some*, meaning some apple sauce. He might say, *I want more than Jack has*, meaning I want more apple sauce than Jack has. When these words are used with the force of pronouns, they are never form-words. It is when they are used as modifiers that their significance is weighed. The significance is not weighed in every case. The emphatic *some*, although it is a modifier, is not a form-word. For instance, the sentence *Some girls go there* illustrates the emphatic *some* and logically has a great deal of meaning. Here the word *some* also has strong stress. In the sentences *Give him some more water*, or *Give him some water*, the *some* has weak stress and can be well left out without loss of clearness or force. *Some* in the first illustration is used as an adverb, for it modifies *more*. In the second it is an adjective.

Since we have already mentioned adjectives in connection with the pronoun, it is well to consider them now as a part of speech. Adjectives which express permanent attributes, or qualities, are always words of meaning. For instance, in mentioning snow it is the attribute *white* that we immediately summon to consciousness. The word *snow* suggests to most people the quality of whiteness. Thus one can see that the modifying word can become more important, logically, than the word that is modified. The modifier is generally put before the noun it modifies and takes a stronger stress than the word it modifies. Adjectives usually convey definite pictures. It is quite obvious that the success of a written description depends, to a large extent, upon the choice of the adjectives. Under the heading of pronouns the adjectives that might be form-words at times were discussed. Of course, if one considers the articles *a*, *an*, and *the* as adjectives, then there are a great many form-words among the adjectives, numerically speaking, for *the*, *a*, and *an* are used more often than other words.

As articles are always form-words, I shall consider them separately. Articles are syntactically adjectives in that they always modify another word. Every object must be spoken of either in a definite way, as *the man*, or in an indefinite way, as *a man*, or in a collective way, without the article, as in *Man must have food.* This use of the article is not found in most foreign languages. In Latin, for instance, *homo* means *the man*, *a man*, or *man*. Such words as *ille*, "that," or *unus*, "one," are not necessary. Although articles do always modify other words, they are not permanent attributes which belong to one particular object, but can be placed before one object as well as another. There is a difference in the articles. There are two kinds, the definite and the indefinite. The definite article is *the*. It is related to a pronoun in that it refers to some particular thing. If I say *the bird*, I mean a bird of which I have been speaking. In other words, the definite article is put before a noun to show that the idea expressed by the noun has already been stated or is obviously implied. The article refers to the previous statement, which is necessary to complete the meaning. If, on the other hand, the idea is new, the noun expressing it is modified by the indefinite article. The indefinite articles are *a* and *an*, which select a noun from many others, but without identifying or defining it, as the definite article does. For instance, at the beginning of an animal story about rabbits and foxes, the story begins by speaking of *a rabbit* and *a fox*. After the animals have been introduced, they are spoken of as *the rabbit* and *the fox*. The definite article modifying an indefinite class-noun makes it definite. The indefinite *mountains* or *birds* can be made into the definite *the mountains*, *the birds*. Without the article such a word as *birds* expresses the idea of birds in general, while *the birds* implies the birds near us. Note the difference between *The birds are out of the cage* and *Birds should not be kept in cages.*

The history of the articles is interesting. *A* and *an* are derived from the numeral *ān*, "one," in Anglo-Saxon, which was inflected like a strong adjective. Occasionally, though rarely, in Anglo-Saxon *ān* was used in an indefinite sense, as *ān mann*, meaning *a certain man*, *a man*. In this it approached the indefinite article. In most cases, however, the indefinite article was not expressed at all.

In Middle English *ān* developed into a regular indefinite article. It lost its stress and shortened its vowel, becoming *an*. Since this shortening took place before the change of *ā* into ǭ, the article *an* was separated phonetically from the numeral ǭn, "one."

In Middle English *an* dropped its final *n* before a consonant, keeping it before a vowel or *h* + a vowel, as in *a man*, *an ǭld man*, *an hous*. In Early Modern English the full form was kept before *h*: *an house.* We now say *a house, a history*. However, we generally use *an* before *h* in weak syllables, where it is then dropped in pronunciation, as in *an honest man.* A word that is pronounced as if it began with a consonant takes *a* before it, such as *a university.*

A and *an*, having been derived from the word for *one*, are at times now used in the sense of *one.* In the common phrase *a day or two*, which is still used, *a* means *one.* It means one in a great many cases. If a person goes to buy *a* hat, he means to buy *one* hat, an intention accounted for by the fact that no distinction in language is made accurately and definitely at a particular moment. No doubt at first in the Middle English period the two interchanged—that is, ǭn was at times used as an indefinite article and *an* was used in the sense of "one." The forms had not been completely isolated from each other.

The is derived from *sē*, *sēo*, and *ðæt*, called a demonstrative pronoun in Anglo-Saxon. As a strong demonstrative we have retained *ðæt* in *that*, now completely disassociated from the article. *The* may be called a weak demonstrative. No doubt *sē* and *sēo*, by analogy, became *ðē* and *ðēo*, which then developed regularly into *the.* In Anglo-Saxon the definite article was highly inflected for case and number. There were also three genders. In the course of time the definite article lost its values and forms and now, having no meaning, cannot be defined at all.

Among the adverbs, which I shall discuss now, we also find some form-words. Adverbs are words or phrases, attached to verbs, adjectives, or other adverbs, which qualify in the sense either of characterizing or of limiting. They may tell us the manner (*He spoke well*, *with animation*, etc.), the degree (*He ate enough*, *a little*, etc.), the frequency (*He came often*, *twice*, etc.), the time (*Stop now*, *soon*, etc.), the place (*It is there*, *here*, etc.), the cause

(*He stopped consequently*). Such modifiers, if one word only, are called adverbs; if comprised of several words (*in this way, at once, by all means*) they are called adverbial phrases. There is, however, no difference between the function of the phrase and the function of the single word, as in *He acted at once* compared with *He acted immediately*. Though we write *at once* as two words, we do not feel conscious of two words, any more than when we combine them, as in *oftentimes, anywhere*. There are many adverbs which can be used as prepositions, such as *in, up, inside, outside, above, below, down, under*. If one says, *Go in*, or *Go up*, *in* and *up* are adverbs and words of meaning. If, however, one says, *He is staying in the house*, or *He is walking up the mountain*, *in* and *up* are prepositions and form-words. Thus one must be careful to distinguish between adverbs and prepositions. Most adverbs are not form-words. For example, in the sentence, *He walks briskly*, *briskly* has as much significance as the other two words, for it tells the manner in which he walks. There are many ways of walking and *briskly* is one of them. There are a few adverbs, however, such as *quite* and *very*, the significance of which depends upon the intonation of the voice when they are used orally. One may say of a piece of work that is done, *That is very good*, putting great stress on the *very*, and meaning that the work is excellent. On the other hand, one may say, *That is very good*, putting about as much stress on *very* as on *good*, meaning that the work is not "A" work, but "B" work. Again one may say, *That is very good*, putting little stress on the *very*, and meaning that the work is fair. There are persons who in conversation insist on using *very* time and time again, to make a statement emphatic; as, for example: *A very good book is very hard to get because very few are written*. Here it is the intonation of the voice that makes the *very's* forceful. In writing it is usually better, if forcefulness be desired, to omit the *very's*, which have little stress and can be omitted without loss of clearness or emphasis. The sentence quoted above is improved, for written discourse, if recast as follows: *A good book is hard to get because few are written*. Thus, it will be seen that the *very's* are actually devoid of meaning and are therefore only form-words.

As I have shown by preceding illustrations, adverbs of place are usually full of meaning. In one instance, however, the adverb is a pure form-word without any meaning of its own. The word is *there*, similar in usage to the grammatical use of *it* in *It snows*. *There* is not a form-word in *There it is*, for *there* is strong and has strong stress, but in *There is a fire there* the first *there* is weak and a mere form-word, while the second *there* is an adverb of place, receiving strong stress.

There are also what is termed indefinite adverbs, formed by combining indefinite adjectives, such as *any* and *some* with interrogative adverbs and by combining interrogative pronouns with the adverbs *ever* and *soever*, such as *anywhere, somewhere, wherever, wheresoever, whenever, whensoever, anyhow, somehow, however, howsoever*. All of these are not always form-words, but the last four illustrations usually are, for they are not stressed words.

Then there are correlative adverbs which are form-words. They are dependent adverbs, for they go in pairs. By correlation we understand that two or more form-words of similar meaning and function belonging to the same part of speech, and having a mutual dependence upon one another are used together in the same sentence. *As . . . as*, in *He is as old as you; so . . . as*, in *He is not so old as you; the . . . the*, in *The more you give her to do the better she does it*, are examples of correlation-pairs.

There is a connection between adverbs and conjunctions and it is often difficult to distinguish between them. The most unmistakable conjunctions are those which connect independent clauses, or sentences, as wholes, without entering into any special relations with any separate words of which the clauses are composed. In the sentence *John drank water and I drank milk*, we see that *and* does not modify and is not associated with any one word in either clause. But if an adverb introduces a clause as a modifier, not a modifier of a word in the preceding clause, but a modifier of the whole sentence, then the adverb becomes indistinguishable from a conjunction. In the sentence *He telephoned yesterday because he knew I was out*, the clause *because he knew I was out* seems to modify the whole clause *he telephoned yesterday* instead of one particular word in the clause. Then *because* should be regarded as a conjunction, not as an adverb. If, however, we have the sentence

He telephoned while I was out, he might have telephoned because I was out. Then *while* would have to be regarded as an adverb, in one sense of the word, and as a conjunction in another sense. These words, however, are usually considered as conjunctions, although they may not be considered as form-words.

Then there are the independent adverbs which bear a resemblance to conjunctions. Examples of these are *still* and *nevertheless*, as in *Your cakes are good; still (nevertheless) mother's are better.* Compare that with *Your cakes are good, but mother's are better*, where a pure conjunction is used. Note that there is a difference in punctuation. Where the pure conjunction is used, the clauses are usually separated by a comma; on the other hand, where an independent adverb is used the clauses are separated by a semicolon or a full stop. These independent adverbs are also words of reference, for they refer us to the preceding clause or sentence. Pure conjunctions do not do this. The clauses or sentences which independent adverbs introduce always contradict the preceding one. Still the clauses or sentences introduced by these words are independent of the preceding ones. These adverbs always modify the whole clause or sentence, but they do not always stand at the beginning of the sentence. Look at *however*, which may stand at the beginning, the middle, or the end. Of course, it is usually better to place it in the middle of the sentence as a matter of emphasis. One may say, *However, I told her not to go*, or *I told her, however, not to go*, or *I told her not to go, however*. Another example is *nevertheless*, which may stand at the end of a sentence, as in *He said it, nevertheless*. Whether these words are form-words or not depends upon the stress given the word. If the word receives strong stress, then it is not a form-word, but if it receives slight stress and is merely used as a connective, it is a form-word. All pure conjunctions, however, are form-words.

Such words as *and* and *or* are used as conjunctions and conjunctions only. They are pure conjunctions. There are others which we shall call partial conjunctions that serve two functions as in the case of the conjunctive adverb which we have just discussed. They modify and at the same time connect. There are some conjunctions which may be used as prepositions, such as *for*, *since*.

These are also partial conjunctions. There are, in addition to these, phrasal conjunctions, such as *in order that*, *as soon as*, *as if*, and correlative conjunctions, such as *both . . . and* and *though . . . yet*.

T. G. Tucker and R. S. Wallace in their English grammar, both descriptive and historical, define a conjunction as a word (or equivalent of a word), which, not being a relative or interrogative pronoun, links clauses to other clauses, or, not being a preposition, links words to other words. I think that is a fairly complete definition, for conjunctions are purely connective words. They connect without governing, as prepositions do. According to the definition, conjunctions may be word-connecters or clause-connecters; occasionally the same conjuction may be both. In the sentence *John and James cooked the dinner*, *and* is a word-connecter; in the sentence *John killed the bird and James made the fire* it is a clause-connecter. At times one of the clauses may be elliptical or contracted as in *He is small but wise*, a statement that may be expanded into *He is small but he is wise*, showing *but* as a clause-connecter. It is, however, better to consider a conjunction as a word-connecter, for in such a sentence as *Three and four make seven*, the expansion of the thought into *Three makes seven* and *Four makes seven* would be an absurdity.

Conjunctions, however, are employed to connect clauses more often than words. They are classed according to their meaning as affirmative, alternative, adversative, concessive, conditional, temporal, and causal, which include conjunctions of cause, effect, and purpose. There are also the correlative conjunctions, which go in pairs.

An affirmative conjunction is a conjunction which connects words or clauses of equal value without introducing any special kind of connection. The chief one is *and*. The partial conjunction corresponding to *and* is *also*, as in *I also will come*. *Too* is used in spoken English, as in *I will come too*. *Likewise* and *as well as* are used in the same way. There are in addition to these a great many affirmative partial conjunctions, such as *furthermore*, *moreover*, *now*, etc., which often add explanatory material to what is being said.

An alternative conjunction is a conjunction which allows one and one only of two or more words or clauses to be considered. There must be a selection. The chief alternative conjunction is *or*. When one asks, *Will you go to school, or will you not?* the speaker expects the one addressed either to go to school, or not to go to school. Of course, he does not know which alternative will be chosen.

An adversative conjunction adds something which does not follow naturally from what has just been said. It stops the natural progress and introduces a barrier, so to speak. When one starts from home with a tennis racquet and balls going toward a tennis court, an observer naturally expects that person to play tennis, but if he does not, the natural sequence is broken and the observer would say, *He left home with a tennis racquet and balls, but he did not play tennis*. If, however, he had played, the remark would have been a different one: *He left home with a tennis racquet and balls and played a good game of tennis*. *But*, the chief adversative conjunction, usually connects two opposing statements, one of affirmation and one of negation, as in *She is intelligent, but not pretty*. There are several partial conjunctions which are used adversatively, such as *still, nevertheless, however, only*.

A concessive conjunction is a kind of adversative one. It may be made a division of adversative conjunctions. The most important concessive conjunctions are *though* and *although*. The only difference between an adversative and a concessive conjunction is one of reference. The former refers the reader or listener to what has already been said, while the latter causes him to look forward to what is going to be said, as is shown in *Although I am fond of dill pickels, I know they are not good for me*.

A conditional conjunction is one that introduces a condition. The chief one is *if*, an example of which is *If you go, I shall not*. *Unless* is a negative conditional conjunction equal to *if not*, as is shown in *Unless you go, I shall not* = *If you do not go, I shall not*. There are also several phrasal conjunctions of condition, such as *in case, provided that, supposing that*, which are often shortened into *provided, supposing, suppose*. There are also some words with the condition included in them, such as *otherwise* in *We must write the letter now; otherwise, we shall write in vain.* That sentence, of course, means *If we do not write the letter now, we shall write in vain.* There is a difference between *otherwise* and *unless.* In using *unless* the negative refers to what is going to be said; in using *otherwise* the negative refers to what has already been said. In addition to the phrasal conjunctions that have been mentioned there are others which include a condition. One is a concessional condition expressed by *even if,* as in *Even if he is bad, you need not punish him;* another is a comparative condition expressed by *as if,* as in *He looked as if he had been frightened.*

A temporal conjunction is a conjunction of time. The words are often confused, for it is hard to tell whether the word is an adverb or a conjunction, or a preposition or a conjunction. Such words as *when, as,* and *while* give trouble because they are often used as adverbs; such words as *before, after, since, till* give trouble because they are often used as prepositions. The confusion with the adverb has already been discussed at the end of the discussion of adverbs. The conjunctions formed from prepositions are used in the same way as the adverbial conjunction and give the same difficulty, for they are not pure conjunctions. An illustration is shown in *He came before I had written the letter* and *Sit there till I have eaten my breakfast.* It is hard to tell whether *before* and *till* modify the whole clause or one word in the clause.

A causal conjunction is one that shows cause, as its name implies. The two chief conjunctions of cause are *because,* which states a direct cause, and *for,* which gives a reason. *We took food, because we thought there would be none at hand* shows the cause of taking food. *He thought it would rain, for the barometer had fallen* gives the reason why he thought it would rain. *Since* and *as,* which are usually thought of as conjunctions of time, are also pure conjunctions of cause.

The chief conjunction of effect is *therefore. I saw no reason for moving; therefore I stayed still.* Conjunctions of effect are partial conjunctions, or conjunctive adverbs.

The chief conjunction of purpose is *that.* The emphatic form is *in order that,* an example of which is found in the expression *We work in order that we may live,* which is ordinarily written *We work that we may live.* Purpose is expressed in the negative by *lest*, which means *so that . . . not.* For instance, the sentence *The man took the pistol from the boy lest he should shoot himself* has the same meaning as the sentence *The man took the pistol from the boy so that he should not shoot himself.*

Turning to correlative conjunctions, which are similar to correlative adverbs in that they consist of two or more form-words which have a mutual dependence upon one another, one finds that they are usually the emphatic forms of the simple conjunctions. Two of the correlative conjunctions *both . . . and* and *not only . . . but* have the same meaning as *and*, but are more emphatic. For instance, the sentence *Both Mary and Audrey went* merely means that Mary and Audrey went. The emphatic form of the alternative conjunction is *either . . . or* and *neither . . . nor*, which is the negative of *either . . . or*. *I demand neither a statement, nor money* is the same as *I demand not either a statement or money*. The correlative *though . . . yet* is the correlative of concession. *Though he is rich; yet he is honest* is a good example. The man's wealth is admitted but we are warned against inferring that the man is not honest. Another correlative pair is *whether . . . or*, which expresses an alternative condition, as in *I do not know whether I shall do that or not.*

It may be well to state that the conjunctions just discussed are of two kinds—the coordinate conjunction and the subordinate conjunction. The coordinate conjunctions, such as *and*, *both . . . and; or*, *either . . . or; nor*, *neither . . . nor*, and *but* are coordinate, for they join words and clauses of equal rank. All the other pure conjunctions and all dependent adverbs are subordinative, such as *though*, *although*, *though . . . yet; if*, *unless*, *whether . . . or; because*, *since*, *as*, *that; when*, *while*, *before*, *after*.

In addition to these conjunctions there are also detached conjunctions, which are placed at the beginning of a paragraph, or at the beginning of a sentence, joining what has been said in preceding sentences to what is to follow. These conjunctions are nearer to coordinate conjunctions than to subordinate conjunctions, for they join two ideas of equal importance. They, along with the pure conjunctions, are form-words. Whether the partial conjunctions are form-words or not depends upon the stress and significance in each individual case.

The other principal words of relationship are prepositions, which are words showing relation of a noun or pronoun to a word of action or to some other noun or pronoun, as *Put it on the table* and *The book on the table is mine.* As I have shown in a previous discussion, most prepositions can be used as adverbs. A few can also be used as conjunctions. There are a few, however, that are not used as adverbs, such as *of, to, for.* Of course, it is true that *of* (ov) is the unemphatic form of the adverb *off.* In Anglo-Saxon and Middle English *of* was used in the sense of "of" and "off," but in Early Modern English the weak "of" was gradually restricted to the less emphatic meaning and the strong "of" took on the adverbial meaning and was written *off* to distinguish it from the preposition *of.* At present the connection between them has been completely forgotten. *Off* and *too* are the adverbs corresponding respectively to *of* and *to* in Anglo-Saxon. *Off* and *too* have diverged so much from *of* and *to* that there is no longer any association between them. The Anglo-Saxon prepositions are closely allied to the adverbs. For that reason most of them can be used as adverbs without any change of form.

Prepositions were also formed from other parts of speech. *Across* is formed from the noun *cross*; *along* from the adjective *long*; *excepting* and *except* from the verb *except.* The same is true of many others. Some, which may be called compound prepositions, were formed from joining prepositions and adverbs, such as *into, upon, throughout.*

In addition to these, there are phrasal prepositions, such as *by means of, for the sake of, with regard to,* consisting of a noun governed by a preceding preposition and followed by another preposition, which governs the following noun. Logically the noun is governed by the whole phrase, but grammatically only by the preposition before it. For instance, in *I will go for the sake of mother,* the noun *mother* is governed grammatically by *of,* but logically by the phrasal preposition, *for the sake of.*

Prepositions, not being words of meaning themselves, govern nouns and pronouns in the objective case. The grammatical function of a preposition is to make the noun or pronoun it governs into a modifier, as in *a man of intelligence* and *Go to the store.* The phrase *of intelligence* is used like an adjective in that it modifies the noun *man*, telling what kind of man he is. The phrase is equivalent to saying *an intelligent man.* The phrase *to the store* is used like an adverb, modifying the verb *go*—telling the person where to go. Prepositions are used in place of inflections, most of which were lost in the Middle English period. The English language is not a highly inflected language. During the Anglo-Saxon period it had a great many more inflections than it now has. As time has passed inflections have been dropped and words of relationship used. Word-order now counts for a great deal. Of course, it is not so important as it is in the Chinese language, which depends entirely upon the position of the words, for it has no inflections at all. It is called an isolating language. The English language still has a few inflections, although it is mainly an isolating language. One can always tell a noun in the genitive case on account of the *'s* or *s'* which are added, respectively, in the singular and plural. This inflection may be eliminated by means of the preposition *of.* Thus *the boy's father* may be changed into *the father of the boy,* a construction which oftentimes prevents awkwardness or ambiguity, especially in the plural. Prepositions are not always placed directly before the word they govern, as one would think from the name itself, especially in speaking. For instance, one hears in conversation *Whom are you speaking to?* much more often than one hears *To whom are you speaking?*

There are certain prepositions which have become attached to verbs so that they are a part of the verb. The verb is then called a verb phrase, such as *look at, laugh at, think of, attend to.* In order to find out if the preposition is a real part of the verb, change the verb which resembles the transitive verb in meaning from the active to the passive voice, as *You were not thought of, It was not attended to.*

All prepositions which are pure prepositions are form-words. If they have become an integral part of a verb they are not form-words, but have a significance of their own, such as *laugh at,* which has an entirely different meaning from *laugh.*

In contrast with prepositions, verbs are words with a great deal of meaning. Verbs usually express action and change, as *I eat, I run*. They always form the nucleus of the predicate. In fact, in the English language, predication cannot be expressed in any other way. One of the main verbs which, however, is devoid of meaning is the verb *to be* when it is used as a means of joining the subject to its attribute. To use it alone with the subject conveys no sense. For instance, *She is* calls for something else to complete the statement, such as *She is a teacher*, or *She is pretty*. Even then it has a grammatical function, for it has the inflections of a verb which enables it to express distinctions of time. It is necessary for a complete statement in instances similar to those given above. In English one has to say *He is sad* instead of *He sad*, in order to make sense. In Latin it is possible to omit the verb, as in *pulchra puella*. *Pulchra puella* has the same meaning that *Puella est pulchra* has, *The girl is beautiful*. In English, although the verb *to be* has a grammatical function, it does no more than connect, just as a conjunction does, and is thus a form-word.

There are other verbs which serve the purpose of connecting subject and predicate and are often thought of along with the verb *to be*, but have also definite meanings of their own. Such words are *become, turn, appear, seem, look*. These verbs cannot stand alone, but they have in them the idea of "change" as is shown in such a sentence as *He became governor*.

The verb *to be* in addition to being used as a main verb in a sentence can also be used as an auxiliary verb, a verb divested of independent meaning and helping another verb express tense, mood, or voice. In this capacity it shows itself again as a form-word, as in *She is crying*. There are, in addition to the verb *to be*, other auxiliaries, the chief of which are *have, do, must, will, would, shall, should, can, may, might*. Auxiliaries are empty words in the sense of expressing an idea in themselves. They only assist in denoting the relations of other words. They are mere pointers, help-words. In most instances they also receive weak stress. Just as prepositions took the place of old inflections, so the auxiliaries have replaced the special changes of form which indicated future and past action in a verb. The future is shown in *shall, will*, and in subordinate sequence after a past tense in *would*, as in *He said he would go*, his own words being *I will go*; also in *may*, *might*, *can*, *should*, *would*, the forms used in the subjunctive mood. The weak forms and weak stress of these auxiliaries, or help-words, always occur before the nucleus verb, as in *I shall come*, where *shall* receives weak stress. In such sentences as *I think I shall*, the *shall* receives more stress, for it is used alone. It absorbs the stress of the omitted word *come*. The sentence means *I think I shall come*. Of course, as in the case of the prepositions, the combination and the order of the words determine whether these weak stressed auxiliaries may at times receive strong stress. Also if one wants to make a statement emphatic, he will say, *You must go*, stressing the *must*.

The origin of the auxiliary *do* can be traced back to Anglo-Saxon. It was continued in the Middle English period and used in the Modern English period without at first having any distinctive meaning. It was used as a means of convenience, wish, clearness, or enphony. It is now used almost entirely as an emphatic form, with extra stress on the *do*. It is always used in questions. Instead of changing the order of the subject and object, one may use *do* at the beginning of the question. For instance, *Do horses eat oats?* is used instead of *Eat horses oats? Do*, like other auxiliaries, is used only with verbs of full meaning. It cannot stand alone, although it frequently receives great stress. Thus it must therefore fall also into the class of form-words. Of course, there is a verb *do* which possesses independent predicative value, as in *Every day I do my work*, the meaning of *to do* being *to perform*, or *to execute*. The same is true of *have*, which means to possess, as in *I have a pencil*. It is then only when verbs are used in the auxiliary sense that they are form-words. If they are used as main verbs they have full meaning.

The only part of speech left to consider is the interjection, which is never a form-word.

In the examination of the parts of speech in search for form-words, we find that there are two kinds of form-words, the modifying, as is shown by the article *the* in *the ball*, and the connective, as is shown by the verb *to be* and by conjunctions. The relations between words in sentences are shown mainly by connectives, which are form-words. The relation may be, one either of coordination, or of subordination. Coordination is shown either by word-order or by the use of form-words, as in *The dogs, cats, and birds were in the room.* There the words, *dogs* and *cats*, are connected only by their position, while *cats* and *birds* are connected by the form-word *and*. Subordination implies the relation of modified and modifier.

CHAPTER III

ARTICLES

IN THIS chapter and the two following chapters, devoted respectively to the article, preposition, and conjunction, I shall endeavor to classify the different methods that have been used in the law courts to arrive at decisions concerning the meaning of form-words, upon which the cases turn. There are hundreds of cases which revolve around the denotation of words. To render a just verdict, the law courts must find out as nearly as possible the meaning of the words or phrases involved. Each case, of course, presents a new problem, but each case involving the definition of a work falls under one of thirteen general classifications: (1) Literal interpretation; (2) Interpretation based on intent; (3) Interpretation based on putative intent; (4) Interpretation suggested by fact; (5) Common meaning; (6) Specialized meaning; (7) Technical meaning; (8) Interpretation suggested by technical terms; (9) Dictionary meaning; (10) Etymology; (11) Historical development; (12) Context; (13) Circumstances.

I shall discuss briefly each of these classifications, on which hinge decisions given in law courts. First of all, I shall define classifications (1), (5), (10), and (11), for there might be confusion in the mind of the reader as to the differences suggested by the nomenclature. Classification (10), etymology, has to do with the origin or derivation of a word as shown by its analysis into elements. The etymological study of a word deals with its original constituent elements. *Aggravate* goes back to the Latin, *ad*, "to," + *gravare*, "to burden," akin to *gravis*, "heavy." Therefore the etymological meaning would be *to increase the weight of*. The indefinite article *an* is derived from the Anglo-Saxon word *ān*, meaning *one*. Thus the etymological meaning of *an* is *one*. Consequently, in the cases decided according to etymology, the judges have gone back to the original meaning of the word as shown in the parent language, whether it be Latin, Anglo-Saxon, French or some other one.

In the case of literal interpretation, classification (1), I have considered what the word actually denotes in its usual construction, according to the authorities on standard English; that is, I have chosen the standard meaning, which is not exaggerated or embellished in any way and have eliminated all connotative value. For example, think of the word *nice*. Etymologically, it would mean *ignorant*, as it comes from the Latin word *nescius*, "ignorant," being formed from *ne*, "not," + *scius*, "knowing." One of the customary literary interpretations, however, would be *discriminating*, a standard meaning, according to authorities on English words. Think of the word *around*, for example, which is *a* + *round*. Etymologically *a* means *on* or *in* (from the Anglo-Saxon *an*, *on*, which meant *on* or *in*) and *round* means *wheel* from the French *rond*, a derivative from the Latin *rotundus*, which came from the Latin *rota*, meaning *wheel*. Thus, *around* means *on a wheel* or *in a circle*. The literal interpretation, however, would be *on every side so as to encompass or encircle*, the standard import of the word.

The common meaning, classification (5), differs from the literal meaning and the etymological meaning in that it is the one understood by the masses, the one accepted in ordinary speech. Examine the word *nice*. The common meaning is *pleasing*, or *delightful*. In the case of *around*, the common meaning is *near* or *in the neighborhood of*, as in *He is staying around New York*. After a word has been used by the masses for a century or so, the common meaning often becomes the literal meaning.

Classification (11), historical development, traces the history of the word, noting the different meanings that have been recognized from century to century, without going back to its original meaning, where the roots would be concerned. The etymological meaning deals with the roots. In the case of *of*, one of its former meanings, though not its original meaning, was *by*.

Classification (2), interpretation based on intent, is self-explanatory. The decision was based on the intended meaning of the word. People in speaking often intend to say one thing and say another, for they are not careful to use the correct word. For instance, *between* may be used in the sense of *among*. In the decision, then, *between* would take on the intended meaning, "among."

Classification (3), interpretation based on putative intent, is somewhat similar to classification (2), except that it goes much further back. The meaning has to be sought in a hypothetical situation. The court has to think what really would have been intended had such a situation arisen. For example, *a* might mean *one* or *more than one*, as shown in the illustrative cases. If a case arises in which there is no law governing the situation, the court has to imagine what the ruling would have been had there been a law.

In classification (4), interpretation suggested by fact, the word takes on a meaning according to the facts of the case. For instance, *at* may take on the meaning of "within," if the facts of the case show that a railroad, described as ending at a place, actually ends within the place.

When a case is decided according to classification (6), specialized meaning, the word has a meaning which is assigned to a particular use or function. For instance, *across* in the expression *across country*, used in steeplechasing, has a definite meaning understood in that sport. To run a race *across country* is to run a certain distance in the country, overcoming all obstacles.

Classification (7), technical meaning, refers to meanings which are peculiar to any trade, profession, or the like, especially in terminology or method of procedure. For instance, in tax laws *within* takes on the meaning of permanence. For a man to be considered within a state, he must be there permanently.

Classification (8), interpretation suggested by technical terms, is somewhat similar to classification (7). The technical terms surrounding the word cause it to take on a peculiar meaning. In one of the cases given in this dissertation *or* takes on the meaning of "that is" because of the fact that *floor cloth canvas* and *oil-cloth foundations* are technical terms referring to one and the same thing.

When a case is decided according to classification (9), dictionary meaning, the dictionary is referred to and the definition found there is used.

In classification (12), context, the decision is made according to the meaning the word acquires in relation to the subject matter. Examine the passage, "Be it enacted that the judges of all district courts . . . shall continue in office until the first day of April, on which day their term of office shall end. The successor . . . shall continue in office for five years from the first day of April. . . . " *Until* signifies "up to and including" the first day of April, according to the context, based on the words *on* and *from* in the statute. *On* designates a particular day, the one named. *From* is a word of exclusion; thus excluding the first day of April as the beginning of the term of the new judge.

In classification (13), circumstances, the import of the word is determined by the surrounding circumstances. For instance, if a farmer agrees to let a railroad be constructed through his farm but before signing the agreement demands that the words "at the back of the garden" be inserted (a survey having been made which went through the garden), the word *at* then signifies "without" instead of "within," its frequent meaning. There was certainly some reason for the farmer's demanding that the words be inserted.

At the end of the discussion of each word is given the linguistic principles used and concerned in the making of the decisions. An attempt has also been made to show how much or how little of common, everyday English is used by the lawyers in the courtroom.

THE ARTICLES

In the beginning, I have considered the articles, starting with the definite article *the* and continuing with the indefinite articles *a* and *an*. For each word has been given, first, the classifications formulated on the basis of court decisions, and, secondly, in consecutive order, cases illustrative of these classifications.

The

In studying the cases that turn on the word *the*, I have discovered six methods used by the law courts. The word is defined according to: (1) Literal interpretation; (2) Interpretation based on intent; (3) Interpretation suggested by fact; (4) Common meaning; (5) Specialized meaning; (6) Context. There is presented in consecutive order a case illustrative of each of the foregoing methods.

Case 1.—On May 7, 1906, a case arose in Louisiana concerning the adoption of children. The administrator of the succession of

Eugene Dupre having filed the account of his administration, the tutor of the minor, Helen Coleman, filed an opposition claiming that his ward should be placed on the account as heir to one-fourth of the succession, in her quality of adopted child of the decedent.

Wishing to adopt a child, Dupre and wife went before a notary and passed an act (as the phrase is in Louisiana), which they and the notary thought conformed with all legal requirements of the law concerning the adoption of children. It was as follows:

"An act providing for the manner of adopting children.

"Be it enacted by the Senate and House of Representatives of the State of Louisiana, in General Assembly convened: That any person above the age of twenty-one years shall have the right by act to be passed before any parish recorder or notary public, to adopt any child under the age of twenty-one years, provided, that if such child shall have a parent, or parents, or tutor, that the concurrence of such parent or parents or tutor shall be obtained and as evidence thereof shall be required to sign said act."

In this case the child was a foundling without a tutor. Sister Veronica, the Mother Superior of the St. Vincent's Infant Asylum, signed the act. The contention of the administrator was that the act should have been signed by the child's parents, who were presumably living; or by a tutor, if the parents were dead.

The judge said that the law, without doubt, was intended to cover the whole subject-matter; that the title was: "An act providing for the manner of adopting children." He also said that manner was described as *the* manner; not a manner, or one of the manners, or part of the manner; but *the* manner; that is, the exclusive manner.

It was decided that Helen Coleman was heir to one-fourth of Dupre's estate.

This case was decided upon the basis of the literal interpretation of *the*.[1]

Case 2.—The grand jury of Shelby County, Tennessee, at the June term of the circuit court, in 1840, returned an indictment against Demsey Sanderlin, which was in the following words:

"State of Tennessee }
Shelby County } Circuit Court, June Term, 1840.

"The grand jurors for the State of Tennessee, elected, impanelled, sworn, and charged to enquire for the body of *the county aforesaid*, upon their oaths, present, that Demsey Sanderlin, late of *said county*, laborer, on 4th day of June, one thousand eight hundred and forty, with force and arms in the county, unlawfully did keep a tippling house, and then and there did vend and retail spirituous liquors in less quantities than one quart, and by the quart, intended to be drank on the premises, against the form the statute in such case made and provided, and against the peace and dignity of the State."

The jury found Sanderlin guilty. He was then fined fifty dollars.

The defendant appealed to the Supreme Court. One of the things he insisted upon was that the venue was not sufficiently laid in the indictment, as state and county were first written in full and twice thereafter referred to as "the county aforesaid," and then by the words "the county."

The court said that the use of the words "the county" in an indictment for a misdemeanor was a sufficient designation of the county first mentioned, as the use of the definite article *the* necessarily meant that county, the name of which had been repeated three times immediately before.

The judgment was therefore affirmed.

Without doubt, it was the intent of the grand jury in the indictment to signify Shelby County each time county was used; thus the decision was based on the interpretation of intent.[2]

Case 3.—In Iowa, Amundsen brought action to recover rent from the Standard Printing Company upon a lease made. He issued on May 7, 1903, an attachment upon a printing press. Then various labor claimants, eleven in all, filed claims for labor performed within ninety days previous to the levy of the attachment. Judgment was rendered establishing the labor claims and declaring them superior to intervener's lien according to the statute, which provided that "when 'the' property of a person shall be seized by any process of any court . . . the debts owing to employés for labor performed within ninety days next preceding the seizure of such property, shall be a preferred debt and paid in full."

The court said that the definite article *the* sometimes had the meaning of "all of the" and the law required that "all the property" of a debtor should be seized before labor claimants could have preference.

In this instance, all of the property was seized; the labor claimants would not have had another chance of getting their pay. If part of a man's property is left, he is supposed to pay his laborers by the use of that part; if nothing is left, it is a fact that he will not be able to pay those who have already worked for him. Thus *the* must have the meaning of "all of the" in the above quoted law, the interpretation being suggested by fact.[3]

Case 4.—On October 10, 1865, the Adams Express Company, of which Dinsmore was president, received from Demas Barnes and Company, in New York, for transportation to Mr. Wetzell at St. Louis, one package containing three gross or cases of Shallenberger's pills, of the value of $340.50, each case being worth $113.50. The contract under which the transportation was undertaken had the following provision: "nor in any event shall the holder hereof demand beyond the sum of fifty dollars, at which the article forwarded is hereby valued, unless herein expressed, or unless specially insured by them and so specified in this receipt, which insurance shall constitute the limits of the liability of the Adams Express Company." Only one of the three cases of pills reached the plaintiff. When delivered to the express company, the three boxes were severally addressed to the plaintiff and were wrapped together in a single package by a paper cover, likewise addressed to the plaintiff. The plaintiff demanded fifty dollars for each of the boxes lost. "The article" to be forwarded was valued at fifty dollars and consisted of 432 pills, all in one package, addressed to the plaintiff.

The court said that the plaintiff might as well have claimed fifty dollars for each pill.

Judgment was therefore rendered in favor of the express company.

The decision was based on the common, ordinary meaning of *the* as designating a particular object. It was impossible for each of the three separate boxes in the one package to be "the article forwarded."[4]

Case 5.—The plaintiffs, Mary E. Noyes and James Loveridge, executors of the last will and testament of Elisa Hearsey, offered the will, dated July 11, 1874, to the surrogate of the county of New York for probate. The Children's Aid Society and St. Luke's Home, legatees under a former will, filed objections thereto. At the trial the unsuccessful contestants applied for allowances, and an order was made granting to the proctors for the Children's Aid Society an allowance of $2,500 and $764.65 disbursements, and to the proctor for St. Luke's Home $750. From this order Mary E. Noyes, executrix and the principal legatee, and James Loveridge, executor, appealed to the General Term of the Supreme Court, which reversed the order of the surrogate.

The law upon which the surrogate acted was one giving the surrogate the right to give costs to *the* party entitled. The court said that the Surrogate's Court might give allowances in lieu of costs and that the surrogate might award them to the party who, in his judgment, was entitled to them and not always to the party who was technically successful—that is, not to the one who obtains a decree in his favor upon the question contested, but to the party whose behavior in the circumstances provoking the litigation, whose situation in relation to the estate, or the particular subject in controversy, was such that it was equitable and just that he be remunerated for his expenses in the litigation, for *the* party meant "any" party, just as Shakespeare meant any man when he said, "The man that hath not music in his soul is fit for treason," etc., and not one man only.

In this case *the* has a specialized meaning. It means "any" and not one particular thing.[5]

Case 6.—In Iowa, in 1893, the Home Insurance Company of New York issued to Mr. Born two policies of insurance on certain real and personal property. The plaintiff's barn and a considerable portion of his personal property were destroyed by fire. Before the fire the plaintiff had given several chattel mortgages, all of which he had paid off except one. In applying for his insurance he did not ask for coverage on the property under mortgage. The Insurance Company contended that under the following law the policy was forfeited when the mortgage was given:

"A policy insuring both real and personal property provided that if the property should thereafter become mortgaged or incumbered, the policy should be void, and also declared that it should be forfeited if other insurance was taken 'on any of said property.'"

The court said that *the* referred to the whole property mortgaged, for the words which referred to other insurance, "on any of said property," indicated it; the use of *the* in one instance and "any" in the other surely indicating an intention to express something different.

Thus the policy was not forfeited by the mortgage of a portion thereof and judgment was rendered in favor of Born.

The subject matter determined the decision here. Without the latter part of the clause and the use of the word "any," the former part would have taken on a different meaning.[6]

As for *the*, the most frequently used word in the English vocabulary, there are two linguistic classifications under which the illustrative cases fall: (*a*) The generalizing value; (*b*) The specific meaning.

(*a*) Both uses of *the* are customary in every day speech.

The cases that illustrate the generalizing value are (1), (3), (5), and (6).

Case (1), the decision of which turned upon the title of the law, "an act providing for the manner of adopting children," shows that *the* becomes inclusive in that it takes in all cases of adoption; the case where the child had parents, the case where the child had a tutor, and the case where the child had any other kind of guardian, as in this case Mother Superior of an infant asylum. It is exclusive in that it refers to the particular manner of adopting children, but inclusive in that it has the generalizing value of taking care of more than just the specific cases mentioned in the law.

This means of making a statement is common. If a home economics teacher should say to her class, "This is the way to make your dress," she would give the general directions for making a dress which would include all of the dresses of the students in the class, but would not be the specific directions for any one particular dress.

Cases (3) and (6) show the generalizing value of *the* in "the property." One possession, such as a horse, would be the property of a man, but in these cases *the* includes all of the possessions, not just part of them. We speak of the clothes of a man if we are speaking of his entire wardrobe; we also designate several suits of the man as the clothes of this man, not meaning, of course, all of the clothes of the man. Thus "the property" may mean one possession of a person or it may mean more than one, or all of the possessions of that person, as it does in these cases.

Case (5) shows the generalizing value of *the* in that it takes on the import of "any." This usage of *the* is general. One may say: "The student who cheats in that way should be expelled," signifying any student who cheats in that way and not one particular student; "A scholarship will be awarded to the boy who makes the highest grade in Latin," the *the* not designating one particular boy, but "any" boy who makes the highest grade.

(*b*) Ordinarily, if *the* is mentioned or discussed as a separate word, it is thought of as the definite article pointing out a particular person or thing. This specific meaning is shown in cases (2) and (4).

In case (2), Shelby County, Tennessee, was first mentioned at the head of the indictment; then farther on *the* county was referred to. *The* in that case designates one particular county—Shelby County—and not "any" county. The misdemeanor happened in Shelby County; therefore no other county could be considered.

Also, in case (4), the phrase "the article forwarded," included in the contract, which read: "nor in any event shall the holder hereof demand beyond the sum of fifty dollars, at which the article forwarded is hereby valued," means that particular object which was being shipped. Here, too, *the* has the specific signification. It is a demonstrative.

Thus, we see that the law courts have to deal with *the* in its customary use, to determine whether it has the generalizing value or a specific meaning.

A

The indefinite articles *a* and *an* will next be considered. In this section attention is to be centered on *a*, for which I have found the following five classifications: (1) Literal interpretation; (2) Interpretation based on intent; (3) Interpretation based on putative intent; (4) Interpretation suggested by fact; (5) Common meaning.

Case 1.—In 1912, Moynahan brought action to recover fees as an official stenographer in one of the parts of the Supreme Court of the State of New York for transcribing and furnishing from day to day several copies of his stenographic notes taken at the trial in 1904 of one Totterman, who was charged with and convicted of murder in the first degree.

The Code of Civil Procedure, Section 86, provided that each stenographer specified in the act, on request, must furnish, with all reasonable diligence, to the defendant in a criminal case "a copy," written out at length from his stenographic notes, of the testimony and proceedings, on payment, by the person requiring same, of the fees allowed by law; that, if the district attorney, or attorney general required such a copy in a criminal case, the stenographer was entitled to his fees therefor, which should be a county charge, and must be paid like other county charges.

There was another law, the General Construction Law, Section 35, which declared that words in the singular number include the plural, and in the plural include the singular.

Moynahan contended that the latter section could not be applied to Section 86, so as to authorize the district attorney to require more than one transcript of the testimony for his use at the expense of the county, and that, in view of such section, the district attorney had no inherent power to incur such expense as might result from ordering two or more transcripts of the testimony in an important criminal case.

It was held that Moynahan should receive pay for the extra transcripts made.

Thus the literal interpretation was given to *a* in the Code of Civil Procedure. "A copy" meant "one copy."[1]

Case 2.—Perry, Ryer and Company imported two marble statues, each carved from three pieces of marble. The goods were assessed for duty at 50 per cent *ad valorem*. Perry contended that they should have been assessed at 15 per cent *ad valorem* according to the provision in paragraph 454 of the Tariff Act, which read as follows:

"The term 'statuary' as used in this act shall be understood to include only such statuary as is cut, carved, or otherwise wrought by hand from a solid block or mass of marble, stone, or alabaster, or from metal, and as is the professional production of a sculptor only."

The court said that, no doubt, the qualifying statement was to restrict paragraph 454 to statuary made from solid marble, etc., as distinguished from statuary made by molding from composition stone or similar materials.

It was decided that "a solid block or mass of marble" was not limited to statuary made from single blocks, for many of the best statues, especially those of heroic size, are executed from more than one piece of marble, but included certain statues, each carved from three solid blocks of marble.

In this case *a* meant more than one; it meant three. The decision was based on the interpretation of the intent of the indefinite article in the law under discussion.[2]

Case 3.—In Arkansas, on February 8, 1895, the Legislature passed an act providing for an additional judge for the Sixth Judicial Circuit, and for the splitting up of that circuit into the First and Second Divisions. The reason for this action was that the population and judicial business had increased so much that the courts provided by law could not promptly protect the people.

On February 12, 1895, the governor appointed Joseph W. Martin "as judge of the circuit court for the Second Division of the Sixth Judicial District." Then the state, through its attorney general, applied for a writ of quo warranto on the ground that Martin had no right to hold office as judge.

The state contended that the act was in conflict with Section 13 of Article 7 of the Constitution, which read as follows: "The state shall be divided into convenient circuits, each circuit to be made up of contiguous counties, for each of which circuits a judge shall be elected, who, during his continuance in office shall reside in and be a conservator of the peace within the circuit for which he shall have been elected." It was contended that the letter "a" before the word "judge" in the section above was a limitation upon the power of the Legislature to provide for more than one judge in a judicial circuit. The judge read Section 6 of the same article, Article 13: "A judge of the supreme court shall be learned in the law" and Section 16 of the same: "A circuit judge shall be learned in the law." Then he asked if the word *a* in those sections meant one, and only one, judge. If it meant one he wanted to know to which one it referred. The state replied in one of its arguments that if a sack of flour were ordered, it was understood that one sack, and only one, was wanted.

Finally, it was decided that there should be two divisions of the court, and two judges holding court in the same circuit at the same time, each judge performing all the duties of a circuit judge for that circuit while thus engaged in holding the court.

It is difficult to place this case under one general classification, for it is evident that many different elements entered into the decision. One of the main reasons for the decision was circumstances; that is, the practical need. It was impossible for the people of an over-populated district to receive justice as they should. Then analogies were made to special meanings of *a* in other laws. What I think really happened was that the court tried to imagine what the makers of the law would really have intended in such a situation. It is true that the law-makers did not make provision for an over-populated circuit, but the idea was to find out what they would have said if they had realized such a condition might exist at some time. For this reason I have put this case under the classification entitled "putative intent."[3]

Case 4.—Below is a memorandum signed by James Brown and his wife, Anne Brown:

"Lynn, April 14, 1866. $50. Received of John and Michael Hurley the sum of fifty dollars in part payment of a house and lot of land situated on Amity Street, Lynn, Mass. The full amount is $1700. This bargain to be closed inside of ten days from date thereof."

Mr. Brown, the husband, died while the transaction was pending. Then Mrs. Brown tried to hold the house and lot. She contended that the words "a house and lot" in the memorandum were not definite enough, for there were other houses and lots on the same street. She owned, however, no other house and lot on the street.

The court said that she might as well have said "my house and lot," for the description could refer to no other.

Judgment was therefore rendered in favor of Hurley.

In this case *a* took on the meaning of "my" for since she owned only one house and lot, the description could refer only to that one which was hers. Thus the decision was based on interpretation suggested by fact.[4]

Case 5.—In 1885, in England, there was an appeal against an order of the York County Court, whereby it was declared that a distress levied upon farming stock and other chattels of Sanders by the appellant (Sergeant), for rent due to Rhodes, was an illegal distress. The case turned on the article *a* preceding county court in the Agricultural Holdings (England) Act of 1883, which declared that "no person shall act as bailiff to levy any distress or other holdings to which the act applies unless authorized to act as a bailiff by a judge of 'a' county court." In this case the bailiff was given authority to levy the distress by a judge from the county other than the one in which Sanders lived.

The court said that grammatically, the words "a judge of a county court" meant the judge of any county court, for "a county court" did not mean a particular county court.

It was decided that *a*, as used in the phrase "a county court" was not intended to specify a particular county court, but should be construed as meaning any county court.

The decision was based on the common meaning of *a*, the construction used here. If one asks for *a* book, he means any book.[5]

In Webster's New International Dictionary, published in 1926, *a* is defined as "one or any—without special emphasis on the number." The letter *A* was derived from Anglo-Saxon *ān*, "one," the same word as the numeral. For a long time it was used as *ān* "one," but for reasons of euphony it lost the *n* before words beginning with the consonant sound. Gradually it lost its definite meaning of "one" and became indefinite. It is now known as one of the indefinite articles, which may signify "one" or "any." The word *any*, meaning one indifferently out of a number, goes back to Anglo-Saxon *ǣnig*, a variation of *ān*.

The cases given here illustrate two classifications. (*a*) *A* definitely meaning "one"; (*b*) *A* used as an indefinite adjective. Cases (1) and (4) belong to classification (*a*); cases (2), (3), and (5) to classification (*b*).

(*a*) In case (1), "a copy" meant one copy only. There *a* had its original meaning "one." Case (4), however, shows a slight variation of the same meaning. "A house and lot" referred to "one house and lot" since Mrs. Brown owned only one house and lot on the particular street. Nevertheless, the phrase implied one house that was hers; thus taking on the import of "my." Although *a*, in this instance, meant "my," it belongs under classification (*a*) for there was only one house and lot. This meaning of *a* is common. One may say, if one is in a group that needs a red pencil for certain figures, "I must get a red pencil," signifying one red pencil. In ordinary speech *a* also includes "my" in its meaning along with "one." If a girl is going out and says to another, "Hand me a hat," she certainly means one hat and implies that she wants her own hat, thus giving the signification of "my" to *a*, unquestionably the meaning, if there is only one hat and that one hat belongs to the girl.

(*b*) More often *a* has the indefinite meaning, although it did originally mean "one." A person says, "Give me a book to hold this paper down," meaning any book. This meaning is shown in case (5), in which "a county court" refers to "any county court." Used in its indefinite sense *a* may take another form as in cases (2) and (3), meaning any without special emphasis on the number. In case (2), *a* meant three; in case (3), *a* meant two. If a girl should say that she wanted a dress made from a piece of red satin, she would not signify that all the material required would have to be in one piece. The goods might be in several lengths, each length used for a particular part of the dress. The same signification was found in speaking of the statues made from a solid block. The complete statue did not have to be carved from one slab of marble, but did have to be carved from solid marble. If a father should say that he wanted his son always to have a good teacher, the father would not mean that he wanted his son always to have one teacher. Here *a* would apply to any number of teachers, for it is used in its indefinite sense. So it was in case (3), in which *a* judge meant "two" judges.

An

The word *an* is defined according to: (1) Interpretation based on intent; (2) Etymology.

Case 1.—In 1899, the Plastic Fireproof Construction Company brought an action against the city and county of San Francisco to recover damages for the infringement of a patent. The Fireproof Construction Company, through Mr. Calvin Brown, in its application for the patent stated: "My invention relates to improvements in roofing and sheathing buildings and other structures, and the object thereof is to obtain an artificial slate of durable and incombustible quality to take the place of, and to be used for the same purpose as natural slate."

The court said that *an*, as used in a claim for a patent for *an* artificial slate, fairly implied that the claim was for material having form and dimensions, and not for a new substance in mass.

It was decided that a mere carrying forward of the original thought, a change only in form, proportion, or degree, doing the same thing in the same way, by substantially the same means, with better results, was not such an invention as would sustain a patent. Thus the patent was not granted to the Fireproof Construction Company.

The decision was based upon the meaning implied in *an;* that is, the interpretation suggested by intent—the intent of the Fireproof Construction Company in their application for the patent.[1]

Case 2.—In 1894, the town of Greece in the county of Monroe, New York, had two overseers of the poor. On May 15, one of them applied to a justice of the peace of the town to inquire who was the father of a child likely to be born a bastard, and chargeable to said town. The two overseers did not meet, and the application was the sole act of one of them. A warrant was issued and the defendant was adjudged to be the father of the child. The defendant made an appeal to the Court of Sessions. He said the application was made by but one of the overseers of the poor of the town, without consultation with the other overseer. The statute under which the proceedings were brought provided as follows:

"When a bastard, chargeable to the public, is born, or is likely to be born, application to be made to a justice of the peace or police justice. If a woman be delivered of a bastard or be pregnant of a child likely to be born such, and which is chargeable to a county, city, or town, a superintendent of the poor of the county, or an overseer of the poor or other officer of the almshouse of the town or city where the woman is, must apply to a justice of the peace or police justice in the county to inquire into the facts of the case."

The judge said that the power to institute proceedings was not conferred upon the board of overseers of the poor of the town, for there was no such board, nor upon all of the overseers of the poor, but upon "an overseer," one of the overseers of the town. He said the term "an overseer" was the equivalent of either or of any of the overseers, for *an* originally meant "one" and was seldom used to denote plurality.

It was therefore held that the statute providing that *an* overseer of the poor may bring an action to inquire into the facts of a bastard case authorized "one" overseer to bring such action. Thus, the action of the overseer was legal.

The decision was based on the etymology of *an*.[3]

Some of the same assertions may be made of *an* that were made of *a*, for both were derived from the Anglo-Saxon word *ān*, "one," the same word as the numeral. For a long time it signified "one."

Unlike *a*, it kept its original spelling and is used before words beginning with a vowel sound for the sake of euphony. Although it did not lose its original form, it gradually lost the definite meaning of "one" and became indefinite. Along with *a*, it is now known as one of the indefinite articles which may mean "one" or "any." The word *any*, meaning one indifferently out of a number, goes back to Anglo-Saxon *ǣnig*, a variation of *ān*.

The same linguistic classifications also hold true for *an:* (*a*) *An* definitely meaning "one"; (*b*) *An* used as an indefinite adjective.

(*a*) Case (2) illustrates classification (*a*), in which "an overseer" refers to "one overseer." If a person says, "An abbey is on the hill," he means that one abbey is on the hill. This use of *an* is frequent in everyday speech.

(*b*) The employment of *an* as an indefinite adjective or article is illustrated in case (1), in which Brown speaks of inventing "an artificial slate of durable and incombustible quality. . . ." In daily speech a person may say that he is going to produce an unusual apple by means of grafting. This application of *an* is the same as that in case (1)—*an* used as an indefinite adjective or article.

Thus we see that the common import of the indefinite articles as well as that of the definite article must be considered in the law courts.

Chapter IV

PREPOSITIONS

THE preposition, I find, gives the law courts far more difficulty than any other of the three parts of speech with which I am concerned. A preposition shows relationship, but the relationship is not clearly defined. Therefore the words, though small in size, give a great deal of trouble because of their latitude of meaning. In the volumes of "Words and Phrases" I found cited more than 150 cases that turned on the one preposition *about*.

Following the method pursued with the articles, I have formulated for the prepositions classifications based on judicial decisions, and then have cited in consecutive order illustrative cases. Forty-one prepositions have been studied in their aspect of form-words, and this study has been presented in alphabetical order, beginning with *about*.

About

The word *about* is defined according to: (1) Literal interpretation; (2) Interpretation based on intent; (3) Interpretation suggested by fact; (4) Common meaning; (5) Specialized meaning; (6) Technical meaning; (7) Dictionary meaning; (8) Context; (9) Circumstances.

Case 1.—In England, in 1868, John Lane, of Cirencester, made a will in which he bequeathed to his two sons, John and George, all articles which at his decease should be "in or about" his dwelling-house or "in or about" his mill.

On April 15, 1871, Mr. Lane ordered a cargo of wheat from a firm at Gloucester. The firm received a note, dated May 2, 1871, and on May 4 delivered at the Gloucester Railway Station 1,920 bushels of wheat consigned to Mr. Lane who died on that day. Later the firm delivered the rest of the order. The representatives of the testator's sons claimed they were entitled to the money received from the sale of the wheat.

It was decided that the money did not belong to the sons, for the wheat had never been in Mr. Lane's possession and at the time of his death was in transit and could not be considered "in or about" the mill.

The court, in this case, gave a literal interpretation to the will, although it is evident that the father's intention was to give the wheat, or the money for it, to the two sons, for the wheat would soon have been "in or about" the mill. The fact was that the wheat happened to be in transit at the time of the father's death. Here the literal interpretation conflicts with the real intention.[1]

Case 2.—In Alabama, in 1879, Powell was working with others in another man's field, which was located more than a mile from his own house. There he sold liquor from a jug which he had with him. He had no license as a retailer from a proper legal authority. Thus he was convicted for selling liquor without a license according to the law which stated that one was guilty of a misdemeanor who sold liquor in small quantities which was drunk "on or about the premises." Powell pleaded that the liquor was not drunk on or about his premises, but it was decided that the liquor was about the premises.

The interpretation of this case was based on the intent of the law. Literally, the liquor was not "on or about" the premises. The purpose of law, however, is to protect society. The body of lawmakers who made the law had the welfare of society at heart. If the court had allowed Powell, who sold liquor in another man's field, to go free, it would have been defeating the law, for the very evil which the prohibition against drinking "on or about the premises" was made to prevent would have been produced. The court, realizing that fact, interpreted the law according to its intent; thus enlarging the meaning of *about*—making it extend over into another man's field.[2]

Case 3.—In Alabama, Diffey carried a pistol concealed in a hand basket, which he carried in his hand or on his arm from his home to the station on the street railway, a distance of three or four hundred yards. After he entered the car he put the basket on the seat beside him. He was convicted for carrying a weapon concealed "on or about" the person.

This case illustrates the interpretation suggested by fact. The weapon certainly was not on the person, but it was near enough to be accessible. Then *about* took on the meaning of accessible; it was defined in terms of interpretation suggested by fact. The fact was that the pistol was near at hand and could be used at any moment. The purpose of the statute against carrying concealed weapons was to prevent a weapon from being connected with a person in such a manner that it might be easily and promptly used without other persons' knowledge of its presence.[3]

Case 4.—In New Hampshire, Banks conveyed, by lease, to Thompson and his brother a mill privilege, called the Leather's Privilege, giving them certain rights, among which was that of laying logs, boards, and the lumber "on or about" the mill grounds.

Banks would not allow Thompson to lay logs, etc., on property adjoining the mill grounds, which also belonged to Banks. As a result, Thompson brought action of covenant broken against Banks.

It was decided that the lease did not give the lessee permission to occupy lands of the lessor lying outside the mill privilege.

This decision was based on the meaning of *about* in common conversation. The judge said the word *about* might frequently have the meaning of "around; on the outside of; without the limitations; etc."; yet it frequently in common conversation meant "through or over, in various directions, or in various parts of the whole promiscuously," and that to travel about the country meant to go from place to place in the country and not out of it. He concluded by saying that if a man should scatter or lay his lumber all about his mill-yards, one would expect to find it somewhere in the limits of the yard and not on the outside of it.[4]

Case 5.—A contract was entered into between Peterson Bros. and James Hood. It provided as follows: "Santa Rosa, Sept. 22nd, 1902. In consideration of one ($1.00) dollar, paid to me in hand, I sell and promise to deliver to Chaix and Bernard at James G. Hood's winery at Santa Rosa, Cal., about 250 tons grapes, more or less tons of grapes, at the stipulated price of $27.00 per ton cash after delivery. Grapes to be of sound quality. Seller: Peterson Bros. Buyer: James G. Hood."

Chaix and Bernard accepted 256.81 tons and then notified Peterson Bros. that they would not accept any more. There were left 166.15 tons, which Peterson Bros. sold for only twenty dollars per ton. The difference in price amounted to $1,093.08. Then there were ten tons that became decayed and valueless on account of the refusal of acceptance.

Peterson Bros. tried to show that 250 tons, more or less, meant all the grapes grown by seller, for the terms had by custom among buyers and sellers of wine grapes a local and peculiar signification, which meant all grapes grown by the seller. The additional quantity was 166 tons, or 60 per cent more than the contract called for.

The court said that the engagement was to furnish goods of a certain quality to a certain amount and that the addition of the qualifying words *about*, *more or less*, and the like, was only for the purpose of providing against accidental variations arising from slight and unimportant excesses or deficiencies in number, measure, or weight.

Judgment was rendered in favor of the defendant.

The decision was based on the common meaning of *about* among mercantile men—a specialized meaning which is well understood in the connection in which it is used. The *about* is introduced for the purpose of protecting the seller who is expected to fulfill his contract by a delivery of the specific quantity within a reasonable limit.[5]

Case 6.—In Rhode Island, Annie Campbell owned a tract of land in Pautucket, on which she was erecting a dwelling house. She mortgaged a portion of that tract to Emma Hawkins on February 1, 1894, and mortgaged the whole tract to the Co-operative Building Bank on April 18, 1894. On July 15, 1896, Myron Hawkins took possession of the land mortgaged to Emma Hawkins.

In February, 1903, the Co-operative Building Bank proceeded to plot the tract into streets and lots. The mortgage to Emma Hawkins was as follows: "Beginning at a point 'about' 315 feet distant from Dudley Street and 363 feet from Main Street, said land runs westerly. . . ."

In attempting to apply the description to the land, the Co-operative Building Bank took as the place of beginning a point exactly 363 feet west of Main Street, and exactly 315 feet south of Dudley Street. According to that measurement, the dwelling house extended more than seven feet beyond the lines of said lot into the Bank's land. The Bank threatened to cut off the part of the building extending across the line, or to barricade that part so that it could not be used by tenants.

Between October 22, 1906, and November 22, 1906, Emma Hawkins had the house moved back within the lines of the lot. The Co-operative Building Bank brought an action of trespass against Emma Hawkins. The jury returned a verdict for the plaintiff for $682. The defendant's motion for a new trial was based on the word *about*. The justice presiding at the trial in the Superior Court ruled that this word should not be held to render the description uncertain, but should be considered as equivalent to the word "at." The judge said: "As to the word 'about,' used in the grant, I am of the opinion that it does not make the land uncertain. It has always been determined that the word 'about' signifies in an entry or grant 'at,' unless something can be shown to evidence a contrary intention." The judgment was therefore affirmed.

This case was decided according to the technical meaning of *about* in entries and grants. In entries and grants, according to the judge's decision, *about* takes on the meaning of "at" and denotes certainty instead of uncertainty.[6]

Case 7.—Wompelmeir and Company held three notes on Moses, amounting to about $900. On December 16, 1869, before either of the notes had matured, complainants filed their attachment bill in the Chancery Court at Nashville, Tennessee, alleging that the "Defendant is about to remove the stock of goods he has on hand, and which is all the property he owns in the world" and praying that the goods be attached to satisfy their claim.

The Chancellor dismissed the attachment bill because the proof failed to show that the defendant was about to take his property out of the state. The complainants appealed. The burden of proof was on the complainants to sustain their allegation, for the defendant not only had the furniture in his store, but also owned property in Nashville.

The judge said that in a statute allowing an attachment when a debtor is "about" to remove his stock, *about* must be taken in its common acceptance as defined by lexicographers—"near to in action, or near to in the performance of some act." He also said that Moses' stock could not have been attached, for his real estate was worth $10,000 and his stock from $3,000 to $4,000 but his indebtedness was much less.

The decree of the Chancellor was therefore affirmed with costs.

The decision was based on the dictionary definition of *about:* "near to in action or near to in the performance of some act."[7]

Case 8.—In Arizona, in 1924, William Hoffman brought action against the United Eastern Mining Company for damages for injuries received from a fall from a tower twelve feet high located about equidistant between the Big Jim Mine and the mill of the United Eastern Mining Company, which was constructing an aerial tramway between the two, the distance between the mine and the mill being about one mile. Hoffman was foreman of the work.

Hoffman claimed that according to the Employer's Liability Law he was entitled to damages. The statute included a number of dangerous occupations, such as:

"(6) All work of construction, . . . alteration or repair where wires, cables, switchboards, or other apparatus or machinery are in use charged with electrical current.

"(7) All work in the construction, alteration, or repair of pole lines for telegraph, telephone or other purposes.

"(8) All work in or about quarries, open pits, open cuts, mines, ore reduction works and smelters," etc.

Hoffman claimed that the work he was doing upon the tower was work "in or about . . . mines . . .," falling under subdivision 8 of the statute. He was not working in the defendant's mine, but was half a mile away from the mine, working upon a tower not then in use in mining or otherwise, but to be utilized later when the tramway was completed. The question was whether this latter work was "about" the defendant's mine.

The court said that *about* in the context in which it was used was intended to mean work of the general character done or carried on in the danger zone incident to operating a mine, but not work away from the mine and dangers or hazards incident thereto.

The court held that Hoffman was not engaged in hazardous work *about* the mine within the Employer's Liability Law; *about* meaning work of general character done or carried on in the danger zone incident to operating the mine. Therefore the case was reversed. At the first trial judgment was rendered in favor of Hoffman, and the United Eastern Mining Company appealed.

The case was decided upon the basis of context. From the subject matter of the Liability Law, it was evident that the employees were to be protected in dangerous places. All of the other occupations listed were perilous ones. Thus it would naturally be assumed that the part mentioned in regard to mines also referred to the danger zone.[8]

Case 9.—Lingham agreed to ship cattle by the steamer N. H., "sailing from New York about the middle of September." The vessel was at sea when the contract was made. On September 14, Lingham inquired the steamer's probable sailing day and was told that it was about September 27, a date to which he made no objection. On September 22, when he was notified that the steamer would sail on the twenty-ninth, he declined to ship cattle by her, on the ground that his contract did not require him to ship at so late a date. Bennett, the ship owner, held that having construed the indefinite phrase, "about the middle of September," to mean as late as the twenty-seventh of the month, and Lingham having acquiesced therein, and that, too, on a day before the middle of September, Lingham should not say that a tender on the twenty-ninth was not a compliance with the contract.

It was decided that the refusal to ship was a breach of the contract and that Lingham was liable for damages resulting from not shipping on the N. H.

The decision in this case was determined by circumstances, which extended the meaning of *about* to "from the middle to the end of the month."[9]

The word *about* is universally used, for the average person who is not discriminating in his speech has a tendency to use words that have latitude of meaning, *about* being one of them. If a man makes an appointment for eight o'clock, he usually says, "I shall be there about eight o'clock." He gives himself a number of minutes before or after the hour so that if he fails to arrive at the appointed time, he will not have to apologize. Thus the word *about* is convenient as well as inexact. It is the inexactness of the word that causes trouble.

The many cases that turn upon this word illustrate the following linguistic classifications: (*a*) Limited meaning, (*b*) Extended meaning; (*c*) Definite meaning. Cases (1), (3), (4), (5), (7), and (8) illustrate the limited meaning; cases (2) and (9) illustrate the extended meaning; and case (6) illustrates the definite meaning.

(*a*) Case (1) turned upon the meaning of "about the mill." The wheat was not in the millyard, nor in the immediate neighborhood of the mill; but many miles away at the time of Mr. Lane's death. The decision shows the limited meaning of *about*. If the wheat had been in contiguity or proximity to the mill, it, or its value, would have been given to the two sons. There were certain limits, however, within which the wheat had to be.

This use of *about* is very common. If a person says, "Jane is about the house," he means that Jane is either in the house or in the yard adjoining the house or in the garden or some similar place on the premises. Jane can be seen or called from the house; she is near.

In case (3), Diffey was convicted because he had a concealed weapon about his person. The pistol was within certain limits, for it could easily be reached at any moment. If the weapon had been beyond his reach, he would have been set free. This use, too, is commonplace. One often asks, "Have you much money about you?" The questioner means to ask if the person has much money in his pockets, or in his wallet, or in any other place where a person might carry money. He is not concerned with the amount in the bank, which might be only a few steps away.

The phrase "about the mill grounds" in case (4) limited Thompson to putting logs on the inside of the mill grounds. In ordinary conversation, if a person says, "John is walking about the room," he means that John is walking to and fro in the room and not outside the room.

Case (5) also shows the limited meaning of *about*, in that "about 250 tons" does not mean 416.15 tons, all the grapes grown by one man. If a man asks for about fifty chairs to be put into a classroom, he does not want 60 per cent more, especially if the room is small.

Case (7) illustrates another phase of the limited meaning of *about*. Here *about* is used before an infinitive, which signifies present, and not future action. "About to remove" means "on the point of," or "in the act of" removing. The action is limited to present action. If I say, "I am about to sign this paper," I mean that I have not begun, but I am just ready to sign it. The use of *about* before an infinitive is common.

Case (8) limits *about* to the danger zone of the mine. Similarly, in everyday speech, a mother may say to a maid, "If the baby is about the fire, lock him in the nursery." If the baby were playing in an adjoining room where there was no fire, the mother would not expect the nurse to lock the baby in the nursery. The danger of the fire causes the mother to make the statement and as long as the baby is safe, locking is not necessary.

(*b*) At times the meaning of *about* is not limited, but is extended as is shown in cases (2) and (9).

In case (2), "about the premises" was extended over into another man's field, in order to carry out the intent of the law. This extension of the signification of *about* is also used in daily speech. A teacher may make the following statement, "Any student who fights about the schoolhouse shall be expelled." If, then, two boys should fight at recess, the teacher would expel them although they were two miles away on ground not contiguous to the school, or near the school. The meaning of *about* is extended beyond the school ground in order to promote good behavior at the school.

Case (9) shows "about the middle of September" extended to "about the end of September." Suppose that a tailor was making a suit for a man and that it was to be delivered about five o'clock. If the man stopped in at four o'clock for the suit, and the tailor told him he had not quite finished it, but would deliver it about ten o'clock that evening, and if the man raised no objection, then the tailor would expect the man to be satisfied if he delivered it at eleven o'clock instead of ten. Here, too, the import of *about* is extended by circumstances.

(*c*) Although we think of *about* as an indefinite word, it at times takes on a definite meaning. In case (6) "at the point 'about' 315 feet distant from Dudley Street" shows *about* taking on a definite import and meaning "at." The measurement was made exactly 315 feet distant from Dudley Street. If a person should walk into a store and ask for about a quart of oil, the merchant would understand that he wanted a quart of oil and would measure out a quart.

Thus we see that the law courts deal with *about* as it is used in ordinary conversation. The courts must decide whether the word has a limited meaning, an extended meaning, or a definite meaning, all of which are commonly used.

Above

The word *above* is defined according to: (1) Interpretation based on intent; (2) Common meaning; (3) Specialized meaning.

Case 1.—In New Jersey, the Mechanics and Laborers Savings Bank was incorporated by an act of the Legislature, approved in 1869. The charter of the bank provided that, "said corporation shall invest no money . . . on bond and mortgage except on real estate worth at least double the amount of the sum invested, above all encumbrances."

The bank failed and W. B. Williams, receiver for it, brought action against the officials of the bank. It was shown that a real estate loan of $1,120 had been made. The security was a house and two lots worth $4,500, already encumbered by a mortgage for $2,700, which was also a lien upon two other lots worth $1,500. The mortgager was married, but his wife did not join in the mortgage. Many other similar loans were made in opposition to the charter of the bank.

The judge said that there did not seem to have been the least inquiry into the propriety, honesty or legality of the methods used until after it was discovered that the bank had been ruined and that the defendants could not excuse imprudence or indifference by showing honesty of intention coupled with gross ignorance or inexperience, or coupled with an absorption of their time and attention in their private affairs. He also said the words of the charter meant that in investing in real estate the property should be worth at least double the amount of the sum invested and double all encumbrances, the word *above* signifying "in excess of" so that such real estate should be worth at least double the investment and double the encumbrances.

The court held that since the landed security was not worth twice the encumbrances and twice the whole investment, the entire investment was illegal.

The decision in this case was made on the basis of the interpretation of the intent of the charter; that is, the intent of the word *above*. According to the charter, the bank was supposed to insure itself against loss of any kind. In order to do that, no chances were to be taken. Thus, if investment was made in real estate the property was to be worth double the amount of the sum invested and double all encumbrances. With that margin there would not be much danger of loss.[1]

Case 2.—In Georgia, the fifth section of the Act of 1806 provided that it should not be lawful for "any person or persons, at any time or times, to build any bridge, or keep any ferry on the river Great Ogeechee, within five miles, either above or below the said bridge, which is hereby exclusively vested in the said Joseph Hill, his heirs and assigns."

The McLeods, who claimed under Joseph Hill, averred in their bill that the defendants kept a ferry, and proposed to erect a bridge on the Great Ogeechee, at Fort Argyle, within five miles of their bridge, erected under the grant to Hill, and sought an injunction. The question was: should the distance of five miles be measured in a straight line from the bridge of the complainants to the ferry of the defendants, at Fort Argyle, or should the line of measurement pursue the meanderings of the river? The plaintiffs contended that the measurement should be by a straight line and the defendant contended that it should be by the meandering of the stream. The river, in passing from Fort Argyle to Hill's Bridge, made a considerable curve, and the distance between those two points, in a direct line, was less than five miles, while the distance, if measured on the stream, was about ten miles.

The court said if the Legislature had stated only that it was illegal to build any bridge or keep any ferry within five miles of Hill's Bridge, it would have been clear that the distance was intended to be measured in a straight line. The Legislature stated, however, that it was not lawful to build any bridge or any ferry *on the Great Ogeechee River*, within five miles, either above or below Hill's Bridge and that, according to usage, speaking of distance on the earth from one place to another was understood to mean distance measured on the usual line of travel and of distance from the earth to a fixed star was understood to mean distance measured in a straight line.

The court held that the distance of five miles was to be measured on the course of the river.

The decision was made on the basis of the common meaning of *above* in the sense in which it was used; that is, usage determined its interpretation. In common parlance, *above*, used in connection with a stream, follows the meanderings of the stream.[3]

Case 3.—In Missouri, in 1920, the Landau Grocery Company brought action against Hart *et al.* and prayed judgment for damages of $500. The plaintiff agreed to buy one car of "one pound picker beans" from the Michigan Bean Jobbers Association. The memorandum of the sale read: "We confirm sale made to you this date by Ford and Doan. Quantity—One car pound pickers pea beans. Price—$2.63 per bu. Less freight at St. Louis. Above grade or no sale. Time of shipment: Prompt. Terms: Michigan Bean Jobbers Association rules and grading on beans to govern."

The Landau Grocery Company alleged that the defendants failed to perform the agreement on their part and refused to deliver the beans so purchased by the plaintiff, though the plaintiff was ready and willing to receive and pay for them.

The beans were sent out immediately by the defendants to the plaintiff who rejected them. The defendants sold them elsewhere and considered the contract as null, because of the statement "above grade or no sale" in the memorandum.

M. J. Hart, one of the defendants, testified that the term "above grade or no sale" was a trade term, understood in St. Louis, used in contracts when there was uncertainty as to the goods being dealt in, as where a car of beans is in transit, or where there may be a difference of opinion between the buyer and the seller as to the quality of the beans. He contended that the phrase meant that, if the beans shipped should not meet the grade specified, there was no sale, and both parties to the contract would be relieved.

"One pound picker," under the rules of the Michigan Bean Jobbers' Association, meant that there was one pound of bad beans, or dirt, or split beans to the bushel.

Judgment was rendered in favor of the defendants.

This decision was based on the specialized meaning of *above* in St. Louis, which had its own definite meaning there in regard to the beans, since it implied that the beans shipped should meet the grade specified, in order to make the contract valid.[3]

The cases cited here with reference to *above* illustrate two linguistic classifications: (*a*) The physical meaning; (*b*) The figurative meaning.

Both uses of *above* are customary in everyday speech. Case (2) belongs to classification (*a*); cases (1) and (3) belong to classification (*b*).

(*a*) In case (2), *above* was used in its physical sense—that is, I mean one thing is placed above another in its material relationship. If I place one block on top of another, the top block is *above* the bottom block. In case (2), *above* is employed in the physical sense, for it is concerned with material relationship, the distance of the bridge from the ferry. It was, however, not employed in the vertical sense; that is, the bridge was not to be placed five miles *above* the ferry in a vertical direction, but five miles up the river, the distance of five miles to be measured in a horizontal direction. In ordinary conversation we speak of one thing's being above another in that sense. A person will say, "You have to cross a bridge above this point," meaning at some distance in a horizontal direction. Case (2) also illustrates the customary use of *above* in measuring distances, showing that "five miles above the ferry" meant to follow the meandering of the river instead of measuring a straight line of five miles. This interpretation is true of all distances measured on roads or rivers. If I say, "Seven miles above this house you will find a church," I mean seven miles measured along the highway. That meaning is understood by all.

(*b*) The figurative sense of *above* is employed just as often as the physical one. Cases (1) and (3) illustrate this symbolical use.

In case (1), *above* takes on the meaning of "in excess of," or "more than," a signification often employed. One speaks of a man's holding office above five years, meaning more than five years. There is no place relationship here; the meaning is all mental.

Case (3) also illustrates a metaphorical meaning, which is also a common one. The beans were to be "above grade"; that is, they were to be superior to, surpassing others, in quality. This connotation is often used. A man may say of another, "His character is above reproach," meaning that his character is a superior one and cannot be censured.

Thus we see that the cases illustrate ordinary uses of *above*.

Across

The word *across* is defined according to: (1) Literal interpretation; (2) Interpretation based on intent; (3) Common meaning; (4) Specialized meaning.

Case 1.—There was an ordinance in the city of Chippewa Falls, Wisconsin, prohibiting railway companies from permitting any locomotive to stand or remain *across* any street or alley longer than five minutes—a period of time sufficient to couple and separate cars. On December 15, 1903, the Chicago, St. Paul, Minneapolis and Omaha Railway Company let one of its locomotives remain for about half an hour on Canal Street in such a way as not to obstruct public travel, yet so that the head of it reached slightly into the cross street, called A Street. Mr. Crowley, while lawfully using such streets for travel, riding on a load of wood drawn by a team of horses, in passing from A Street to and along Canal Street, was compelled to drive around the head of defendant's train. While he was doing so, exercising ordinary care, defendant permitted steam to escape from the locomotive, which frightened Crowley's horses, causing them to jump sideways, to tip over his load and thereby throw him to the ground, seriously injuring him. Crowley brought action for the violation of the ordinance and claimed damages of $2,500. The plaintiff was non-suited. The plaintiff then appealed to the Supreme Court.

It was held that the train was not *across* the street in any sense of the term, that the ordinance was not violated, and that the railway company was not liable for the noise made by the escape of steam, the noises being incident to the operation of railroads.

In interpreting the ordinance providing that trains should not be allowed to stand or remain *across* any street longer than a certain time, it was held that the ordinance was not violated where a train stood so that one end reached slightly into the street, but not in such a way as to obstruct public travel. The judgment appealed from was therefore affirmed.

The decision was based on the literal interpretation of *across*. Since the train was not entirely obstructing the intersecting street, the railway company was released from the charge.[1]

Case 2.—W. R. Felker sued the Texas and Pacific Railway Company, the St. Louis, San Francisco, and Texas Railway Company, and the St. Louis and San Francisco Railway Company to recover damages for delay in the transportation and for rough handling of a train of cattle from Iatan, Texas, to Henryetta, Indian Territory. The defendants pleaded that each road had limited its liability to its own line; that the cattle were poor and weak and not fit for shipment; that the damages, if any, to the cattle grew out of their weak and bad condition, rather than out of any negligence upon the part of defendants. A trial resulted in judgment against each of the defendants. They appealed.

The envelope containing the deposition of the witnesses, Smith and Warner, bore the following indorsement: "Received this package on the 4th day of November, 1904, from the hands of E. T. McDowell, the officer before whom they were taken, and forwarded the same on the 4th day of Nov., 1904, by due course of mail, as directed. R. H. Jenness, P. M., per Shick, postmaster at Okmulga, Indian Territory." A motion was duly made to quash the depositions, upon the ground that the postmaster's receipt was not in compliance with the Revised Statutes of 1895, and for the further reason that the officer before whom the answers were made had not written his name *across* the seal as required by the statutes. The only proposition submitted under the assignment calling in review the action of the court in refusing to quash the deposition was the sole question of the failure of the notary to write his name *across* the seal of the envelope.

The statute provided that an officer taking depositions should seal them in an envelope and should write his name *across* the seal. In this case the officer did not write his signature directly across the seal, but across the edge of the lap or cover forming the seal and on to the portion of the cover containing the mucilage which formed the seal.

The court said that the intent of the statute was sufficiently complied with.

The judgment of the district court was therefore reversed and the cause remanded for a new trial.

The decision was based on the interpretation of intent. It was not the intent of the lawmakers to require that the signature of the officer be written literally *across* the seal, if it were near enough to be considered across the seal.[2]

Case 3.—In Missouri, the Missouri Packett Company brought action against the Hannibal and St. Joseph Railroad Company to recover damages for injuries to their steamboats caused by the vessels' striking upon the piers of a railroad bridge across the Missouri River. The verdict and judgment was for the Missouri River Packett Company. Then the Hannibal and St. Joseph Railway Company appealed in 1887.

The Act of Congress of July 25, 1866, authorizing a bridge to be constructed across the Missouri River at the city of Kansas, required that there should be a distance of 160 feet between the piers of the bridge and that the distance should be obtained by measuring along a line between those piers drawn perpendicularly to the faces of the piers and to the current of the river. As such a line drawn between the piers of this railroad bridge measured only 153 feet and a fraction, instead of the required 160 feet, the Missouri River Packett Company contended that it was not a lawful structure within the meaning of the act.

The court said that unless the word *across* were qualified by some prefix, such as diagonally or obliquely, there was attached, in ordinary use, but one meaning, and that was a direction opposite to length. The judgment was therefore affirmed. The court held that the mere fact that the bridge had not been constructed as required by the statute rendered the railroad company liable, regardless of whether improper construction caused the accident.

The decision was based on the common meaning of *across*. If a person hears the word *across* he thinks of direction opposed to length.[3]

Case 4.—Evans was the owner of a certain mare, called Matilda, and one Wm. Ryley was the owner of a certain brown mare, then late the property of the defendant, Pratt. An agreement was made between Evans and Pratt for a race. The following memorandum was made:

"Pratt and Evans

"Thomas Holyoake, Esquire, umpire.

"Frederick Pratt bets Thomas Evans £100 to £25, P. P. (play or pay), Mr. Ryley's brown mare (late his property) beats Thomas Evans' mare Matilda, four miles across a country, thirteen stone each. To come off 1st March, 1841. The umpire's decision to be final.

"Thomas Evans.
"Frederick Pratt."

Mr. Holyoake decided that Mr. Evans' mare won. The defendant refused to pay the £100. Then the plaintiff brought action against defendant and proved by Mr. Holyoake, the umpire, that the race mentioned in the memorandum was run on the day appointed; that Mr. Ryley's brown mare came in first, but that he, the umpire, decided that the plaintiff's mare was the winner, as the former had passed through a gateway instead of going over the hedge, as required by the rules of steeple-chasing.

The judge said that the words "across a country," as used in an agreement for a steeple chase was not an expression of which the court could take judicial notice, but that the evidence showed that the words meant that the riders were to go over all obstructions and not avail themselves of open gates. The parties had agreed that the decision of the umpire should be final, and he decided in favor of the plaintiff.

The jury therefore returned the verdict for the plaintiff with damages of £100.

In this case, *across* took on a specialized meaning, one particularly known in steeple-chasing. To run a race "across country" meant to run a certain distance in the country and to go over all obstructions.[4]

When a person hears the word *across*, he immediately thinks "from side to side," "crosswise of or in a direction opposed to length." This meaning is the definite, limited meaning of *across*. The word, however, is not always used in this restricted sense, but, like many others, has an extension of meaning.

The cases given here illustrate *across* used in the limited sense and also in the enlarged sense. Therefore the linguistic classifications are: (*a*) Limited meaning; (b) Extended meaning. Cases (1) and (3) belong to classification (*a*); cases (2) and (4) to classification (*b*).

(*a*) In case (1), we find the limited meaning. The train was not actually crosswise of the street, obstructing the passage of vehicles, although its head reached slightly into the street. This occurrence is a common one in daily life. If a child happens to be standing at the edge of a path, which accommodates only one person at a time, and a man passes, the man does not say that the child is actually across the path, for he is not hindered from passing.

Case (3) shows that *across* means the perpendicular distance from side to side in a direction opposite to length. This usage is frequent in everyday speech. If I should tell a boy to measure the distance across a street, he would measure the perpendicular distance from side to side. It would never occur to him to make the measurement diagonally or obliquely unless I specified it.

(*b*) At times *across* has the extended meaning, as is shown in cases (2) and (4). In case (2), the name was not written directly across the seal, but on the edge of its cover. In daily speech this signature would be considered across the seal. If a person should draw a circle and ask a boy to write his name across the circle, the boy would not understand that his name was to be written directly through the circle. With his name, he might form a chord instead of a diameter and think he had written across the circle. Neither would the person who asked the boy to write across the circle expect him to write directly through the center with geometrical precision.

Case (4) shows another variation of the extended meaning of *across*. It is used in the expression "across the country," signifying a distance in any direction to be covered and including the hurdling of any obstacles along the way. This use of the word is found in steeplechasing. It is a term well understood by all who are interested in that sport. This meaning given to *across* is a specialized one.

After

The word *after* is defined according to: (1) Literal interpretation; (2) Interpretation based on intent; (3) Common meaning; (4) Context.

Case 1.—In Pennsylvania, John and Solomon Menges brought action, on October 6, 1868, against Henry Frick and others on an account for lumber furnished by the plaintiffs to the defendants. The question to be considered was whether the plaintiff's action was barred by the Statute of Limitations. The last item of timber in the account sued on was delivered on October 6, 1862, and the action was begun on October 6, 1868. The law provided that actions for accounts should be commenced and sued "within six years next after the cause of such actions or suit, and not after."

It was decided that the action was not barred by the Statute of Limitations.

The decision was based on the literal interpretation of *after*. The last item of timber was delivered on October 6, 1862. One year after that date would have taken the time to October 6, 1863; then six years after the cause would have taken it to October 6, 1868, which date would have still been within six years after the cause of action, the delivering of the timber.[1]

Case 2.—In Georgia, John Atwell died leaving a will in which he devised a negro slave to his daughter, Elinder, and directed that "after her death, if no lawful issue" the slave should be divided among his children. The question came up as to the meaning of the clause, "after her death, if no lawful issue." It was construed to mean at or immediately after the death of the daughter.

The decision was based on the interpretation of the intent of John Atwell. *After* took on the meaning of "at." It was not intended that the division should take place until the death of his daughter. Of course, it does not mean that the division should take place simultaneously with the death of the daughter, but as soon after as convenient.[2]

Case 3.—Edward King's will bequeathed, after the payment of debts and funeral expenses, certain things and certain amounts to different persons.

It was decided that the clause "after all my debts are paid," when used in a will where it is followed by a devise, indicated an intention that the lands devised should be subject to the debts.

The decision was based on the common meaning of *after*, which is "later than." The debts were to be paid first and then the property was to be distributed as Edward King devised.[3]

Case 4.—In Connecticut, Joshua Lyon, at the time of his death, owned an estate. He made his last will and testament on July 11, 1837, and died on the night following, October 1, 1841, leaving seven children and heirs at law, one of whom was Phebe Sands, one of the plantiffs. Another was John Lyon, the defendant.

The plaintiffs claimed to recover the demanded premises from John Lyon, who was to receive them according to the will, provided he should comply with certain conditions, which was the payment, in one year next after Joshua Lyon's decease, of $100 to each of a certain number of heirs.

October 2, 1842, fell on a Sunday. On Monday, October 3, Lyon tendered to the plaintiffs, as well as to the other heirs, $100, as requested in the will. All refused the money.

The court held that *after*, like the words "from," "succeeding," and "subsequent," in a devise of property to a beneficiary on condition that he shall pay to another a certain sum within one year "after" the testator's decease, or "from," "succeeding," or "subsequent to" his decease, where it is not expressly declared to be exclusive or inclusive, is susceptible of different significations, and is used in different senses, with an exclusive or inclusive meaning, according to the subject to which it is applied. The court further held that as the term would be deprived of some of its proper significations, if one invariable meaning were affixed to it in all cases, its true meaning, in any particular case, must be collected from its context and subject-matter, which are the only means by which the intention can be ascertained.

It was therefore decided that the defendant had, by the terms of the devise, a full year allowed him for paying the money; and therefore was not bound to pay it on the Saturday preceding the day on which the year expired.

From the context it was thought that Joshua Lyon wanted John Lyon to have the property. One interpretation would give him the property; the other would deprive him of it. The will was so construed as to prevent the latter interpretation. Lyon was given a year in which to pay a certain amount of money and since the year ended on Sunday the thing to do was to pay the sum on the Monday following.[4]

The word *after* has both a physical and figurative signification. The former meaning is "behind in place." I may say, for example, "I walked along the street and saw that one house after the other had a porch." The latter meaning, the figurative, is the meaning that gives the trouble in the law courts. Not a case could be found that turned on the meaning of *after* in its physical sense. All of the cases were concerned with time; that is, one thing happening subsequent to another. Thus, all the cases belong to the linguistic classification: (*a*) The figurative meaning.

In case (1), *after* has the meaning of later, with certain definite limitations shown by the context. The statement is "within six years next after the cause of such actions." Here *after* can be at any time before the expiration of the six years. In this case it is definite, in that the suit must begin within six years, but indefinite in that the suit may take place at any time within that period. This use is frequent. A man may say, "Within two weeks after May 1, I shall pay," meaning he will pay at some time later than May 1, but not more than two weeks later.

In case (3), *after*, in its figurative sense, has a certain definiteness about it, for the bequests were to be given to the person named in the will when the debts were paid. They were, of course, to be given subsequent to the paying of the debts. So it is with *after* in case (2). The money for the slave was to be divided among the children immediately following the death of the daughter. This meaning of *after* is common. If a mother is going out and is leaving her daughter home alone, the mother may say to the daughter, "After my departure, lock the door," meaning that the daughter shall lock the door immediately subsequent to her departure.

In case (4), we also see the figurative meaning of *after* as later in time. This use, too, has a certain definiteness, as in case (1), where the limitation was one year. Certain money was to be paid in one year next after the testator's death.

Against

The word *against* is defined according to: (1) Interpretation based on intent; (2) Interpretation suggested by fact; (3) Common meaning; (4) Specialized meaning; (5) Context.

Case 1.—At an election on November 4, 1884, the electors of Montgomery County, Kansas, voted upon a proposition to issue $50,000 in bonds, to be used in the building of a courthouse and jail. When the vote was counted the board of canvassers found that 2,683 votes had been cast in favor of the proposition, and 2,652 against it. Accordingly, the board declared that the proposition had been adopted. E. B. Clark, who was an elector of that county, applied to the judge of the district court for a temporary injunction restraining the county commissioners from issuing the bonds declared by them to have been voted.

The controversy arose over seventy-six ballots cast in two election precincts, which the plaintiff claimed should have been counted against the proposition, but which the election boards refused to count because of their informality. The rejected ballots bore at the bottom in printing, and underneath the names of the candidates for national, state, and county offices, the words "for the bonds." A pencil line had been drawn through those words and immediately beneath the words so marked was written in pencil the word "against." The order of the county commissioners, submitting the question to the electors of the county, provided that all those voting in favor of the proposition should write or print on their ballots the words "for the bonds," and those voting against the proposition should write or print on their ballots the words "against the bonds." If the rejected ballots had been counted as negative votes the proposition would have been defeated by a majority of forty-five votes.

The judge said that it was not imperative that an elector, in voting upon a proposition to vote bonds, should use the exact language prescribed in the order submitting the proposition and that any words of similar import which showed with a reasonable degree of certainty the intention of the voter were sufficient. He also said that the drawing of a pencil mark through the printed words which would make the vote affirmative showed that the voter did not wish his ballot to be recorded for the bonds and that the writing of the word *against* below the cancelled words showed he was voting against the bonds.

It was therefore held that the ballots were intended as negative votes.

The decision was based upon the interpretation of the intent of the voter. It was evident that the voters intended to vote against the issuing of bonds, or they would not have crossed out the words "for the bonds" and have written *against* below.[1]

Case 2.—The Leffler, Thiele and Company made the following contract with Lobsitz:

"For your services you are to receive $125 per month and 2½ per cent commissions on all accepted shipments up to $50,000; above $50,000 your commission is to be 5 per cent. Against the above we are to send a check for $50 each week to Mr. I. Lobsitz 1616 So. State St., Syracuse, N. Y. . . . We are also to pay your traveling expenses at the rate of about $6 per day while you are on the road."

The plaintiff worked from December 15, 1905, to September 7, 1907. The defendant sent the check for fifty dollars every week until June 1, 1907, and gave the notice of three months, as required by the contract to terminate it. The plaintiff sought to recover the fifty dollars per week commencing June 1 up to and including September 7, 1907, while the defendant sought to recover the amount claimed to have been overpaid on the contract.

Judgment was rendered in favor of the plaintiff, for it was decided that *against* in the phrase, "against such amount $50 was to be paid each week," meant "towards," and that the fifty dollars was for paying the salary and commissions already earned and not to be returned in part. In other words, it was decided that the plaintiff was to be paid at least fifty dollars per week for his salary and commissions.

In this case, the decision was based on the interpretation suggested by fact. The fact was that fifty dollars was sent each week to the wife. No company advances more than it thinks the employee will make, in the expectation that part of the money will be returned if the employee should not be successful. Since that amount was paid each week for a certain length of time and since there was a provision in the contract for a higher commission beyond a certain amount of work done, it was evident that the fifty dollars was to be a part of the whole, but not the whole or more than the whole. Thus *against* took on the meaning of "towards."[2]

Case 3.—In Indiana, in 1873, John C. Prather was indicted for assault and battery with intent to murder. The indictment charged that the defendant "in and upon one Ransom P. Baldwin did feloniously, purposely and with premeditated malice, make an *assault*, and then and there, *at* and *against* the said Ransom P. Baldwin did feloniously, purposely and with premeditated malice, shoot a certain pistol, then and there loaded with gunpowder and leaden ball, which he, the said John C. Prather, then and there had and held in his hand with intent," etc., "to kill," etc.

In 1875, the indictment was quashed, on motion of the appellee, and the State took exception. The sufficiency of the indictment was, therefore, the only question to consider.

The appellee insisted that the facts alleged, in describing the offence charged in the indictment, did not constitute an assault and battery, within the meaning of the statute defining that offense. He contended that the allegation that the appellee shot at and against the said Baldwin, etc., did not charge the "touching" necessary to make an assault and battery.

The court said that to push or run against a person implied, in common parlance, a coming in contact or in collision with the person so pushed or run against.

The court held that the indictment sufficiently charged an assault and battery and that the word *against*, as used in the indictment, would have to be taken in its usual acceptation in common language.

The decision was based on the common meaning of *against:* "coming in contact with."[3]

Case 4.—In Kentucky, in 1891, Malone was convicted under the General Statutes stating: "Whoever shall unlawfully take or detain any woman against her will, with intent to marry such woman, or have her married to another, or with intent to have carnal knowledge with her himself, or that another shall have such knowledge, shall be confined in the penitentiary not less than two nor more than seven years." The evidence showed that John Malone, between seven and eight o'clock at night, stealthily went into the room where Annie Durne, a girl between thirteen and fourteen years of age, was sleeping, and without waking her removed the bedclothes and exposed her person and his without awakening her. He, contending that he had been intoxicated and had got into the wrong room without knowing that the girl was there, appealed. It was necessary to show that the carnal knowledge was had against the will of the woman.

The court said that the appellant had certainly taken possession of the girl for the purpose of carnally knowing her; and although she was asleep, and therefore incapable of exercising her will in the matter, yet it was in law a detention or taking of her against her will.

The judgment was therefore affirmed.

The decision was based on the specialized meaning of *against* in the phrase "against her will"—that is, the meaning of it in law. The act certainly was not with her will. Since she was asleep and not capable of exercising the will, the act was against the will.[4]

Case 5.—In New York, in 1882, J. J. Hogan brought action, as administrator of Mary Ann Hogan, against Mary Curtin, administratrix of the will of Daniel Curtin, deceased, to procure a judgment establishing the right of the plaintiff, as administrator, to a legacy of $16,000, given to Mary Ann Curtin by the will of her father, Daniel Curtin. The fourth clause of the will was: "I give, devise and bequeath to my daughter, Mary Ann Curtin, the sum of $16,000 to be paid to her by my said executors upon her attaining the age of twenty-one years, with the consent of her mother and my said executors, and in case my said daughter should die unmarried, before attaining the age of twenty-one years, then the share hereinbefore bequeathed to her shall go to and belong to my said sons, James and Francis, share and share alike; and in the event of my said daughter, Mary Ann, marrying against the consent of my said executors and her said mother, then my will and desire is, that instead of the said sum of $16,000, hereinbefore bequeathed to her, she shall only receive from my said executors the sum of $5,000, in full, for her share of my estate."

Mary Ann married with the consent of the executors, but without the consent of her mother. The question was, whether the marriage, under the circumstances stated, was a breach of the following condition: "if the daughter should marry against the consent of my said executors and her mother," etc. The plaintiff contended that a marriage without the mother's consent was not a marriage against her consent.

The judge said that the testator evidently used the word *against* in the last sentence of the fourth clause as the correlative of "with" in the first sentence, for in the first sentence, he gave the legacy with consent and in the last he abridged it in case of her marriage against consent, using that word as the synonym of "without." He said it was also rendered clear by the language of the eighth clause, which provided for the maintenance of the daughter by the executors out of the proceeds of the real estate until twenty-one, and until she got married "with their consent and that of her mother, as hereinbefore stated."

The court held that Mary Ann's marriage without the consent of her mother was a breach of the condition and that she forfeited her right to the legacy, except for the $5,000.

The decision was based on the context. By reading the whole will it was possible to determine that *against* meant "without," a meaning made clear by the first part of the fourth clause and by the eighth clause.[5]

For *against* there are two linguistic classifications under which the illustrative cases fall; (*a*) The physical meaning; (*b*) The figurative meaning. Both uses are customary in everyday speech.

(*a*) Case (3) illustrates the physical meaning. The allegation that Prather shot at and against Baldwin shows *against* in its physical aspect. It has the meaning of actually coming in contact with; that is, one physical thing is in opposition to another. In this case one physical body was in opposition to another. This use of *against* is common. If a person hits a wall, he says, "I ran against the wall"; if a child runs into a man in playing, the man says, "The child ran against me."

(*b*) Cases (1), (2), (4), and (5) illustrate the figurative meaning. In case (1), *against*, which meant "against the bonds," did not mean physical opposition to the bonds, but a mental opposition to them. This use is frequent. During any political campaign, we hear such statements as "Mr. Smith is against Jones," meaning that Mr. Smith will not vote for Jones, for he thinks some one else should have the office.

Case (2) shows another variation of the figurative meaning. It takes on the meaning of "towards." A certain salary plus a commission was to be paid to Lobsitz. Then the contract read: "Against the above we are to send $50 each week to Mrs. I. Lobsitz." What could *against* mean except "towards"? This interpretation is taken over from its physical meaning. To run against the wall, a person runs towards the wall and keeps running towards it until he hits it. This idea of "towards" is also used in daily speech, especially between merchants and their customers. If a customer owes a merchant $560 and pays him $360, the merchant often says, "against the $560, I shall credit you with $360," meaning "towards" the $560 originally owed.

Cases (4) and (5) show still another variation of the figurative meaning. In case (4), the man takes advantage of the girl while she is asleep and not able to exercise her will. There is no active opposition; neither is there any consent. It is naturally supposed that the girl would have objected if she had been conscious, especially since the case was brought against the man. This idea of *against* is shown in the statement often heard, "If you are not for me, you are against me." That is, if the person does not declare himself for a particular individual or cause, his silence puts him on the other side. Of course, the fact that the girl was asleep makes the case slightly different. At the same time, there was no assertion for the act, and there could be none against it, because of the girl's unconsciousness. In ordinary life when every person is conscious of what he is doing, similar occasions arise. If a topic is being discussed and it is proposed to adopt a certain policy, to which every one agrees except one man, it is thought by all that he is opposed to the act, although he does not assert himself against it. This non-assertion is implied opposition in a figurative sense.

Case (5) shows a variation of the implied opposition in a figurative sense. The girl married with the consent of the executors, but without the consent of the mother. Here *against* took on the meaning of "without." This usage is frequent among many persons, especially among minors and those in subordinate positions. If both father and mother object to a young man, with whom their daughter associates and if the mother says to the daughter, "You must not marry James against your father's consent, for you will be disinherited," should she marry James without her father's consent she would be disinherited just the same. The father would be opposed to the marriage and he would consider his daughter marrying against his consent when she failed to get it before she entered matrimony. There would be no physical opposition, but there would be a great deal of mental opposition.

Thus we see that the courts consider the uses of *against* in common conversation.

Along

The word *along* is defined according to: (1) Literal interpretation; (2) Interpretation based on intent; (3) Interpretation suggested by fact; (4) Common meaning; (5) Technical meaning; (6) Dictionary meaning; (7) Etymology; (8) Context; (9) Circumstances.

Case 1.—In Massachusetts, in 1899, action was brought by W. H. Quigley against A. B. Clough to recover damages for personal injuries received from a barbed-wire fence, running diagonally across a yard from the house to the corner of the street. The Statutes of 1884 prohibited the construction of barbed-wire fences along a sidewalk upon a public street. That prohibition was the basis of Quigley's action. The court decided in favor of Clough. The plaintiff took exception, but the exception was over-ruled.

The decision was based on the literal interpretation of *along*. The barbed-wire fence was not "by the length" of the street, but diagonally across the yard from the house to the corner of the street.[1]

Case 2.—In New York, in 1892, Alice Burt and others brought action against the Lima and Honeoye Falls Railroad Company to enjoin the defendant from constructing its road along a highway. The defendant moved to dissolve the injunction according to the Laws of 1890, which permitted a railroad company to construct its road "across, along, or upon" any highway.

The defendant proposed to construct and operate a steam locomotive railroad from Lima to Honeoye Falls, a distance of four miles, and the road was to be operated in the highway between the two villages. The plaintiffs, owners of abutting land, objected.

The court said that the law permitting a railroad company to construct its road "across, along, or upon" any highway meant only a casual or incidental occupation and use of the highway and did not authorize a company to build its entire railway along the highway.

The motion of the defendant was therefore denied.

The decision was based on the interpretation of the intent of *along* in the law. It was not thought that the Legislature would give a railroad company the right to lay the whole length of its tracks in a highway, but that the Legislature could grant that privilege for a short distance, if necessary.[2]

Case 3.—In Maine, in 1895, Jairus Martin brought action against the Grand Trunk Railway of Canada to recover damages for an injury to his wood and timber caused by fire from locomotive sparks. The declaration in his writ contained no averment of negligence on the part of the defendant but was based on the Revised Statutes, which read as follows: "When a building or other property is injured by fire communicated by a locomotive engine, the corporation using it has an insurable interest in the property along the route for which it is responsible, and may procure insurance thereon." The defendant filed a general demurrer to the declaration, which was over-ruled. The counsel for the defendant agreed that the declaration failed to allege that the property injured was situated "along the route" of the railway, as required by the law, and that the railway should not be held responsible.

The court said that the property should be deemed "along the route" if it were so near the railroad as to be exposed to the danger of fire from the engine and that it was alleged that the fire was in fact communicated by the defendant's engine to the plaintiff's land, and that the growth of wood thereon was in fact greatly injured by burning.

The court held that the defendant's responsibility was limited to property "along the route" and that it was to be deemed "along the route" if it was so near the railroad as to be exposed to the danger of fire from the engine.

In this case the decision was based on an interpretation suggested by fact. Here *along* took on the meaning of "as in the vicinity of," for the fact was that the timber of Mr. Martin was damaged by a spark from the engine, although the timber did not border directly on the railroad. It was only just that the plaintiff should recover as much as a man whose timber was adjacent to the railroad would.[3]

Case 4.—In New Hampshire, in 1920, Alvah Downes was indicted for operating an automobile in the business of transporting passengers for hire along a regular route contrary to the Laws of 1919.

Section 1 of the law read: "Every person, form or corporation operating any motor vehicle other than a street car upon any public street or way in the business of transporting passengers for hire, and receiving and discharging passengers along a regular route over which the vehicle is operated, is hereby declared to be a common carrier and as such shall be subject to the provisions of this act so far as applicable thereto."

Downes received and discharged passengers only at the termini of the route. The state claimed that he received and discharged passengers "along a regular route upon which the vehicle was operated" within the meaning of the statute. The question presented was to determine whether the defendant's business was within Section 1.

The court said that Downes did not receive or discharge passengers along the route between termini as street cars do and thus was not guilty of receiving or discharging passengers along a regular route within the meaning of the act.

Downes was therefore discharged.

The decision was based on the common meaning of *along*. Because he did not receive and discharge passengers at any point on the road over which he drove, but at the ends of it, Downes was not considered as violating the law. When a person speaks of running along a road, he means in ordinary language passing over the road.[4]

Case 5.—In New Jersey, in 1877, an action of ejectment was brought to recover a small strip of land, which was one-half of what had been a public street, in front of a lot which Salter had conveyed to a certain person, and which lot had come, by divers mesne conveyances, to Jane and Richard Jonas. The deed described the premises as running thence along the northerly line of Johnson Street south, etc., and thence north, twenty-three degrees and forty minutes west, fifty feet, to a stake in the said easterly line of Rowland Street, etc.

After Rowland Street had been used for some time, it became useless, in consequence of another street's having been opened, and the defendants proceeded, thereupon, to take in and enclose the land to the middle line of the street in front of the lot.

The judge said that the established inference of law was that a conveyance of land, bounded on a public highway, carried with it the fee to the center of the road, as part and parcel of the grant.

The court held that the defendant's deed covered the land in the street which was in dispute as there were no express words of exclusion.

The decision in this case was based on the technical meaning of *along* used in deeds to land bordering on highways, roads, or streets. In such cases *along* does not mean "by the side of"; but "to the center" of the highway, road or street.[5]

Case 6.—In Virginia, in 1892, the Postal Telegraph Cable Company brought action to acquire a right of way along and upon the right of way of the Norfolk and Western Railroad Company. The statute provided that telegraph companies might construct their lines "along and parallel to any of the railroads in the state." The plaintiffs insisted that the law gave them the right to go upon the railroad land, which had been acquired for railroad purposes; the defendants contended that the telegraph company had no right to go upon their land, but only alongside their right of way, and not on it.

The court said that the lexicographer's definition of *along* is" by the length of," as distinguished from "across" and that it was not ambiguous.

The decision was therefore rendered in favor of the defendants.

The decision in this case was based on the dictionary definition of *along:* "by the length of."[6]

Case 7.—An action was brought in 1853 by Mr. Pratt against the Atlantic and St. Lawrence Railroad Company to recover money for damages done to growing timber by fire communicated from the defendant's locomotive engine. The question was, whether or not a railroad corporation was answerable for damages occasioned by fire communicated by their locomotive engines to wood and timber growing along the route of their road.

The suit was sought to be maintained under the Statute of 1842, which provided that "when any injury is done to a building or other property, of any person or corporation, by fire, communicated by a locomotive engine of any railroad corporation, the said corporation shall be held responsible in damages to the person or corporation so injured." The same section provided that railroads should have an insurable interest in the property for which they may be so held responsible, in damages, along the route, and might procure insurance thereon in their own behalf.

The court pointed out that the railroad company, under the provision, was not liable for an injury to property, in which it had no insurable interest; and that it only had such interest in property that lay along its route. He then referred to Webster's Dictionary and found under the word *along* the following: "Sax. *and-lang* or *ond-lang;* Fr. *an-long*, *le-long*. See Long. The Saxons always prefixed *and* or *ond*, and the sense seems to be by the length, or opposite the length, or in the direction of the length." The first definition he found was, "By the length; lengthwise; in a line with the length; as the troops marched along the bank of the river, or along the highway." He then said that the words "along the route" would describe buildings near and adjacent to the route of the railroad, so as to be exposed to the danger of fire from engines, but without limiting or defining the distance.

Judgment was rendered in favor of the plaintiff.

The decision was based on the etymology of *along* as found in the dictionary. It is derived from the Anglo-Saxon *and*, or *ond* plus *lang* or *long*, meaning "long."[7]

Case 8.—In Connecticut, Isaac Church brought an action against Silas Meeker for trespass, for entering upon land on the shore of Long Island Sound, and for taking and carrying away seaweed from it. The plaintiff had to prove what land belonged to him in order to see if the defendant trespassed.

The plaintiff referred to a deed of 1828 which gave the boundaries of "a certain piece of sedge-flat in said Norwalk, at the great marsh, so called," which was also described as being "a narrow strip of land lying near the spreading place, so called, on said marsh, extending along the seashore about 200 rods to the land of Daniel Betts at the bluff, or near thereto."

First the definitions of sedge-flat and shore were found: a *sedge-flat* being "a tract of land below high water mark" and *a shore*, according to Bouvier's Law Dictionary, being "that space of land on the borders of the sea which is alternately covered and left dry by the rising and falling of the tide—or that space between high and low water mark."

The court said that for quantity of land, *along* meant "by," "on," or "over," according to the context, and that here it meant "on."

The highway was the place from which the defendant took the sedge. The judge said that the east line of the highway should be located at high water mark, where the sedge-flat was described as ending.

The defendant took sedge that had been piled up longer than twenty-four hours. It had to be removed within that time. The defendant therefore was held not liable.

The decision was based on the subject matter of the deed. The sedge-flat was also described as a strip of land lying along the shore. After the definitions of sedge-flat and shore were considered, it was found that the two terms referred to the same land. Thus *along the shore* took on the meaning of "on the shore."[8]

Case 9.—In Iowa, in 1902, a case arose concerning the meaning of the Code of 1897, which enacted that the board of supervisors of any county should have power, on its own motion, to change and establish a highway along a stream, when it can avoid bridging such stream. Stahr and others brought certiorari proceedings to determine the legality of the action of the board in vacating a highway and establishing another on its own motion. The vacated highway crossed a deep ravine which required a bridge about eighty feet in length and the shifting soil required an occasional lengthening of the bridge and constant attention to keep it in a safe condition for public travel. The newly established road was fifty rods north of the bridge and at the east section line at a still greater distance from it.

The judge said that the purpose of the statute was to avoid expensive bridging and thus it was evident that if a highway could not be established close to a stream to avoid that difficulty, it could be established within a reasonable distance of it (if in the vicinity of the stream), and at the same time be within the spirit of the statute.

The court held that the statute did not require the road to be constructed on the immediate bank of the stream, but within a reasonable distance.

The decision was based on the circumstances. The former road had been expensive because of the shifting soil which made the lengthening of the bridge necessary at times in order to insure safety to the travelers over the road. Thus the meaning of the word *along* was extended to express a distance of fifty feet and more than fifty feet in a few places.[9]

There are for *along* two linguistic classifications: (*a*) Restricted meaning—"by the length of"; (*b*) Extended meaning—signifying "by the length of."

(*a*) Cases (1), (2), (4), and (6) show *along* with its restricted meaning, "by the length of." In case (1), Clough was not convicted because of the limited sense given to *along* in the law concerning barbed-wire fences. It was used in its original sense "by the length of." This meaning is the one that is usually suggested when a person mentions the word alone. If a man says, "Put a hedge along the yard," he means, put a hedge by the length of the yard at its outer edge, and not diagonally across, or in any other direction.

Case (2) also shows *along* with its restricted meaning "by the length of." Therefore, the railroad company was not allowed to operate a steam locomotive in the highway for the distance of four miles. If a person says the railroad runs along the highway, he does not mean that it is on the highway, but parallel to it, or by the length of it.

In case (4), Downes did not receive and discharge passengers by the length of the road as street cars do; therefore he was freed. In ordinary conversation we speak of street cars taking on passengers along the street, meaning by the side of the street, or by the length of it.

Case (6) also shows *along* with the same meaning. "Along and parallel to any of the railroads in the state" has the meaning of "by the length of" the railroad property, a very common usage. If a farmer wants to put a fence around his field, which borders on railroad property, he will order the fence to be put "along" the railroad.

(*b*) The word *along* does not always mean definitely "by the length of"; oftentimes it has an extension of meaning as seen in cases (3), (5), (7), (8), and (9). In cases (3) and (7) *along* does not apply only to the land that is adjacent to the railroad, but to all land imperilled by fire from the engine, regardless of the distance. It thus has the meaning of "in the vicinity of." It is often used in this manner. If a farmer says, "Cut down the weeds along the garden fence," he means cut down all the weeds in the vicinity of the garden fence, and not only those adjacent to the fence.

Case (5) shows that *along* means "to the middle of the street." It has the meaning: "by the length of" plus half the street itself. This meaning is understood by many persons, especially by those owning property adjacent to a highway, street, etc. The land does not stop at the side of the road, or by the length of the road, but extends to the center. This signification is given to the word in law.

In case (8) *along* means "on." "Along the seashore" is "on the seashore." Of course, the phrase "on the seashore" includes reference to the seashore itself. *Along* implies an extension from the edge of the seashore over the whole seashore, a sense in which *along* is frequently used. If a person says, "I was driving along the road," he means he was driving on the road and not to the right or left of the road.

Case (9) extends the meaning of the word *along* to express a distance of fifty feet beyond the stream in places in order to insure safety and avoid expense. This interpretation shows *along* again taking on the meaning of "in the vicinity of." This use of the word is customary. If a boy sets traps for animals at different places near a stream, he says that they are set along the stream, although they are not at the edge of the stream.

Alongside

The word *alongside* is defined according to: (1) Dictionary.

Case 1.—In Kansas, in 1923, action was brought by the Board of County Commissioners of Mitchell County against the City of Beloit to recover one-half the cost of a hard-surfaced road. The plaintiff recovered and the defendant appealed.

The road was a quarter of a mile in length constructed along the boundary of Beloit. The city opposed the construction and notified the county commissioners that it would not be liable for any part of the cost incurred.

The county proceeded to build the road under the Laws of 1921, which provided that "When a benefit district hard-surfaced road is constructed alongside the corporate limits of any city, the city shall pay fifty per cent of the cost of the construction thereof," etc.

The court said that Webster's Dictionary defined *alongside* as "along or by the side."

Judgment was therefore affirmed.

The decision was based on the dictionary definition of *alongside:* "along or by the side."[1]

The preposition *alongside* has not given the law courts much trouble. The linguistic classification for the illustrative case given here is: (*a*) Definite meaning.

In this case *alongside* has the definite meaning of "along or by the side of," since the road was constructed along or adjacent to the boundary of the city. The road was not at variable distances from the city limits, but was next to them all the way. This use of *alongside* is common. If a man says to a boatman, "Bring the boat alongside the rock," he means by the side of the rock.

Among

The word *among* is defined according to: (1) Literal interpretation; (2) Common meaning.

Case 1.—In Alabama, in 1917, James Word brought action against the Dwight Manufacturing Company for personal injuries caused by electricity. Judgment was rendered in favor of the plaintiff and the defendant appealed.

One of the courts charged that the company negligently allowed its dangerous wire "to sag down among the wires of the telephone company." The company contended that *among* meant "in the midst of" or "mingled with" and that the allegation was not supported by proof that the wire sagged down to twelve inches or less above the telephone wires.

Judgment was therefore reversed and the cause remanded.

This decision was based on the literal interpretation of *among*. Because the wire which caused the injury was not mingled with the wires of the telephone company, the decision of the lower court was set aside.[1]

Case 2.—In Rhode Island, in 1898, W. H. Holder and others applied for an opinion as to the construction of a will. The testatrix had directed her executor, as soon as practicable after her death, to sell certain real estate and, after payment of expenses of sale, to distribute the remaining proceeds, as follows: "Two-fifths thereof to my cousin, Mrs. Mary A. Holder; the balance to be divided equally among my cousin George Stone and his wife, Mary Stone, and my friend, Fannie Northup."

The judge said that the three-fifths of the proceeds of the real estate constituting the balance after payment to Mrs. Holder were taken in equal shares by the legatees named, to wit, George Stone, Mary Stone, his wife, and Fannie Northup, according to the use of *among*.

The court held that where a will directs a balance of testator's estate "to be divided equally among" certain legatees, such balance is to be taken in equal shares by such legatees.

The decision was based on the common meaning of *among*, implying that each person concerned should have an equal share.[2]

The linguistic classifications for *among* are: (*a*) Physical meaning; (*b*) Figurative meaning.

(*a*) Case (1) illustrates the physical meaning of *among*. The fatal wire was not in the midst of and mingled with the wires of the telephone company; that is, the wire was not in the physical presence of the wires of the telephone company. Commonly, we hear such statements as, "The apple was among the oranges." The apple was surrounded by oranges, in the midst of them, having their contact.

(*b*) The figurative meaning of *among*, derived from its physical meaning, is shown in case (2). This figurative meaning is usually employed in expressing a relation of dispersion and distribution. It is also usually followed by a plural or collective noun. Wills offer a good example of this use of the word, as shown in the case given here. The money was to be divided into three equal parts, one each for George Stone, Mary Stone, and Fannie Northup. If a man has twenty dollars which he is going to divide equally among the children, he will say, "Divide the money equally among the children," meaning that he wants each child to have four dollars.

Thus, it is evident that it is the everyday use of *among* with which the court has to deal. (See *between*.)

Around

The word *around* is defined according to: (1) Common meaning.

Case 1.—In 1915, the First National Bank of Canyon, Texas, brought action against H. H. Hawkins to foreclose a chattel mortgage on 1,000 head of grown sheep and 700 head of spring lambs, all branded O around the hip bone and located about sixteen miles west from Hereford on a place known as the Bob Mount Place. The First National Bank sued out a writ of sequestration, which was placed in the hands of the sheriff of Deaf Smith County, who executed the writ on November 22, 1913, by sequestrating as the property of H. H. Hawkins:

"520 ewe sheep, branded O, paint brand on either hip or side, each valued at $2.00 per head, or a total of $1,040.00; also 364 ewe sheep branded O paint brand, on either right hip or side, each valued by me at $2.00 per head, or a total of $728.00; . . . The total value of all property levied on is $2,662.00."

Hawkins sought to quash the return of the sheriff on the writ of sequestration because the sheep were not branded in the manner called for in the mortgage. The chattel mortgage described the sheep as all branded "O around the hip bone," while the sheriff's return on the writ of sequestration recited a levy upon certain sheep branded " 'O' with a paint brand on either hip or side." Hawkins admitted that the right sheep were seized, but insisted that the brand described in the mortgage was a circle around the hip bone. The First National Bank, on the other hand, contended that the brand did not necessarily encircle the hip bone, for the meaning of *around* was "near" or "in the neighborhood of."

The court therefore held that, as Hawkins did not claim the wrong sheep had been levied upon, the writ could not be quashed on the ground that there was a variance between the mortgage and the return, for the term *around* might be construed to mean "in the vicinity of the hip bone" instead of encircling it.

The decision was based on the common meaning of *around:* "in the neighborhood of."[1]

When a person hears the word *around* he immediately thinks of "encircling." Our idea of *round* is derived from the image of a circle. The word, however, very often has an extended meaning as in the case given here. The linguistic classification for this case is: (*a*) The extended meaning of *around* in its definite physical sense. We find the use of *around* as "near," or "in the vicinity of," a common meaning in ordinary speech. One often hears, "He lives around Fourth Street," meaning he lives near Fourth Street. If a person is hunting something, he says, "I know it is around this place somewhere," meaning the object being looked for is near.

At

The word *at* is defined according to: (1) Literal interpretation; (2) Interpretation based on intent; (3) Interpretation suggested by fact; (4) Common meaning; (5) Specialized meaning; (6) Technical meaning; (7) Dictionary meaning; (8) Context; (9) Circumstances.

Case 1.—In 1833, in Yorkshire, England, a case was brought by Vaux against a clergyman named Vollans for willfully absenting himself from his benefice, without license or exemption. One calendar month before the commencement of an action for penalties against a clergyman for non-residence, a notice in writing of the intended writ and cause of action was delivered to the bishop's deputy registrar at his own house, and carried by him the next morning to the registry office, and there left. Vollans held that this act was not sufficient to satisfy the statute, which required such notice to be delivered to the bishop of the diocese, by leaving the same "at the registry" of his diocese.

It was decided that, according to the statute, the notice should have been left *at* the registry of the bishop's diocese.

The decision was based on the literal interpretation of *at* in the law. Practically speaking, the notice was left at the registry of the bishop's diocese, for the bishop's deputy saw that it reached the registry the next morning, but it had not actually been left there.[1]

Case 2.—In 1877, Catharine Stewart brought an action of ejectment to recover a small triangular strip of land, the title to which depended upon the location of a disputed boundary line. She claimed that it began at or near the north side of a buttonwood tree; the defendant, Patrick, claimed that it began at the center of the tree. The deed read: "Beginning at or near a tree at the westerly corner of said lot . . ." Patrick contended that the tree had grown during the forty years since the deed had been made.

The court said that a conveyance of land describing its boundaries as beginning *at* a certain tree did not necessarily fix the point at the center of the tree, but that the deed might be interpreted in conformity with the practical effect given it by the parties; thus the description in the deed was sufficiently accurate for all practical purposes and the line located at the outer surface of the tree was not inconsistent with the terms of the deed.

The decision was therefore in favor of the plaintiff.

The decision was based on the interpretation of the intent of the party who made the deed. The party did not intend to fix definitely the boundary at the center of the small tree, but somewhere in its vicinity.[2]

Case 3.—In 1861, Mason, an owner of land on Bridge Street in Brooklyn, brought action to restrain the Brooklyn City & N. R.

Company from proceeding to construct their road through the street. He alleged that the construction and use of the railroad were not authorized by law and would be specifically injurious to him as an owner of adjacent property.

According to the act of 1854, if the railroad began and ended within the city, the common council were forbidden to give assent to its construction or use without the sanction of the adjacent owners; they could assent, however, if the railroad did not terminate within the city.

The articles of association of the defendants stated that the subscribers associated themselves together "to form a company for the purpose of constructing a railway in the counties of Kings and Queens." The third article stated the object of the company to be "to construct a railroad with its appurtenances, to commence in the city of Brooklyn at some convenient point, and to terminate at Newtown, Queens County; the railroad to be located in Kings and Queens Counties, its length to be about twenty-five miles."

The plaintiff urged that certain acts of the defendants showed that the road which they were organized to build was in reality to begin and end within the city of Brooklyn, or that they had confined themselves to such a road by the location which they had made of their route, and had no right to construct any other. He also exhibited a map which they had filed, showing the road between two points in Brooklyn but not reaching the boundary of the city.

The judge said that the map could not be of the road they chartered to construct, but only a portion of it, for if the road ended in Brooklyn, it could not be in Kings and Queens Counties, according to the charter. He also said it had to go into Newtown, for if it were terminated at the limit or boundary of Newtown (which was also the boundary of Brooklyn), the road would be restricted wholly to that city and Queens County would be eliminated.

Judgment was therefore rendered in favor of the defendant.

The decision was based on the interpretation suggested by fact; *at* took on the meaning of "in" or "within." According to the charter the railroad had to end within Newtown, as Newtown was on the boundary line of Brooklyn. Thus "at Newtown" meant "in Newtown." If it did not end in Newtown the railroad would not enter Queens County at all.[3]

Case 4.—In 1838, at Little Rock, Arkansas, John Graham was convicted and fined for playing faro and for winning money. He brought a writ of error concerning the validity of the indictment, the legality of the judgment, and the jurisdiction of the city court. One of the questions involved the place. Graham contended that the indictment should have been "in" or "within" instead of *at* the city of Little Rock.

The judge said that the word *at* in common parlance was frequently used to note the situation or place where a person or thing was, or where something happened. To say, for example, that a person resided *at Washington City*, or *at New Orleans*, was equivalent in each instance to stating that the person spoken of resided "in" the place named. The word *at* was used by the Legislature to convey the same idea, he explained, when they said the Superior Court should be holden "at Little Rock, the seat of government"; a phrase illustrating the fact that *at* and "in" were often used as synonyms in the laws as well as in ordinary language.

It was decided that the indictment was good and valid.

The decision was based on the common meaning of *at*, which often takes on the meaning of "in."[4]

Case 5.—In Illinois, in 1926, Sam Washington was convicted of murder and his punishment was fixed at death. He appealed, contending that the verdict which fixed his punishment "at death" was so uncertain and indefinite that it did not authorize the court to enter a judgment directing that his life be taken. He contended that *at* meant "near to" or "in proximity to" and that, when punishment was fixed at death, any punishment provided by law except the actual taking of human life was meant.

The judge said that when one spoke of a point in space, *at* meant "near," "in proximity to," or "in the vicinity of"; but when one spoke of time, *at* meant "upon the stroke of" and when *at* was used in speaking of relations it meant "in a state or condition of." When a person, for example, says the sun rose at 5:22 a.m., he means it rose on that instant, and not near that time; or when a person says that a nation is at war he does not mean that conditions exist which may lead to war, but that a state of war then exists. Thus the judge concluded that when punishment was fixed at death the convicted person would be dead when the punishment had been inflicted and that the former verdict was in proper form.

Judgment was therefore affirmed.

The decision was based on a specialized meaning of *at*, used in the phrase "at death" in regard to punishment. In this case death and punishment take place simultaneously.[5]

Case 6.—In Alabama, Jasper Christian, convicted of assault with intent to murder, appealed.

Will Riley with six other men went to Christian's house at midnight. Three of the men went to the house and asked if Jack Truitt were there. Christian told them he was not and that he did not know where they could find him. They asked Christian to go down the road, but he refused. Then they told him they were going to search his house. He would not allow them that privilege unless they showed a search warrant, which they did not have. Christian barred the door and took down his gun. The seven men surrounded the house, some of them forced open the door and Will Riley was in the act of entering with a gun in his hands, raised in a shooting position, when Christian shot him in the hip.

The court said that in law a man's house was regarded as his castle—his place of refuge—and from it he did not have to retreat and that if an assailant violated the sanctity of another's dwelling by following him to it and pressed upon him, the assailed, being in his own house, was regarded as "at the wall" and was justified in using such force as was necessary to repel the assailant and to defend himself and family, even to the taking of life.

Judgment was therefore reversed in favor of Christian.

The decision was based on the technical meaning of "at the wall." In law *at* has its own significance in special cases.[6]

Case .7—On March 7, 1895, Scott O'Connor applied to Charles Nadel for a loan of $5,000. He gave Nadel mortgage over his land, "known as the town property of the Attalla Iron and Steel Company, situated at Attalla, Etowah County, Alabama."

O'Connor refused to pay the money when Nadel demanded it. He said that Nadel should not get the property outside of Attalla, for *at* meant "in."

The judge said that from the description of the property it was plain that the property mortgaged was not property belonging to the Attalla Iron and Steel Company, but property that once belonged to that company and merely known by that name afterwards. He also said that, according to Webster's Dictionary, the preposition *at* denoted primarily "nearness, presence, or direction toward"; and that thus a mortgage on property "known as the town property of said Attalla Iron and Steel Company at Attalla" was not necessarily limited to property in this town, but might also include neighboring property.

Therefore the decision was rendered in favor of Nadel.

The decision was based on the dictionary definition of *at:* "near."[7]

Case 8.—In New York, in 1882, David Lee brought a case against Ann Lee over the title of a deed. David Lee held that the title of the grantee to the portion of the road lying in front of the premises conveyed was not free from doubt. His contention was that the established law, in relation to country lands, that the owner of lands abutting on a highway owned to the center of the highway and that in conveying said land the owner intended to convey his interest in the road, applied to this case unless it could be rebutted by a description showing a decided intention on the grantor's part to exclude the road from the conveyance. The description was as follows: "Beginning on the east side of the Bloomingdale road at the southwesterly corner of lot No. 2, and running thence along the southern boundary of the same south fifty-seven degrees, east nine chains and twelve links to Low Benson's land . . . to the Bloomingdale road aforesaid, thence along the said road five chains to the place of beginning. . . ."

The judge said that it was a well-settled rule that when a boundary of land was described as beginning *at* a road, without qualifying words, the boundary was the center of the road, and not the side thereof, but that in this case the east side of Bloomingdale road at the southwesterly corner of lot No. 2 was made the monument of the beginning and then the actual distance by chains and links to Low Benson's land was another monument and that the measurement was finally taken back to the Bloomingdale road.

The decision was therefore rendered in favor of David Lee.

The decision was based on the context, which contained exclusive terms. If the description had read: "Beginning at the Bloomingdale road at the southwesterly corner of lot No. 2," the title would have taken in one-half the road. The phrase "on the east side of Bloomingdale road," however, excluded it.[8]

Case 9.—In Tennessee, Beller conveyed to the Knoxville, C. G. and L. Ry. Company, upon consideration of the benefits expected from the building of a road through his farm, a right of way over his premises upon condition that the road run at the back of his garden. The question arose, whether the road should be constructed within or without the garden.

The court said that the provision for the construction of a road "at the back of the garden," in the absence of anything else, might imply (considering that *at* was more generally used to mean "within" than "without") that it was to be constructed within the garden, but that circumstances should be considered, for it might also mean without and back of the garden.

In this case, the farm contained more than 300 acres. The garden was immediately behind the dwelling and was about 100 feet square. The land owner was anxious to have the road located over his premises and to induce the abandonment of a rival line some distance away. A preliminary survey was made and it went through the garden, near his residence. He then refused to sign the deed for the right of way unless the words "at the back of the garden" were inserted.

It was decided that the road should not run within the garden, but back of it and entirely without (without being here equivalent to outside of).

The decision was not based on the phrase "at the back of the garden" alone, but on all surrounding circumstances; especially the fact that the landowner refused to sign the deed unless the words "at the back of the garden" were inserted. Before he demanded the insertion of the phrase a survey had been made which went through the garden. That being the case, it is evident that the words "at the back of the garden" were inserted for some purpose. Thus *at* took on the meaning of "without."[9]

Ordinarily the word *at* has an indefinite sense. It does not signify to one's mind a particular spot and no other. The word, however, is not always indefinite in location, for sometimes it takes on a very precise meaning, pointing out one particular place or thing. Thus the two linguistic classifications under which the illustrative cases fall are: (*a*) The indefinite meaning; (*b*) The definite meaning. Cases (2) and (7) belong to classification (*a*); cases (1), (3), (4), (5), (6), (8), and (9) to classification (*b*).

(*a*) In case (2), *at* does not signify the center of the tree as the definite spot of beginning the boundary, but has its usual meaning of "near," and the fact that the tree had grown a few inches during the intervening forty years did not alter the sense. The use of *at* as shown in this case is common. One says, "I shall meet you at the old oak tree," meaning near the tree, not on any definite spot. Case (7) shows the same meaning of *at*, for here *at* Attalla means "near" Attalla and not "in" it. If there is a cotton gin near a small town, by the name of Jonesville, the farmer will say, "I am going to take my cotton to the gin at Jonesville." The gin does not have to be inside the town limits to justify the farmer's use of *at*.

(*b*) The definite meaning of *at* is illustrated in case (1), in which the notice had to be delivered *at* the registry of the bishop and not at the house which belonged to the bishop's deputy registrar. Thus, *at* may be applied to one specific place. If a girl asks a boy to leave her books at the library, she means the library, and not any building near the library.

Case (3) shows *at* taking on the meaning of "within," since *at* Newtown denotes "within" Newtown. This meaning, too, is often used in common parlance. If a man says, "Mr. Smith lives at Ithaca," he means that Mr. Smith lives in Ithaca. The same idea is conveyed by case (4), where *at* Little Rock means "in"

Little Rock. Of course, this meaning of *at* does not refer to a specific spot, but to some place definitely "within" instead of "near."

Case (5) show *at* meaning "upon the stroke of" or "simultaneously." The punishment was to take place simultaneously with death. In daily speech one says, "The clock struck at twelve o'clock," meaning on the very moment when both the minute and hour hands reached twelve.

Case (6) also shows *at* with a definite meaning, but with a definiteness of a different kind from that pointed out in the preceding cases. In this case, it had a technical meaning. It is used in the phrase "at the wall," understood in the field of law. In the phrase, *at* carries a definite significance. A person attacked "at the wall" is in his own home—a definite place. He is also definitely protecting himself, or himself and family, against assailants.

In case (8), *at* signifies beginning the boundary on a definite spot—on the east side of the Bloomingdale road. Often, especially in the case of boundaries, *at* designates a particular spot; as when monuments are mentioned. If a person is going to measure a certain part of a wall for some reason, he may receive the following directions: "Begin at the desk on the right side and measure to the opposite wall." Here the place of beginning is definite. It is understood that the measurement should start at the right side of the desk, not in the center or on the left side, but still *at* the desk.

Case (9) shows *at* definitely meaning "without" (in the sense of "outside of"), also a frequent use of the word. If a man says, "The city built a road at the front of my lot," it is understood that the city did not build the road within the lot, but in front of it.

Thus we see there are many variations in common speech of the definite use of *at*.

Before

The word *before* is defined according to: (1) Literal interpretation; (2) Interpretation based on intent; (3) Technical meaning; (4) Circumstances.

Case 1.—The Barnard Company, the plaintiff's assignor, owned a patented device to be applied to computing scales of which the Computing Scale Company of Ohio was a manufacturer. In 1907, the Barnard Company granted to the defendant the exclusive license to use their invention; $5,000 was paid then, and it was agreed that a second payment of $5,000 royalty should be paid on January 20, 1909, unless the defendant had given and the licensor had received notice of a cancellation of the contract before that date. The defendant sent a telegram to the licensor on January 20, 1909, at 12:32 p.m.

It was decided that as the cancellation was neither sent nor received before the date specified the defendant should make the second payment.

The decision was based on the literal interpretation of *before:* "preceding in time." The cancellation was not made earlier than January 20.[1]

Case 2.—The Code of Civil Procedure provided that in an action for personal injuries, the court in granting an order for examination of the plaintiff before trial may, on application of the defendant, direct that the plaintiff submit to a physical examination by physicians to be designated by the court, and that, if the plaintiff be a female, she be entitled to have such examination *before* physicians of her own sex.

Action was brought by Rose Potter against the village of Hammondsport, New York, in 1906, to determine the meaning of this law.

It was decided that the phrase "before physicians of her own sex" meant that the examination should be made by them, and not merely in their presence.

The decision was based on the interpretation of the intent of the law. The makers of the law intended that females should be examined by female physicians.[2]

Case 3.—In Oregon, Thomasin owned a mining claim and offered Baum an interest for about $300. Baum told him he had no money but he thought that he could place it *before* capital. Thomasin told him if he would do that he would give him a third interest in the two claims. Baum gave him twenty dollars with which to increase the drilling. Later Baum had Thomasin and Cantile, the partner of Thomasin, sign a statement giving him one-third interest in the claims. Baum, however, was to induce one or more persons with capital to purchase, or to make advances upon some such consideration as an interest in the mine, or to furnish means for its development and operation.

Baum brought action for one-third interest in the claims. The decision, however, was against him, for he had not placed the mine *before* capital.

The decision was based on the technical meaning of *before*. An agreement to place another party's interest in a mining claim *before* capital involves calling the attention of some one with capital to the claim and inducing him to invest in it.[3]

Case 4.—In Iowa, in 1886, Everett took passage on the Chicago, R. I. and P. Railway, at a small station named Weston, intending to travel to Council Bluffs, a distance of ten miles. He did not procure a passenger ticket and the conductor demanded ten cents in addition to the ticket rate. As the plaintiff refused to pay it, the conductor stopped the train and forcibly ejected him. Then Everett brought action to recover damages for the alleged wrongful act of the conductor.

In 1874, a law had been passed providing that "a charge of ten cents may be added to the fare of any passenger, where the same is paid upon the cars, if a ticket might have been procured within a reasonable time before the department of the train."

Everett claimed that he went to procure a ticket and that the window was closed. It was not closed until the engine of the train passed the office window. Weston was a very small station where there was only one man to attend to the ticket office and to the business on the train, such as the loading of the mail. Everett was also thoroughly acquainted with the kind of office it was. He had come into the village and had lingered at a store, until he heard the whistle blow.

The court said that it would be unreasonable to expect the defendant to keep two men at a place of that size.

It was decided that "before the departure of the train" did not require that the office remain open up to the instant the train moved off.

The decision was based on circumstances—the kind of office it was and the fact that Everett knew the nature of the station.[4]

If a person hears the word *before,* he immediately thinks of "in front of." If a word has a physical meaning, it is that meaning which comes to the foreground of consciousness, for the mind has a mental picture of that signification. From that mental picture words often take on figurative meanings. Thus *before* does not always show material relationship; it also takes on different figurative significations. Hence the two linguistic classifications for the selected cases are: (*a*) Physical meaning; (*b*) Figurative meaning. Case (2) belongs to classification (*a*); cases (1), (3), and (4) belong to classification (*b*).

(*a*) In case (2), we find the physical meaning of *before.* This illustration, however, does not suggest the usual physical meaning of "in front of," but a variation of it. The woman was not to be placed directly in front of women physicians and examined, though she might have been in front of them. There was, however, just as much chance of her not being so situated. This case really shows an extension of the usual physical meaning, for the woman to be examined had to be in the physical presence of the physicians. *Before* thus took on the meaning of "by" and "in the presence of," a meaning implying a physical relationship which does not represent one object placed in front of another. This use, however, is general. A person says, "I am going to appear before the board of examiners," meaning that he will be in their presence.

(*b*) But *before* has the figurative meaning just as often as it has the physical one In case (1), *before* refers to time, a common use of the word. If a person says, "I shall come before May 1," he means that he will arrive previous to that date, not on that date, or after it.

Case (3) shows the figurative signification taking a technical turn. Baum was to place the mine *before* capital, not, however, in the actual presence of capital. He was to appear before a man with money and get him so interested in the mine that he would give his money for the development and operation of it. Employed in this sense, *before* is understood by persons interested in development projects of one kind or another.

Case (4) shows *before* having the same meaning as case (1). It refers to time. "Before the departure of the train" meant prior to its departure. Often *before* means "preceding in time." We may say, "The heroic couplet was used before Pope's time," meaning prior to Pope's day.

Behind

The word *behind* is defined according to: (1) Interpretation based on intent.

Case 1.—In England, on July 12, 1726, John Dobin made a will in which he devised as follows: "Item, I give and devise unto my son *Philip Dobin*, his heirs and assigns for ever, all that messuage and tenement wherein I now live: but my will is that in case my said son *Philip Dobin* shall happen to die *leaving no issue behind him*, then my said wife (meaning his then wife Joan Dobin) shall receive and take the rents, issues, and profits thereof, and dispose of the same at her will and pleasure, . . . and after her decease, or marriage as aforesaid, then the lands so devised to *Philip* as aforesaid I give and devise the same for want of issue by him as aforesaid unto my son *James Dobin*, his heirs and assigns forever . . . But in case my son *James Dobin* shall happen to die before my son *Philip*, and the said *Philip* shall not leave any issue of his body begotten, then my will is that my said lands shall be sold and equally divided between my six daughters and their issues."

Philip Dobin entered into possession of the land and sold it. Later he died leaving no issue behind. The plaintiff, Porter, was the only child of Elizabeth, one of the daughters. The defendants, the Bradleys, were claimants under the purchaser and the testator's grandson by his eldest son.

The court said that leaving no issue "behind him" necessarily imported that the testator meant at the time of his son's death and that the subsequent parts of the will conveyed the same idea since the devisor mentioned the event as likely to happen in the life-time of his widow, or of his younger son or daughters.

It was decreed that the land should be disposed of according to the will, for Philip died without issue.

The decision was based on interpretation of intent. The testator intended that if at Philip's death there was no child to inherit Philip's property, it was then to go to the wife, or to the other son James, or to the daughters.[1]

If a person hears the word *behind*, he immediately thinks of one object back of another object, for that is the mental image that comes to the foreground of consciousness. The word has a physical meaning—the opposite of "before," which also brings a definite picture to the mind. If I say, "Mr. Smith is sitting directly behind me," I mean he is sitting back of me. If he were sitting before me, he would be in front of me, so that I should be able to see him. If he were *behind* me, I should have to turn around in order to see him. As in the case of "before," *behind* also has a figurative meaning, derived from its physical signification. The illustrative case given here falls under that linguistic classification: (*a*) The figurative meaning.

In this case the issue left *behind* the testator is spoken of, *behind* showing not a matter of physical relationship, but a state of affairs after the death of the testator. It deals not with things later in space, but later in time, for the testator left no issue after his death. It has the element of time combined with the state of conditions as they exist. This employment of *behind* is not infrequent. One sometimes hears at the death of a man, "Did he leave money behind him?" meaning did he leave any money after his death for his heirs.

Below

The word *below* is defined according to: (1) Interpretation of intent; (2) Common meaning.

Case 1.—Action was brought in Maine by Oliver Donnell and another against Curtis Joy and another for erecting and maintaining in tide waters a weir alleged to be "below low-water mark, in front of the shore or flats of the plaintiffs without their consent."

The defendants admitted all the allegations, except that the weir was situated within the locality described by the statutory phrase "below low-water mark," inasmuch as it was on land which was exposed at low water. They contended that to be subject to the penalty it should be attached to land from which the tide did not wholly recede, or, in other words, "under" or "beneath" the water.

The court said that the preceding definition of "low-water mark" was the definition of lexicographers, but that "below low-water mark," as used in the statute, which declared that no fish weir should be erected in tide waters below low-water mark in front of another's shore or flats, did not necessarily mean that the soil in which such weir should be erected, to be contrary to the act, should be under water at all stages of the tide, but might become the subject of the penalty if erected on public flats situated beyond or near the middle of the channel and the low-water line of the flats.

The statute read as follows: "No fish weir shall be erected in tide waters 'below low-water mark' in front of another's shore or flats without his consent, under a penalty of $50, to be recovered in an action of debt."

Judgment was rendered in favor of the plaintiff.

The decision was based on the interpretation of the intent of the law and not upon the literal interpretation in connection with the definition of "low-water mark." The law was made to protect owners of property on the shore from intruders.[1]

Case 2.—In Colorado, in 1878, Ernest Stahl commenced a suit, alleging his ownership of the Lone Tree Lode and complaining that Lee *et al.* had ousted him from it, and still unlawfully withheld the possession.

Stahl's entry in the land-office was dated April 30, 1873. The defendants' patent to the Argentine showed the date of its entry to have been July 3, 1875. The defendants claimed to have made discovery of Argentine in 1865, prior to the discovery of the Lone Tree, and to have complied with all state, federal, and local requirements concerning locations of mines. Stahl denied that claim. The territories described in the two patents crossed each other.

Section 2336 said: "Where two or more veins unite, the oldest or prior location shall take the vein below the point of union, including all the space of intersection." The defendants argued that the words "below the point of union" applied to veins uniting on the "strike" or on a horizontal extension as well as to veins which united on the "dip," or in their downward course; and that the word *below* should be construed as equivalent to "beyond."

The court said that "beyond" was not the ordinary signification of the word *below*, both words being of common use; but that the meaning was plain, simple, and well understood and that it was also well known at the date of passage of the act that veins unite on their horizontal extension as well as in their downward course. The court added that it would not be justifiable to assume that congress committed the palpable mistake of using *below* instead of "beyond," if they really intended to give the preference to the prior location in the case of veins uniting on the "strike," as well as on the "dip," after the point of union was reached.

Judgment was therefore affirmed for the plaintiff, for the jury found no crossing, but found that the two territories united instead.

After it was found that the two veins united, the common, ordinary meaning was given to *below:* "beneath."[2]

In itself, *below* summons to the mind a picture of one thing on top of another. It is, however, not always suggestive of definite vertical arrangement, but often indicates a lower position relatively to some other object or place. It is the opposite of "above." *Below*, like "above," has a figurative meaning. One man may be below another in rank. The illustrative cases, however, all fall under one linguistic classification: (*a*) The physical meaning.

Case (1) shows *below* with one of its common significations. It indicates a lower position in relation to the shore; that is, farther out in the ocean than the shore. This relationship is definitely a physical one, one which is often employed. If a man is measuring the length of a road and putting up mile posts along the way he may say, "Do not put a post below Smith's store," meaning that no post is to be placed beyond Smith's stone, further down the road, a lower position relatively to the store.

The usual conception of *below* is found, however, in case (2). "Below the point of union" means "beneath the point of union." The vein is under the point of union in place. This meaning is similar to the one found in the statement, "The basket is below the table," meaning the basket is under the table.

Beneath

The word *beneath* is defined according to: (1) Dictionary meaning.

Case 1.—One Truman brought suit for the infringement of a patent on breaking-carts. The patent was issued September 14, 1880 to De Witt Putnam. The original application was made May 22, 1880. It was rejected, June 2, the patent office holding that a patent to Jesse Wincoff, October 17, 1871, answered the claim for a two-wheeled vehicle. The inventor amended his claim in order to get a patent. He drew diagrams and described Figure 4: "I have shown the stray F in a single piece, passing transversely under the foot-board, the two ends being connected with the opposite shafts. In either case the operation is the same, the foot-board being sustained by the springs, the same as the seat is, and independent, as far as its connections are concerned, from the axle of the vehicle. This relieves the rider from the disagreeable jar incident to this class of vehicles where the foot-boards are connected with the axles, as is usually done."

In the amendment Figures 1 and 2 were retained, but Figures 3 and 4 were omitted. Putnam stated: "I also amend by canceling the drawing on file and substituting the new drawing filed herewith." The plaintiff, however, contended that those forms were not given up, and that the improvement was without invention.

The only question involved was whether the construction of the strap, or its manner of fastening, was essential. The plaintiff's patent showed that the straps were in a cart in which shafts were placed directly upon the springs, and the foot-board was sustained beneath the axle by straps.

Counsel for the complainant contended that the phrase, "and the foot-board is sustained beneath the axle by straps" meant lower than—nearer to the ground: securing a low cart.

The court said that this meaning of *beneath* was not its ordinary meaning, but that, according to Webster's Dictionary, as a preposition, it denoted "lower in place, with something directly over" and it followed, therefore, that the cart was one with straps beneath the axle and that the carts of the respondent, not being of that construction, did not infringe. The bill was therefore dismissed.

The decision was based on the dictionary meaning of *beneath:* "lower in place, with something directly over."[1]

The illustrative case given here falls under the linguistic classification: (*a*) Physical meaning. It is used in one of its customary senses as directly under, showing that the straps were lower in place than the axle. We often speak of one block's being beneath another, meaning directly under it.

Besides

The word *besides* is defined according to: (1) Literal interpretation.

Case 1.—On October 5, 1886, New York, a case arose concerning the meaning of Mrs. Beckett's will. The will recited: "I leave and bequeath to my niece, Alice McBlair, all the money I die possessed of in several banks and bonds, besides all I bequeath to her in my former will." Mrs. Beckett's sisters said that the will was uncertain.

It was decided that the will was made independent of the other will, determined by the word *besides*, and that the language was sufficiently certain to transfer to the niece whatever money the testator had at death.

The decision was based on the literal interpretation of *besides:* "in addition to, over and above; outside of and separately from what has been previously given."[1]

Etymologically, *besides* is derived from "beside," meaning "by the side of," which shows a definite physical relationship. This physical relationship extends over into another sphere, giving a figurative meaning to the word. The illustrative case given here falls under the linguistic classification: (a) Figurative meaning. *Besides* takes on the meaning of "in addition to" or "over and above," a signification accepted in everyday speech. If a man says, "Besides this book, I shall give you two others," he means he is going to give two books in addition to the one he has already given.

Between

The word *between* is defined according to: (1) Literal interpretation; (2) Interpretation based on intent; (3) Common meaning; (4) Etymology; (5) Context.

Case 1.—Leo Ford and others on July 9, 1852, in Illinois, covenanted to deliver to William Richardson and others, at Peru, 200 head of good fat hogs. Richardson covenanted to pay "$100 at the date of the contract, and $400 between that time and the 1st of September then next." The $100 was paid. Then on September 1, Richardson offered Ford the $400, which the latter refused, saying it was too late. Richardson then brought suit. The question was whether the tender was made in due time.

It was decided that the tender was not made in due time, for the money was to be paid between the first payment and September 1, not on September 1.

The decision was based on the literal interpretation of *between:* the interval which separated July 9 and September 1.[1]

Case 2.—In Georgia, in 1916, Mrs. Bessie Smith, daughter of F. J. Rogers and niece of J. T. Rogers, brought action against the executors of the latter's will, to have the will construed and to recover one-sixth undivided interest in all the estate. J. T. Rogers, in his will, after making certain gifts, had said: "and all the remainder of my estate to be divided equally between the heirs of my deceased brothers, Franklin Jackson Rogers and John Rogers, share and share alike." F. J. Rogers had five children, among whom was Mrs. Bessie Smith; John Rogers had one child, Charles Rogers, who claimed that he was entitled to one-half of the estate.

The whole question was whether, under the will of J. T. Rogers, Charles Rogers should take one-half interest, or one-sixth interest in common with the other five devisees.

The court said that the word *between* primarily denoted two classes of objects, but that that meaning was not observed in ordinary writing and speech.

The court held that the devise was in effect a bequest in remainder, to be equally divided between the children of the testator's deceased brothers, share and share alike, and that it was intended that they should receive *per capita*, and not *per stirpes*.

The decision was not based on the literal interpretation of *between*, but upon the interpretation of intent. It was thought that it was the intent of the testator to have his nieces and nephews receive *per capita*.[2]

Case 3.—Mrs. Julia Morrison of California, in 1891, made a will providing that "the residue of the estate left after the payment of the above legacies to be divided between my sister Mrs. Wann and her daughters, and my brother Stettinius"—this sister having two daughters, and special legacies having previously been made to each of these daughters by name, and to this sister and brother, each of the four receiving the same amount. Stettinius contended that, as the word between was used, the residue should be divided into two parts.

The court said that when *between* and "among" follow the verb "divide" their general use is very similar, and in popular use are considered as synonymous, though "among" denotes a collection, and is never followed by two of a sort, whereas *between* may be followed by any plural number and seems to denote rather the individuals of the class than the class itself generically.

The court also said that, as applied to persons and things, the word *between* primarily referred to two, though Webster's Dictionary gave "among" as a synonym, and in a large number of cases the word was used in wills where a *per capita* devise or legacy was to more than two.

The court held that the residue should be divided into four equal parts.

The decision was based on the common meaning of *between*,

which is often used as "among," when followed by a plural number.[3]

Case 4.—Thomas Record, as executor of F. R. Fields, deceased, brought action against Thomas Fields and others, as legatees under the will of F. R. Fields, deceased. Persilla Turner and Taylor Fields, the only heirs of James Fields, sought to have the will construed so as to divide the residue into two equal parts, one of which should go to them as the heirs of their father, James Fields, and the other to the heirs of William Fields. The heirs of William Fields, being seven in number, wanted it divided into nine parts.

The will read: "The balance of my property and money I want equally divided between the heirs of William Field and James Field deceased."

The judge said that where a testator used technical words, he was presumed to have used them in their technical sense, unless a clear intent to the contrary was apparent and that unquestionably in the will the words conveyed the thought of two parts, the ordinary meaning of the words "equally divided between the heirs of William and the heirs of James." He also said that the true etymological significance of the word *between,* according to Webster's International Dictionary and the Century Dictionary, made it literally applicable to two objects and that there was nothing tending to show that F. R. Fields or the person who drew the will (if other than Mr. Fields himself) was an ignorant man and used *between* in any other sense than its correct one.

Judgment was rendered for two divisions.

The decision was based on the etymology of *between.* The Anglo-Saxon was *betweonum* (*be,* "by"—a form from Anglo-Saxon *twā* [fem.] or *twēgen* [mas.] "two").[4]

Case 5.—Mr. and Mrs. C. C. Kelly made a joint will providing that, in case of the death of either, one's property should vest in the survivor, unless the survivor married again, in which case the property should be divided equally between the survivor and the children born of their union.

The court said *between* was not always to be given a strict etymological signification, "between two," but might, where the context demanded it, be construed as "among."

It was decided that the survivor did not take one-half of the estate and the children the other half, but that the word *between* was used in the sense of "among."

The decision was based on the context of the will.[5]

The word *between* is often misused, for it is confused with "among," which is used when more than two are spoken of. Etymologically, *between* concerns itself with two only. It is derived from the Anglo-Saxon *betweonum* (*mas.*), "two," and akin to the Gothic *tweihnai*, "two apiece." The cases given here illustrate two classifications: (*a*) *Between* restricted to two; (*b*) *Between* including more than two. Cases (1) and (4) belong to classification (*a*); cases (2), (3), and (5) to classification (*b*).

(*a*) In case (4), the phrase "between the heirs of William Field and James Field deceased" implied that the property was to be divided into two parts, one-half of which was to go to the heirs of William Field and the other half to the heirs of James Field. Here *between* had its original meaning, a common use in ordinary speech. If I say, "Divide the apple between James and John," I mean, cut the apple into two parts, giving one-half to James and the other half to John. Case (1) shows a variation of this meaning. The word, however, still involves only two, for two definite dates are given. The money is to be paid between the date of the contract and September 1. This use of *between* is employed when time is involved. No division is made, but an act is supposed to be performed within two definite limits. This use of the word is also common. If John says, on Friday, "I shall write my theme between today and Monday," he means that he will write it some time during that period.

(*b*) Frequently *between* is employed where "among" should be used. This mistake is usually made in expressing dispersion and distribution. In most cases the word is also followed by a plural or collective noun. Wills offer a good example of this misuse. In case (2), the property was to be divided into six parts instead of two; therefore, etymologically, it would have been better to use "among." In case (3), the same is true, for the division was to be into three parts. Likewise in case (5), the division was to be among the surviving parent and the children. Often one hears in daily speech such statements as, "Divide the money between the four children," meaning, of course, give each child one-fourth of the money. The word *between* is used in this sense by persons who are careless in expressing themselves or who do not know the difference between *between* and "among."

Thus we see that the court has to determine whether *between* is used in its original sense, or in the place of "among."

Beyond

The word *beyond* is defined according to: (1) Literal interpretation; (2) Interpretation of intent; (3) Common meaning; (4) Technical meaning.

Case 1.—In 1887, Williams brought action against New York City to be compensated for a small tract which had been wholly or partly appropriated and used by the city as a part of the exterior street or wharf laid out under provisions of the Laws of 1871, which created the Department of Docks for New York City, and authorized the city to prepare plans for improving the waterfront, which when approved, should be the sole plan for building wharves. The city claimed that it had the right, under this act, to take the plaintiff's land without compensating him.

The Act of 1857 authorized the city to fill up and occupy the open space as a necessary incident to the use of the new wharf.

Its second section read: "It shall not be lawful to fill in with earth, or other solid material, in the waters of said port, *beyond* the bulk-head line or line of solid filling hereby established."

The grantees constructed the wharf on the river line; filled in the space between; built the streets required, and went without molestation into the possession of their land and wharf-rights. They became owners of the newly-made land, as well as that already "gained" at the date of the deeds. The new act, however, put all wharves and piers in the hands of the city and not in the hands of individuals. The private owner had no interest in the new bulk-head line.

It was decided that the individuals should be paid for the land they built up, for they built up to the bulk-head line and not beyond it, as required by the Law of 1857.

The decision was based on the literal interpretation of *beyond:* "on the further side of." The land was not built up on the further side of the bulk-head line.[1]

Case 2.—On July 14, 1862, Congress passed an act, the fourteenth section of which read: "There shall be levied, collected, and paid on all goods, wares, and merchandise of the growth or produce of countries beyond the Cape of Good Hope, when imported from places this side of the Cape of Good Hope, a duty of ten per cent. ad valorem, and in addition to the duties imposed on any such articles when imported directly from the place or places of their growth or production."

Hadden imported into New York from Liverpool several packages of raw silk, the growth or produce of Persia and China, upon which the 10 per cent duty was exacted. This duty was paid under protest and suit was brought against the collector to recover the amount.

Hadden objected on the ground that goods which were the products of Persia or China were from countries beyond the Cape of Good Hope with reference to Atlantic ports and were thus chargeable with duty, but with reference to Pacific ports, they were from countries this side of the cape.

The court said that the terms "beyond the Cape of Good Hope" were used to avoid the necessity of enumerating the countries which lie east of the Cape and that "beyond the Cape" and "east of the Cape" were often used in the Acts of Congress as equivalent expressions to indicate the location of certain countries with reference to the position of the lawmakers at the national capital, just as "beyond the Mississippi" was used to refer to countries west of the Mississippi.

It was decided that the phrase "beyond the Cape of Good Hope" was employed as descriptive of the location of certain countries, and not of the relative position of these countries with respect to ports of import.

The decision was based on the interpretation of the intent of *beyond*, as used by the congressmen. It was used in the sense of "east."[2]

Case 3.—On September 2, 1901, the Glenmore Distilleries Company of Kentucky made an agreement with the American Bridge Company to erect a tower for the distillery. The cost was $1,650. The Distillery Company agreed to pay an extra $100 if the tower were delivered earlier—in forty-five working days from September 12. The American Bridge Company was not to be held responsible for delays in transportation, strikes, fires, floods, storms, or for any other circumstances beyond its reasonable control. The tower was not delivered until Januay 12, 1902. The Distillery Company refused to pay the contract price and then the American Bridge Company brought suit for the amount of $1,750, saying that they could not secure material for the tower. They claimed that the inability to secure material was *beyond* their control. The defendants contended that the plaintiffs should have been certain of material, for they knew how quickly the tower was wanted. The delay caused the defendants a great loss.

It was held that the defendants should not have to pay the contract price, for the inability to secure material was not beyond the control of the American Bridge Company if the ordinary sense of *beyond* were considered.

The decision was based on the common meaning of *beyond:* "out of reach, or control."[3]

Case 4.—Murray's Lessee, in 1818, in Georgia, brought an action of ejectment to recover possession of lands lying in that state. The Bakers, the defendants, contended that the lessors of the plaintiff had not been in Georgia since they, or their ancestors, came into possession of those premises. The ancestors of the defendants had possessed the land from 1791.

Georgia's statute of limitations stated that lands sued for must be sued for within seven years after the act was passed or after the title and cause of action accrued to it. The law read: "Provided, nevertheless, that if any person or persons, that is or shall be entitled to such writ or writs, or that hath, or shall have such right or title of entry, be, or shall be, at the time of such right or title first descended, accrued, come, or fallen, within the age of twenty-one years, *feme covert*, *non compos mentis*, imprisoned, *or beyond seas*, that ten such person or persons, and his and their heir, and heirs, shall or may, notwithstanding the said seven years are expired, bring his, her, or their action, or make his, her, or their entry, as he, she, or they might have done before this act."

It was argued that *beyond seas* and "out of the state" had the same meaning. *Beyond seas* was borrowed from a statute in Great Britain.

It was held that the plaintiff, who resided in Virginia, had a right to bring action of ejectment, *beyond seas* meaning "without the limits of the state."

The decision was based on the technical meaning of *beyond seas*, a phrase borrowed from English law, meaning "without the limits of the state."[4]

The word *beyond* is used in both a physical and a figurative sense. If a chair is placed on the farther side of a table, we speak of the chair as being beyond the table. This relationship is a material one. From this definite relationship an indefinite one is derived. One often hears such statements as, "It is beyond my strength," meaning past my strength, a statement in which the use of *beyond* is figurative. The cases given here fall under the two linguistic classifications: (*a*) Physical meaning; (*b*) Figurative meaning. Cases (1), (2), and (4) belong to classification (*a*); case (3) belongs to classification (*b*).

(*a*) In case (1), *beyond* is used in its physical sense. "Beyond the bulk-head line" meant "on the farther side" of the bulk-head line, a common, everyday meaning. If Mr. Smith says, "Put this box beyond the chair," he means put the box on the farther side of the chair. Case (2) also shows *beyond* in its material relationship, denoting the countries on the farther side of the Cape of Good Hope. Case (4) gives a variation of this meaning. It still shows a physical relationship, but does not necessarily mean "on the farther side of." It is used technically in the phrase *beyond seas*. It may mean "on the farther side of the sea," or it may mean just outside the borders of the state, as is shown in this case. It indicates that a person is not in the state, but outside the boundaries. It is a legal term well understood in law. If a person is *beyond seas* he is outside the state, not necessarily in another country.

(*b*) In case (3), we find *beyond* employed in its figurative sense. "Beyond one's reasonable control" does not imply place relationship, but means that a deed to be done is outside a person's control. There is nothing that the person can do about it. For instance, if a storm arises and destroys all the crops, the farmers can do nothing toward stopping the storm, for the natural forces are beyond their control, or outside of their control.

By

The word *by* is defined according to: (1) Literal interpretation; (2) Interpretation based on intent; (3) Interpretation suggested by fact; (4) Common meaning; (5) Technical meaning; (6) Dictionary meaning; (7) Context.

Case 1.—Jones, in 1848, in New York, brought an action of ejectment to recover possession of premises in Ward 16, that constituted the northerly part of a strip of land formerly known as Burling's Lane. In the conveyance, the lot was described as being bounded by exact measurement of feet and inches, on two sides by the side of two streets laid out and opened, and then "southerly *by the northerly line or side of Thomas Burling's Lane.*"

Cowman held that the description limited the grantee, Jones, to the northerly side of the lane and did not carry him to the center of it.

The court charged that whether the road or lane called Bowling's lane was a public, traveled road was immaterial, for by the deed, the plaintiff was bounded by the northerly side or line or Burling's lane, and therefore was not entitled to any of the land included within the boundaries of the lane.

The decision was based on the literal interpretation of *by:* "beside." The lot thus lay beside the northerly side of Thomas Burling's lane.[1]

Case 2.—In 1851, John Blass, a hired worker on a ship, brought suit in St. Louis Circuit Court against the steamboat Robert Campbell. After the boat was out for several days, the plaintiff became ill. The defendant put him ashore at a place belonging to a tribe of Indians, who mistreated him. He thought he should recover damages according to the boat and vessel act, which made steamboats liable for injuries done to persons or property "by" said boat or vessel.

The decision was against the plaintiff, for it was decided that the act meant injuries in which the boat was an agent, such as collisions and the like, and did not embrace the act of the captain in putting an employee ashore in violation of the contract of employment.

The decision was based on the interpretation of the intent of the word *by* as used in the law. It was thought that the law was made to protect persons and property injured by means of the boat itself.[2]

Case 3.—In Massachusetts, in 1870, Mary Griffin made an unlawful sale of intoxicating liquor. She was tried and found guilty. Then she alleged exceptions to the description of the customer, described as "a certain person whose name is not known by the complainant." She contended that the preposition should be "to" instead of *by*, for *by* often meant "through" or "by means of" as in "We shall know by this fellow." The exceptions were overruled, for it was a known fact that she sold the liquor. Therefore the allegation that a person was not known by the complainant had the same signification as the allegation that he was known to her.

The decision was based on an interpretation suggested by fact. As it was a known fact that the liquor was sold, *by* took on the meaning of "to."[3]

Case 4.—Delachamp chartered the ship Lawhill. The agreement contained a clause providing an option of cancelling if the vessel was not "ready for loading by November 20, 1903, at Yokohama." On the morning of that day the charterers gave notice that they cancelled, on the ground that the ship was not ready for loading by November 20. The suit was brought by Ruprecht to recover $5,000 as liquidated damages for the breach of a charter party.

The Lawhill was not ready for loading on November 20 at the beginning of the working day. The cargo was not entirely out until shortly before noon. It was therefore decided that Ruprecht should recover $5,000, the interest, and costs as the common meaning of *by* is "on" or "before."

The decision was based on the common meaning of *by:* "on" or "before."[4]

Case 5.—In California, in 1892, Ott, the owner of a block of land, conveyed to Fraser a portion, "being the north 2 acres of block No. 13 of the W. Company's 4-acre blocks," together with a right of way across "the south half of said block." The block was bounded on the west and south by streets sixty feet wide, and, if measured to the center of the streets, the block contained 4.65 acres, but, excluding the streets, it contained only four acres. The defendant, Ott, held that the title did not extend to the center of the highway.

The action was to quiet Fraser's title to the parcel. It was decided that a deed described as bounded *by* a highway or street should be construed as including the land to the center of the street or highway, according to the Civil Code.

The decision was based on the technical meaning of *by* in such cases as "by a bay, creek, highway, street," etc., a phrasing which gives title to half the water-course, highway, or street, unless words of exclusion are used.[5]

Case 6.—In North Carolina, in 1897, action was brought by the Elizabeth City Cotton Mills against W. E. Dunstan to recover a balance due on the defendant's subscription of $500 to stock of the plaintiff's corporation.

The defendant's stock was sold at public sale for $300 as non-payment of assessments, in accordance with the corporation's by-laws: "Sec. 25. If any stockholder shall fail to pay his installment, when called by the board of directors, for two months the stock of such delinquent may be declared forfeited by the board of directors, and sold for account of such delinquent, publicly, after thirty days' notice, and the net proceeds of such sale be applied first to the payment of all amounts due upon such stock, and the balance, if any, paid to delinquent."

The agreement was that the subscription was not to be binding unless $80,000 was subscribed "by July 1st." The full amount was subscribed at the meeting held on the night of July 1.

The court said that according to the Century Dictionary *by* meant "not later than"; "as early as"; according to the Standard, "not later than"; and according to Webster, "not later than"; "as soon as," and that therefore the condition, "by July 1," meant that the whole amount should be subscribed "not later than" July 1.

It was decided that the defendant lost his stock and had to pay the difference between his subscription and the price for which the stock was sold.

The decision in this case was based on the dictionary meaning of *by:* "not later than."[6]

Case 7.—In Massachusetts, in 1831, a case was brought to determine the boundary of a tract of land, iucluding a town road passing through it. Charles Sibley and Rufus Holden, tenants in common of the land, made a partition by mutual deeds of release, in which the bounds of the tracts so released were described as "beginning at a stake and stones *on the side* of the town road," etc., thence by various courses "*to said* road, thence by said road to the place of beginning." Sibley brought an action of trespass *quare clausum fregit* against Holden. Holden held that the road was not included in the partition, but that the parties still were tenants in common, subject to the public easement.

It was decided that the road was held in common, for the boundary began in one place at a stake and stones "on the side" of the town road. Thus one point in the line was fixed by description to the side of the road. Since that was true, the court thought the other point, "by said road" must be taken at the side of the road and that the soil of the road was not included.

The decision was based on the context—the fact that "on the side" had been used previously.[7]

The word *by* is used in both a physical and a figurative sense. If John says, "James is standing by me," he may mean that

James is standing next to him. There is a definite physical relationship. He may also mean that James is remaining loyal to him. This latter meaning is a figurative one. The illustrative cases given here fall under the two following linguistic classifications: (*a*) Physical meaning; (*b*) Figurative meaning. Cases (1), (5), and (7) belong to classification (a); cases (2), (3), (4), and (6) to classification (*b*).

(*a*) In case (1), *by* means "beside." The lot thus adjoins the northerly side of Thomas Burling's Lane. This relationship is physical juxtaposition, a commonplace use of *by*. If Mr. Smith says, "The book is by the ball," he means the book is physically beside the ball. The same use is shown in case (7) in the description "by said road."

In case (5), we find the physical meaning of *by*, and an extension of the meaning found in cases (1) and (7). The relationship is physical just as *by* in case (1), for the block of land was bounded by the street, which meant the land extended up to the street and also past the boundary of the street to the center of it. This extension of *by* is commonplace in reference to the surveying of land which borders on rivers, highways, and streets. If Mr. Smith's land is bordered by the highway, it is usually understood that his land extends to the center of the highway.

(*b*) The word *by* has the figurative meaning just as often as the physical one. In case (2), *by* denotes "by means of," a usual signification. "He was killed by a gun" means that he was killed by means of a gun.

In case (3), we also find a figurative use of *by* which is common in daily speech. In this case "by the complainant" meant "to the complainant," in reference to a person whose name was not known. One hears such statements as, "He is not known by me," meaning he is not known to me.

In case (4), *by* in its figurative sense denotes "on or before." "By November 20" meant either "on November 20," or "before November 20," a common use. If Mr. Brown says, "I shall be there by Tuesday," he means that he may arrive before Tuesday, but at any rate, he will arrive on Tuesday. He includes Tuesday in the "by Tuesday."

In case (6), we find another figurative meaning given to *by* when used in relation to time. A certain amount of money was to be subscribed "by July 1," which phrase meant that it was to be subscribed "not later than July 1." If a teacher says to a class, "All papers must be in by next Tuesday," he means that he will accept them not later than the class period on Tuesday.

Thus we see that the law courts have to deal with the import of *by* as used in everyday English.

Concerning

The word *concerning* is defined according to: (1) Interpretation based on intent; (2) Common meaning.

Case 1.—Commerford, a citizen of New York, brought a bill against the postmistress of Louisville, Kentucky, to enjoin her from interfering with and delaying the complainant's letters, addressed to him at Louisville, as she had caused him a loss of $5,500 and would cause a loss of a great deal more. The defendant answered by saying that she had been instructed by the postmaster general to keep letters addressed to Commerford, since they were letters and communications concerning lottery, the writing of which was a crime according to the Revised Statute of the United States which read: "No letter or circular concerning lotteries, so-called gift concerts, or other similar enterprises offering prizes, or concerning schemes devised and intended to deceive and defraud the public for the purpose of obtaining money under false pretenses, shall be carried in the mail."

The solution depended upon the construction put upon *concerning*. The judge said that it was obvious that it was not intended to be used in its broadest sense, "pertaining to or relative to," for such construction would include every letter, comprising not only letters written in the interest of the enterprise, but letters of inquiry, letters seeking legal advice, letters written to suppress such gambling, etc., but that it was evidently the intention of Congress to strike at the root of the lottery system by inhibiting those who practiced it the use of the mails for the propagation of their schemes by fining them, with intent to punish guilty promoters of such impostures.

Commerford was therefore found guilty and the bill was dismissed, for the letters were written to promote the lottery business.

The decision was based on the interpretation of the intent of Congress in using the word *concerning* in the law regarding lottery.[1]

Case 2.—Fulkerson was prosecuted for violating a Revised Statute of the United States, which prohibited the depositing in the post office of letters concerning a lottery. The indictment alleged that defendants, on November 9, 1895, "did knowingly deposit, and cause to be deposited," in the post office at Los Angeles, California, "a certain envelope,—which said envelope then and there contained a certain letter concerning a certain lottery conducted by a corporation called the Interstate Mutual Investment Company of Los Angeles, California," and then set forth a copy of the letter.

The defendants demurred to the indictment. They said that the indictment failed to allege that the matter deposited in the post office was in aid of a lottery. The court overruled the demurrer of the defendants by giving the ordinary meaning to *concerning:* "pertaining to," "having relation to."

The court said that Congress, no doubt, intended the ordinary meaning to be given when it made it a crime to deposit a letter concerning lottery.

Thus the decision was based on the common meaning of *concerning:* "pertaining to."[2]

The illustrative cases that turn on *concerning* fall under the following linguistic classifications: (*a*) Limited meaning; (*b*) Unlimited meaning. Case (1) illustrates classification (*a*); case (2) classification (*b*).

(*a*) In case (1), *concerning* has a limited meaning. It applies only to letters which are written to promote a lottery and not to all letters written about lotteries. In common parlance, it sometimes has this meaning. If Mr. Brown says, "Fine any one who speaks concerning deism," he means fine any one who speaks in behalf of deism, but he does not mean fine a man who is ignorant of the term deism and asks the definition of it.

(*b*) More often, *concerning* has the unlimited meaning of "pertaining to," or "having relation to," as is shown in case (2). If John asks, "Did James say anything concerning me?" he wants to know of anything James might have said about him.

Down

The word *down* is defined according to: (1) Literal interpretation; (2) Common meaning; (3) Technical meaning.

Case 1.—In Kentucky, in 1917, Florence Carter and others brought action against the Elk Coal Company and others to recover $6,600, the value of coal alleged to have been wrongfully taken by the defendants from land claimed by the plaintiffs.

The plaintiffs claimed the land under a patent issued to Benjamin Goodin in 1853. The only line in dispute was the fifth line, described as beginning "at a sugar tree at the head of Dean's branch; thence S. 85 E. 350 poles down to spur between Goodin's and Dean's branch to a sourwood." The plaintiffs insisted that the line between the sugar tree and the sourwood should follow with its meanderings the top or crest of the spur that extended from the sugar tree to the sourwood and that lay between Goodin's branch and Dean's branch, running southeasterly from the sugar tree to the sourwood; while the defendants contended that a straight line should be run from the sugar tree to the sourwood.

The courts said that the description of the line did not call for "the top or crest of the spur or the meanders of the spur" and that the surveyors who surveyed the patent did not show a line running with the meanders of the spur.

Judgment was therefore rendered in favor of the defendants and the plaintiffs appealed. The judgment was affirmed.

The decision was based on the literal interpretation of *down;* otherwise the lines would have followed the top of the spur. *Down* means "from a higher to a lower place in a straight line."[1]

Case 2.—In 1858, in Virginia, an action of ejectment was brought by J. B. Brown and others against Benjamin Huger. To determine the boundary of the land the deeds had to be read. The deed of Huger, which was the earlier one, stated that the land had its beginning corner on the Shenandoah River and extended thence down the river, by course and distance, to the point where the Shenandoah unites with the Potomac; and from that point up the River Potomac, by course and distance, to a corner near the last-named river; opposite a small island.

The court said that "down the river" to another point meant down the river according to its windings and turnings and that the stream thus formed the boundary of the granted land of the defendant.

Judgment was thus rendered in favor of the defendant, for the description could not be satisfied by a straight line.

The decision was based on the common meaning of *down* in the expression "down the river." Ordinarily, if a person uses "down the river" he means *down* according to the windings and turnings of the stream.[2]

Case 3.—In 1854, in Virginia, an action of ejectment was brought by James French against General James Bankhead, the officer of the United States in command at Fortress Monroe. The question was whether the United States held land to low water mark or to high water mark. The plaintiff contended that since the deed did not call for a water boundary, but a boundary by courses and distances, the United States was not entitled to claim by a water boundary though in fact the courses and distances called for in the deed were coincident with the high water mark. The deed described the boundaries of the land conveyed as commencing at a tree on the bank of a stream, and extending thence down the creek with the several meanders thereof.

The court said that the fact that the marked corner called for stood four rods from the water did not create any ambiguity in the term "down the creek with the several meanders thereof," but meant the water's edge at low water, a decided natural boundary, and must control a call for corner trees on the bank.

Thus the decision was in favor of the defendant.

The decision was based on the technical meaning of *down* used in descriptions of land by the side of water.[3]

The word *down* is used almost entirely to represent place relationship, a physical sense. The illustrative cases all fall under the following linguistic classification: (*a*) Physical meaning.

In case (1), *down* is used in its ordinary sense representing the distance from a higher to a lower place on the spur; that is, the distance in a descending direction along the spur. The direction was southeasterly, which is always considered *down*, just as north is considered "up." In this case *down* in its measurement is represented by a straight line. This use of *down* is a customary one. If Mr. Jones says, "Measure the distance down the hill," he means measure the distance, in a straight line, from the top of the hill, a higher place, to the bottom, a lower place.

In case (2), we find another use of *down* commonly used in connection with rivers or streams. "Down the river" has the meaning of "along the river toward the mouth or toward the sea." It also implies that the measurement follows the windings and turnings of the river. If Mr. Smith says, "King's land extends down the river to the Georgia line," he means that King's land follows the meanderings of the river until the stream reaches Georgia. In case (3), we find *down* used in the same sense as in case (2). The land follows the meanderings of the stream and has the water as its boundary.

Except

The word *except* is defined according to: (1) Common meaning.

Case 1.—In Alabama, Green Willis, in 1884, had been in possession of a certain tract for ten years. He had bought the land at a sale, which had been described in the administrator's petition as an entire tract "containing in all 596 acres, more or less, less or except the widow's dower, described as follows." Then followed a description of about 200 acres of the land, as given in a previous dower allotment to the widow. At the time of the sale, in 1874, the widow did not object to the land's being sold, which silence in a land suit does not operate an estoppel. In 1884, the widow put in a claim for the land.

The court said that *except* meant "not including," and that since the petition asked for the sake of the entire tract (describing it) except the dower interest or life-estate in a specified part of it, only the life-estate or dower interest was reserved from sale.

Thus the decision was in favor of the plaintiff and she received the land.

The decision was based on the common meaning of *except:* "not including."[1]

When a person hears the word *except*, he immediately thinks of "not including." He assumes that whatever is excepted is left out. It has a definite meaning limited to the object or person mentioned. The illustrative case here falls under that linguistic classification: (*a*) Definite meaning. In the case of the widow's dower, a definite, limited amount of land was not included. In ordinary speech, if John says, "All have gone except Mary," he means that Mary was not included in the party that left. She was omitted.

For

The word *for* is defined according to: (1) Literal interpretation; (2) Interpretation based on intent; (3) Common meaning; (4) Specialized meaning; (5) Technical meaning; (6) Dictionary meaning; (7) Context.

Case 1.—In Nebraska, in November 1898, the electors of Cherry County, in a referendum, approved the proposition to issue $12,000 in county bonds for the purpose of erecting a court house. The question arose as to whether the notice calling the election was published as required by the statute. The notice was inserted in four successive weekly issues of the *Republican* and also in the *Western News-Democrat*, newspapers published in Cherry County. In the *Republican* the first publication was on October 14 and on the day preceding the election the notice first appeared in the *Western News-Democrat*. The election was held on November 8, or before the expiration of the four full calendar weeks after the first publication of the notice. The statute declared: "The mode of submitting questions to the people for any purpose authorized by law shall be as follows: The whole question . . . is to be published for four weeks in some newspaper published in the county."

The attorney general argued that the first publication should have been made at least four weeks, and the last insertion one week, prior to the election.

The attorney general was sustained, because the first publication was not made four weeks before the election.

The decision was based on the literal interpretation of *for four weeks:* "during four weeks."[1]

Case 2.—On August 31, 1844, in Virginia, after a Methodist camp meeting had ended for the day and after the persons in charge had retired to their tents for repose, Jennings procured a tin horn from the preacher's stand and disturbed the congregation resting in the tents. A charge for the disturbance was brought against Jennings in accordance with the statute, which forbade the disturbance of congregations assembled for religious worship. The defendant contended that the disturbance was not during religious worship.

The judge, however, considered the intent of the statute and the purpose for which it was made. He said that the words "if any person shall maliciously disturb any congregation assembled for religious worship" had reference to meeting for the purpose of worship, but did not refer to worship only, but to the time before and after service as well, provided the congregation were assembled for religious worship.

Jennings was found guilty, the decision being based on the interpretation of the intent of the law.[2]

Case 3.—Sawyer, a mill-owner in Milwaukee, sold Tilton 300 barrels of flour at eight dollars a barrel, to be paid for on delivery of each hundred barrels at the Chicago and Northwestern Railway Company's depot in Milwaukee. Plaintiff sent 100 barrels to the depot and the defendant's shipping clerk learned from the teamster, who hauled the first load, that it was "for Tilton." The defendant gave the plaintiff a receipt for the flour, stating that it was received "for shipment." Then the defendant delivered the flour to Tilton without pay and the plaintiff brought suit for the action. The court said that the defendant knew the flour belonged to the plaintiff, for Mr. Watson, the receiving and shipping clerk, acknowledged it. Watson, however, delivered the bill of lading to Mr. Tilton.

The court said the fact that the teamster, who was not the agent of the plaintiff, said the flour was for Tilton did not imply that it was to be delivered by the company to a third person without further instruction from the owner and did not justify the company in delivering it, because *for* was used only in the ordinary sense and did not warrant the inference that the flour belonged to Tilton, but only that it was intended for him.

Judgment was thus rendered in favor of the plantiff for the price of the flour with interest.

The decision was based on the common meaning of *for*, indicating the person for whom something is intended.[3]

Case 4.—Thomas Emerson and Little, in 1810, sold and delivered goods to Frank Roberts, an agent of the Providence Hat Manufacturing Company. Roberts gave the following note: "*Boston*, Jan. 20, 1810. For value received of Messrs. *Emerson and Little*, I promise to pay them, or order, $731.03 in twelve months and grace, *for the Providence Hat Manufacturing Company.* Frink Roberts." The Providence Hat Manufacturing Company refused to pay. It was proved that Roberts was an agent of theirs.

The court said that it would be unjust to a man dealing with the authorized agent of another to have the agent's promise denied by the principal, making it necessary for that man, in consequence, to look only to the agent, who is generally much less responsible.

It was decided that the use of the word *for* in a signature to a contract which *A* signs for B indicates that *A* is signing on behalf of *B*.

The decision was based on the specialized meaning of *for* as used in the case of one person signing a contract for another.[4]

Case 5.—On November 27, 1908, John McGannon, a resident of Seneca, Missouri, died intestate at Tulsa, Oklahoma, having property there worth $280,000, subject to an act entitled "An act providing for a tax on gifts, inheritance, bequests, legacies, devises and successions in certain cases," approved May 26, 1908. The county judge calculated the tax. In the District Court the computations were made differently and decided upon. McGannon brought a writ of error.

It was decided that the county judge was right under the statute, imposing an inheritance tax, fixing the primary rate for class 1 at 1 per cent, and providing, that upon all in excess of $5,000 in class 1, the primary rate should be "increased one one hundred twenty-fifth of 1 per centum for every $100 increase in valuation of such excess" in making the rate for the entire sum of $5,000, $1\frac{1}{125}$ per cent; the word *for* meaning "to be applied to."

The decision was based on the technical meaning of *for* used in the tax law: "to be applied to."[5]

Case 6.—In Missouri, on January 3, 1888, George Weber petitioned the County Court for permission to keep a dram-shop at his place of business in Block 28, at Marshall. The petition was signed by two-thirds of the tax-paying citizens of Block 28. The County Court refused to grant the license, because under the local option law the vote at the election on October 11, 1887, went against the sale of intoxicating liquors. Weber brought suit to compel the County Court to grant him a license. He contended that the election was not valid, since the statute provided that the notice for an election under the local option law should be published for four consecutive weeks. The notice for the election had appeared on September 17, and weekly thereafter. Weber argued that the notice should have been published twenty-eight days, and not twenty-four days, before the election.

The judge said that *for* in the statute had reference to time. He found that Webster defined the word to mean "the space of all time through which an action or state extends; duration; continuance; as to guide the sun's bright chariot for a day." He also said that the statute did not say the notice should be inserted four times in as many consecutive weeks, or that it should be published four times but "for four weeks." Using Webster's Dictionary as an authority, the judge concluded that the period named should cover not less than twenty-eight days.

Judgment was therefore rendered in favor of the plaintiff and the court was ordered to issue the writ.

The decision was based on the dictionary definition of *for:* "duration."[6]

Case 7.—Action was brought by Ready against Sommer and wife for foreclosure of a mortgage, alleged to have become due May 6, 1873. On the trial the defendant offered in evidence a receipt bearing the plaintiff's signature and extending the time of payment. It read: "I have and hereby extend the time for the payment of said two thousand dollars until one year from April 21, 1873, and for said May 5, 1873, one thousand dollar payments each."

The judge said that it was impossible not to understand that the word *for* was applied to the latter date in the same sense as the word "from" to the former date. The meaning was very plain, he contended, notwithstanding the apparent misuse of the word *for*. He turned to the learned author of Wedgewood's Dictionary of English Etymology to show that the word *for*, of itself, was sufficiently explicit, to give effect to the agreement. He stated that the radical meaning of *for* was "in front of," and, in making this application of the word to time, added that "the event of the present moment is before or in front of the train of futurity." He showed that Webster gave as a correct, popular meaning "in place of." The judge then said that either definition gave full expression to the extension of a year from the date of maturity.

The foreclosure began in April, 1874, but, in view of the extension, was premature. The complaint was therefore dismissed.

The decision was based on the context of the receipt given by Ready to Sommer. He spoke of extending the payment of $2,000 until one year from April 21, 1873. Then he added, "and for said May 5, 1873, one thousand dollar payments each." There must be two payments. Since one date was extended for a year, the second, joined by "and," must have been extended a year also, although *for* was used instead of "from."[7]

The preposition *for* is employed often and in a great many different ways. At times it has a definite limited meaning; at others it has an extension of meaning, as seen in the illustrative cases given here. The linguistic classifications are: (*a*) Definite limited meaning; (*b*) Extended meaning. Cases (1), (3), (4), (5), (6), and (7) belong to classification (*a*); case (2) belongs to classification (*b*).

(*a*) In case (1), *for* has a limited meaning denoting a definite length of time. It expresses duration of time, a commonplace use of the word. If Mr. Smith says, "I shall be gone for ten days," he means that he will be away during that period. Case (6) also shows the same use of the word.

Case (3), however, shows a variation of that definite meaning. Here *for* indicates the person for whom the flour is intended. It is definite in that it indicates Mr. Tilton. This signification, too, is commonly employed. If a seamstress is making Mrs. Smith a gift, the seamstress will say, "This gift is for Mrs. Smith," meaning that she intends to give it to Mrs. Smith later.

Case (4) shows the definite substitution of one person for another. The word *for* indicates that the agent is acting in the character of the company. This employment of the word is frequent. If Mr. Jones says, "I am proxy for Mr. Brown," he means he is acting in the character of Mr. Brown.

Case (5) illustrates another definite use of *for*. Tax increase was to be made for every $100, a definite, specific limitation, with *for* denoting "to the amount of." Often one hears such statements as, "Here is a check for ten dollars," meaning "to the amount of ten dollars," a definite, limited sum.

In case (7), we find a very different use of *for*, really a misuse of it, as the word takes on the meaning of "from" in its definite sense. The payment is to be made one year from May 5, designating a limited time, the meaning of which is expressed in the preceding phrase. Then the phrase "and for said May 5," is added, carrying forward the meaning of the first phrase, "from April 21." This use of *for* is not common.

(*b*) In case (2), we find the extended meaning of *for*. "For religious worship" did not have reference to the time of worship only but to the time before and after service as well. Here *for* has the meaning of "for the purpose of," indicating the purpose for which the people had met; therefore it covered more time than was required for the religious service alone, for the worshippers were camping on the ground. This extended meaning of *for* is rather common in daily speech. Such a statement as, "He labored for the good of humanity," shows this.

From

The word *from* is defined according to: (1) Literal interpretation; (2) Interpretation based on intent; (3) Common meaning; (4) Specialized meaning; (5) Technical meaning; (6) Dictionary meaning.

Case 1.—In 1886, in Illinois, citizens of McLeansboro filed a petition for a writ of mandamus to require the railroad company to run its passenger trains to a certain station and to stop there to receive and discharge passengers. The town contended that the obligation to conform with this requirement was imposed by the charters of the St. Louis and Southeastern Railway Company and the Evansville and Southern Illinois Railway Company because of the use of the words "to" and *from* in their respective charters, the use of "to" referring to the building of a railway "to McLeansboro"; and that of *from* to building a railway "from the town of McLeansboro."

It was decided that a railroad charter, authorizing the building of a line of roads "from one town to another" did not require the railroad to come within the corporate limits of either town, but was satisfied by a road extending from the boundary of one town to that of the other. Thus the mandamus was refused.

The decision was based on the literal interpretation of *from:* noting beginning of the road, exclusive of the object mentioned.[1]

Case 2.—In North Carolina, on March 10, 1848, the commissioners of Salisbury passed a town ordinance, prohibiting a "person from Gold-Hill," a place infected with small-pox, from entering Salisbury under a penalty of fifty dollars for each offense. On March 9, Dr. Charles Powe, a resident of Salisbury, was on his way to Wadesborough and passed through Gold-Hill, where he visited a patient, who had the small-pox. Then he went on to Wadesborough. On March 15, he returned to Salisbury, without having been at Gold-Hill since March 9. He knew, however, that the ordinance had been adopted on March 10. The defendant contended that the expression "person from Gold-Hill" was not to be construed so as to include every one who had been in that place, or came from it at any indefinite period before, but to include only those coming immediately or directly from it. Dr. Powe did not come directly from Gold-Hill, nor had he been there after the ordinance was adopted.

After the intent of the law was considered, it was decided that the commissions could not recover. The law applied to persons coming directly from Gold-Hill.[2]

Case 3.—In 1901, in Maryland, James Sindall brought an injunction to restrain a tax put on his property by the mayor and city council of Baltimore. The Acts of the Assembly of 1888 provided that "from and after" the year 1900 certain property annexed to Baltimore should be taxed at the city rate. Sindall had been taxed for the year 1900. He objected, contending that *from*, when referring to a certain point as a *terminus a quo*, always excluded that point. He also argued that the beginning of a point of time within the year 1900 could not then be fixed as from and after the year 1900.

It was decided that Sindall did not have to pay taxes for the "landed property" until after 1900.

The decision was based on the ordinary meaning of *from*, which excludes the *terminus a quo*.[3]

Case 4.—In South Carolina, in 1883, Adam Shuler was indicted, under the General Statute of 1882, for stealing corn in the field of one Riley and upon conviction moved in arrest of judgment, on the ground that the indictment was fatally defective because it charged the corn was stolen "in the field" instead of "from the field" in the language of the statute. The statute read: "Whoever shall steal from the field any grain or cotton, whether severed from the soil or not, shall be deemed guilty of felony; and, on conviction thereof, shall be punished by imprisonment in the penitentiary for not less than one year nor more than five years, or in the jail for not less than three months nor more than six months, or by fine, not less than fifty dollars nor more than five hundred dollars."

The court decided that the real purpose of "from the field"

was to point to a particular kind of property, to wit: the products of, or outgrowth from the field, of the kind designated, before they were gathered by the owner, and not to the stealing of that kind of property in any locality, as a bag of corn, taken from the barn or purchased in the market, carelessly left in the field. The object therefore was to extend special protection to a kind of property which the owner could not carefully guard and protect from theft, as it must necessarily remain exposed in an open field until it could be gathered.

The court said that *from* was necessary and that an indictment charging the stealing of corn in the field was defective.

Judgment was therefore rendered in favor of Shuler.

The words "from the field" in a statute describing the offense of stealing grain or cotton *from* a field has specialized significance, indicating "products or outgrowth from the field." Thus the decision was based on the specialized meaning of *from*.[4]

Case 5.—A bill of sale for goods provided that the vendee should have the proceeds of all sales made "from and after April 1." In 1895, in Iowa, the Chicago Title and Trust Company brought action against J. J. Smith to recover $149.11 with interest from April 5, 1893, alleged to be due as a balance on a contract for the sale of merchandise. Smith denied that he was indebted to the plaintiff. Judgment was rendered in favor of the defendant and the plaintiff appealed.

The case turned on the meaning of "from April"; that is, whether April 1 should be included or excluded. The court said the rule was, "Where time is computed from an act done, the general rule is to include the day; where it is computed from the day of the act done, the day is excluded."

The decision was in favor of the plaintiff, and was based upon the technical use of *from* in computing time.[5]

Case 6.—In California, in 1894, action was brought by J. W. Sefton to obtain an injunction to prevent W. B. Prentice and others from keeping Sefton from attaching his water pipe to the defendant's water pipe. Judgment was rendered the plaintiff and the defendants appealed. In 1811, Prentice had made a contract with F. T. Hill, whose assign Sefton was. The contract, which was the basis of the trial, was an agreement to deliver at a certain place a certain quantity of water to be delivered "through and from a pipe, flume, or conduit, to be constructed" by the appellants. Sefton, having acquired all of Hill's interest in the contract, demanded of Prentice and others that they allow him to attach his pipe to theirs so that by the pressure in the appellants' pipe the water would be carried over the elevation to Sefton's land. The appellants refused to consent. They said that they did not agree to give Hill possession of any part of the pipe, for the purpose of cutting a hole in it and permanently occupying it by his attached pipe, or for any other purpose. They also said that there was not a word in the contract about the furnishing of any "pressure" but that the contract was to deliver the water in such a way as to give Hill a reasonable opportunity to take possession of the water delivered. Sefton put a great deal of stress on the word *from* in the contract. The judge said that *from* simply expressed the general idea of separation as shown in the definitions by Webster: "Out of the neighborhood of"; leaving behind"; "out of"; "the antithesis and correlative of to." The judge did not think that the contract authorized Sefton to cut a hole in the pipe through which the water could flow, and to attach permanently a pipe leading to his own premises.

Judgment was therefore rendered in favor of Prentice.

The decision was based on the dictionary definition of *from*: "out of."[6]

The word *from* is used in both a physical and figurative sense. If Mr. Jones says, "The distance from my home to the school is five miles," he is speaking of the physical distance measured from his home, a definite place, to the school, another definite place. There are material limitations. If, however, Mr. Jones says, "The number of years from this year until 1934 is five," there is nothing physical about the calculation. Nevertheless, the calculation is done in the same way, for the measurement of the time has definite limitations just as the measurement of the road had, but the limitations are not physical. In this temporal sense, *from* is used figuratively. The illustrative cases given here fall under two linguistic classifications: (*a*) Physical meaning; (*b*) Figurative meaning. Cases (1), (2), (4), and (6) belong to classification (*a*); cases (3) and (5) to classification (*b*).

(*a*) In case (1), *from* is used in its physical sense, designating the starting point of the railroad. It is employed as a word of exclusion, showing that the railroad began outside the corporate limits. Usually, *from* is employed as a word of exclusion. If a man says, "Measure the distance from the desk to the table," he means exclude both the desk and table and measure the distance between them. In case (2), *from* is used in its physical sense, but as a word of inclusion as well as one of exclusion. All the persons within the corporate limits of Gold Hill are excluded from Salisbury. It is inclusive in that it involves persons within the corporate limits as well as those near them. One of the definite physical limitations was Gold Hill, but *from* referred to people within the town as well as to those living just at the boundary, as in Case (1). This meaning is also common. If Mr. Smith says, "All the visitors from England are conservative," he means those who come from within England.

Case (4) illustrates *from* in its physical sense, but with still another variation. It is used in connection with a definite place, the field, but the field is the source of the corn, for the corn is growing in it. For the corn to be taken from the field, it must be taken while still on the stalk. This use of *from* is heard in everyday English in such statements as, "If any one goes into my watermelon patch and steals watermelons from it, he will be poisoned, for I have put strychnine in them," the speaker meaning if a person pulls watermelons from the vines and eats them, he will be poisoned, for the strychnine, put into the vine, has gone into the melons. In this case *from* is used as a word of source or origin.

Case (6) shows *from* employed in one of its usual senses. It has the meaning of "out of," denoting separation. The same implication is shown in the statement "I am going away from New York," meaning out of the neighborhood of New York.

(*b*) Often *from* is employed in its figurative sense. Case (4) shows *from* used in this manner in the statement, "from the year 1900." It is used as a word of exclusion but not as a word of exclusion in a material sense. This usage is common. If a man says, "From the day of the game I have not taken a drink," he means, since the day of the game.

Case (5) shows the figurative meaning again given to *from* as a word of inclusion instead of one of exclusion. This use is also known in common parlance. If a man says, "From now on I do not intend to drink," he is including the present as well as the future.

Thus we see that *from* is used in daily speech, both with the physical and figurative connotations.

In

The word *in* is defined according to: (1) Literal interpretation; (2) Interpretation based on intent; (3) Common meaning; (4) Specialized meaning; (5) Dictionary meaning; (6) Circumstances.

Case 1.—In 1897, Spencer Van Bokkelen took out accident insurance with the Travelers' Insurance Company. The policy provided: if "death results from such injuries [injuries resulting 'through external, violent, and accidental means'] alone, within ninety days, the company will pay $10,000 to Caroline Van Bokkelen, his daughter." There was a further provision: "if such injuries are sustained while riding as a passenger in any passenger conveyance using steam, cable, or electricity as a motive power, the amount to be paid shall be double the sum specified in the clause under which claim is made." While the policy was in force Van Bokkelen was killed. He was standing on the platform of a train. In some way he was thrown from the platform and fell upon a bridge, which the train was then crossing, and then upon the ground below. The insurance company paid the beneficiary $10,000. Caroline Van Bokkelen contended that she should have $20,000, the double indemnity, because her father had been a passenger *in* the train.

The court decided in favor of the defendant, by stating that *in* a passenger conveyance there would be little or no danger, while on the uninclosed platform of a railway car there would be great danger when the train was in motion.

The decision was based on the literal interpretation of *in* as used in the policy: "on the inside of."[1]

Case 2.—In 1812, in Pennsylvania, Savary brought an action of debt on a bond, in the penalty of $1,920 with the condition that Goe should deliver to Savary, or his agent or assigns, at the place of embarkation in Brownsville, 1,920 gallons of good merchantable proof whiskey, in good and tight barrels, in all the month of May, 1809. The whiskey was not delivered. The defendant, however, said that he was, in all the month of May, ready, prepared, and willing to deliver the whiskey to the plaintiff, or his agent, at the place of embarkation.

It was decided that "in all the month of May" meant that the seller had authority to deliver the whiskey up till the last hour of May 31, the time intended in the statement. As the whiskey was not delivered, judgment was rendered in favor of the plaintiff.

The decision was based on the interpretation of the intent of *in* in the phrase "in all the month of May."[2]

Case 3.—Clara Blaydes in Iowa made a will by which she directed that the proceeds of her property should, at the expiration of five years after her death, be given to an orphan asylum *in* Muscatine, or, if no such orphan asylum was then in existence there, to a home for old ladies *in* that city. Five years after her death there was a home for old ladies within the corporate limits of Muscatine and an orphan asylum outside the corporate limits, but within a mile of the city. Both the Old Ladies' Home and the Orphan Asylum claimed the legacy. The Old Ladies' Home contended that from the word *in*, the home or asylum would have to be within the corporate limits in order to get the bequest.

The judge said that the bequest to an orphan asylum in the city should not be construed with a strictness limiting the meaning of *in* to "within the corporate limits," but that *in* should be regarded as equivalent to "at," for in ordinary speech *in* and "at" were used synonymously in speaking of cities and towns, or other geographical locations. He also said that *in* or "at" Muscatine would have the same meaning and that no one would consider the geographical lines of the city.

Thus the money went to the orphan asylum, although it was outside the city limits.

The decision was based on the common meaning of *in:* "at."[3]

Case 4.—In West Virginia in 1882, C. D. Uhl granted to the Ohio River Railroad Company "the full and free right of way of the width of fifty feet . . . in, upon, and through the lands of the said Uhl; . . . conveyed for the construction, building, and use of the road of said company." The company contended, in 1902, that the agreement conferred upon it a right of absolute fee-simple estate in the very body of the soil of the fifty-foot strip, the very land itself, carrying with it all minerals, and consequently the right to extract oil from it, just as Uhl could do on his remaining land. The company demanded of him a conveyance carrying the very land itself. Uhl contended that he conferred on the company only an easement, a right to construct a railroad upon the land, and denied the right to carry on upon the land the business of the production of oil, thereby damaging his remaining land irreparably by draining off its oil.

The face of the agreement said that the motive and purpose was to obtain the right of passage for a railroad through Uhl's farm. To accomplish this purpose a "right of way" was granted "in, upon, and through the lands of said Uhl." Thus the judge considered the grant as an easement in fee simple and not as title to the land itself and the oil in it, since the grant was to a railroad, which always wants a right of way.

The decision rendered in favor of Uhl was based upon the specialized meaning of *in* in grants of land for building a railroad.[4]

Case 5.—On July 6, 1895, in New York, Samuel Feree, doing business under the name of the Surface Railway Advertising Company, entered into a contract with the Moquin-Offerman-Hessenbuttel Coal Company. The former agreed to insert an advertisement of a certain size for twelve months in a certain place at a certain price. The following statement was in the contract: "This contract may be discontinued in three months upon payment of $7.50 per month additional." Feree fulfilled his contract and the defendants paid for three monthly installments. At the expiration of the year Feree brought suit to recover the installments for the remaining nine months. The defendants alleged that on November 2, 1895, they had notified the plaintiff that they desired to discontinue the advertisement on and after December 1, and that they offered to pay at the contract rate for two months following October 15, and $7.50 in addition for each of five months, and that the offer was refused.

The court referred to the definitions given for *in* by the Century Dictionary. As a preposition of time they were: "(*a*) Of a point of time, or a period taken as a point; at. (*b*) Of a course or period of time; within the limits or duration of; during. (*c*) Of a limit of time; at the expiration of." The defendants adopted the definition "at the expiration of," but extended the meaning by adding, in effect, the words, "and all times thereafter," so as to carry the option through the remaining nine months of the contract.

Since the time from July 6 to November 2 was a period of more than three months, the decision was in favor of the plaintiff.

The decision was based on the dictionary meaning of *in:* "at the expiration of."[5]

Case 6.—In 1909, in Pennsylvania, Arthur Depue brought action against the Travelers' Insurance Company which had agreed to pay him a certain sum, if his mother, Mrs. Sarah Hope, should lose her life as the result of "bodily injuries effected directly and independently of all other causes, through external, violent and accidental means . . . while in a passenger elevator." The defendant conceded that she died from bodily injuries as were described in the quoted clause, but denied that they were inflicted while she was "in a passenger elevator." The facts were: An elevator was standing at the first floor of the building, with the door, which extended to the elevator roof, wide open. The attendant was elsewhere. The car was operated by a lever on the side wall to the right of a person entering the door, and, while the elevator was stationary the lever was in the center of its arc of operation. To start the elevator it was necessary to push down a button at the center of the arc. This manipulation permitted the movement of the lever to the right or left. The elevator was in perfect condition, both before and after the accident, which no one saw. The building superintendent found Mrs. Hope, hanging head downward into the elevator, her body caught between the roof of it and the floor of the building. One limb, which had been caught at the thigh, was projecting over the floor. When the elevator was released, the woman fell into it on the floor. The court held that since no one knew how Mrs. Hope's death had occurred, judgment should be rendered in favor of Depue, the plaintiff, for $5,000 insurance.

The decision was therefore based on circumstances.[6]

The word *in* has both a limited and an extended meaning as shown in the cases given here. The linguistic classifications are: (*a*) Limited meaning; (*b*) Extended meaning. Cases (1), (2), (4), and (5) belong to classification (*a*); cases (3) and (6) to classification (*b*).

(*a*) In case (1), *in* has a definite limited physical meaning because it applies to the inside of the train only and does not include the platform. If John is standing near a train and does not see James, he mây ask where James is. If he receives the answer, "He is in the train," it is understood that James is inside the train. Were he on the platform John probably could see him.

Case (2) shows *in* with a definite, limited sense, which is also figurative. There is nothing physical about the measurement of time. "In all the month of May" limits the delivery, which could be made at any time from the first hour of May until the last hour. This use is employed in common parlance. If John says, "In all my school life I have never cheated," he means from the first day up until the time he is speaking he has never cheated. He has in mind definite limits in a figurative sense. The same meaning is found in case (5). "In three months" has definite limits. The notice could have been given at any time from the first of the three months until the last of them, but not after the period had expired.

Case (4) differs from the two preceding examples in that *in* is again employed in a physical sense. It limits the railroad company to a certain part of Uhl's land to be used only as a right of way. This use of the word *in* is a specialized one in regard to grants to railroads for the construction and use of tracks. It means a right of way and nothing more.

(*b*) The word *in* does not always have a limited meaning, as is shown in case (3). There "in Muscatine" does not refer to land within the corporate limits, but refers to neighboring land. It has the meaning of "at" in ordinary speech. This use of *in* is common. If Mr. Smith makes the assertion, "There is a factory in Gastonia," he does not necessarily mean the factory is within the corporate limits. He would make the same statement if it were near Gastonia.

Case (6) shows the extended meaning of *in*, but in a different way. A woman with her head hanging downward into the elevator was considered *in* the elevator. This use of the word is common. If John puts his head inside the post office door and James sees him do that, James might make the statement, "I saw John in the post office," although John was not totally inside the building.

Like

The word *like* is defined according to: (1) Common meaning.

Case 1.—In Alabama, the Soule Steam Feed Works sold to the Vinegar-Bend Lumber Company a stacker supposed to be like the one used at the Robertson mill at Chicora. The Vinegar Bend Lumber Company refused to pay for the stacker, on the ground that it was not like the Robertson stacker. They had, however, accepted the stacker, which was very similar to the Robertson type.

The court said that if the defendant accepted the stacker and if, in substantially all respects, it was the same as, or was similar to, or would do the same work as, the Robertson stacker, the meaning complied with *like*, for a difference in a small bolt, lever, or pulley was not a material difference in the construction of the machine.

Judgment was therefore rendered in favor of the Soule Steam Feed Works. The Vinegar Bend Lumber Company appealed, but the judgment was affirmed, the decision being based on the common meaning of *like:* "similar to."[1]

The word *like* may have a definite meaning or an indefinite meaning. If John has just bought a yellow pencil and James wants one of the same kind, James says, "I want one like John's." That use of *like* has a definite meaning. More often *like* is employed in an indefinite sense. For instance, if Mr. Smith says, "John looks like James," he means that there is a similarity between the two. The illustrative case given here belongs to the linguistic classification: (*a*) Indefinite meaning. The stacker was supposed to be similar to the one used at the Robertson Mill at Chicora. The fundamental parts were to be the same, but a slight difference in bolts, levers, or pulleys was not to be considered. This use of *like* is common in ordinary speech.

Near

The word *near* is defined according to: (1) Literal Interpretation; (2) Interpretation based on intent; (3) Interpretation suggested by fact; (4) Common meaning; (5) Context; (6) Circumstances.

Case 1.—Charlotte Kellogg, in 1855, in Massachusetts, brought action against the inhabitants of Northampton to recover damages for a defect in a highway, which she alleged the town failed to keep in repair "at a place near the house of George Kellog." The plaintiff, walking at the spot, was injured. The Statute in 1852 bound the town to keep roads in repair.

It was decided, however, that "at a place near the house of Kellogg" did not describe the spot where the accident occurred with such certainty that the town could be held liable.

The decision was based on the literal interpretation of *near*, which is not definite in its meaning.[1]

Case 2.—In Tennessee, by the Statute of 1869–70, was enacted "That no liquor shop in this State shall be kept open on election days, nor shall any person, on said days, give or sell intoxicating liquors to any person, for any purpose, at or near an election ground." Henry Manis sold to Wilson Johnson on election day

May 13, 1871, some liquor at his house, which was situated one mile or one mile and a quarter from the election ground.

The judge said that if the selling of liquor were permitted at a place which was accessible the law would be a dead letter on the statute book.

It was decided that within a mile and a quarter was within the scope of the operation of the statute, for the purpose of the enactment was to preserve good order and conserve peace.

The decision was based on the intent of *near* in the law, meaning "accessible."[2]

Case 3.—In 1882, in Vermont, O. G. Fassett brought against the town of Roxbury a case for injury on a highway. He was injured while travelling on a highway, "leading from the west, or depot village" in Roxbury to another depot village near a railroad crossing. He said of his injury, "I was thrown from my wagon, and severely injured in my spine near my shoulders so that I have had no use of my arms since that time, but have been, and am now, confined to my bed, entirely helpless, and I was otherwise injured in and about my back and spine, and internally." The defendant contended that the notice did not describe the bodily injuries sufficiently. The statute provided that the part of the body injured should be given in the notice.

The judge said that the spine injured near the shoulders referred to the part of the body between the shoulder blades and that this description was sufficiently definite to designate the part of the body hurt.

Judgment was therefore rendered in favor of the plaintiff, *near* being interpreted to refer to the shoulder blades. The statement referring to the spine near the shoulders designated a definite spot.[3]

Case 4.—In 1820, House brought an action of assumpsit against Griffen to recover money demanded and received for toll at the eastermost turnpike gate, on the Columbia turnpike road, on the ground that the toll was illegally exacted, in consequence of the gate's having been erected illegally at the place where it stood, and without any authority. The turnpike corporation was given the right by the Legislature to erect a most eastwardly turnpike gate, which was to be near the Massachusetts line. The first gate erected was one mile and three quarters west of the Massachusetts line. Later the gate was moved to a spot about one mile distant from the Massachutts border, a place two miles and three quarters from the boundary. The whole length of the road was about nineteen and a half miles.

The judge thought the company should use discretion or common sense in changing and moving the gates and not shift it at their convenience. The court therefore decided that a toll-gate erected two miles and three quarters from the Massachusetts line was not placed *near* that line, within the meaning of the act; and that, therefore, an action lay against the toll-gatherer at the suit of the person from whom he had demanded and received toll, at such gate, to recover the money so unlawfully demanded and received.

The decision was based on the common meaning of *near:* "close to."[4]

Case 5.—In California, in 1911, W. J. Haughawont brought action against Catherine Percival. The judgment was in favor of the former, foreclosing the lien of a street assessment for sewer work done in Los Angeles. The Vrooman Act provided for the posting of notices in street assessment proceedings "on or near the chamber door" of the city council. The court decided that according to the subject matter of the act the fact that the notices were posted on a bulletin board in the city hall in which the council chamber was located was sufficient, because the bulletin board was in plain view from the main entrance of the hall, and so placed as to be likely to bring the notices to the attention of persons visiting the council chamber.

The decision was based on the context of the act.[5]

Case 6.—In Indiana, in 1909, Klitzke Bros. brought action against the Western Union Telegraph Company for damages claimed to be due to the failure of the Western Union to deliver a telegram sent by Klitzke Bros. and addressed to "Miss Julia Ludwig, St. John, Ind." The complaint averred that Miss Ludwig lived near St. John. Under Burns' Annotated Statute of of 1909; "Such companies shall deliver all dispatches, by a messenger, to the persons to whom the same are addressed, or to their agents, on payment of any charges due for the same: Provided, such persons or agents reside within one mile of the telegraphic station or within the city or town in which such station is." The complaint did not state that she lived within one mile of the town.

The judge said that *near* is a relative term and its precise import can only be determined by the attendant facts and circumstances. It was shown that Miss Ludwig lived three miles from the terminal office and the town limits of St. John. Since there was no extra charge on the delivery for the extra distance, it was decided that Klitzke Bros. could not recover. A lower court had given an opinion in favor of Klitzke Bros.

The judgment was reversed because of the circumstances: Miss Ludwig lived outside of the town limits and no provision was made for the extra charge.[6]

The word *near* never brings anything definite to one's mind. It is a word that has a relative meaning which has to be determined by attendant circumstances. Circumstances limiting its meaning will be shown in the illustrative cases given here. These cases fall under two linguistic classifications: (*a*) Indefinite meaning; (*b*) Definite meaning. Cases (1), (2), (4), (5), and (6) belong to classification (*a*); case (3) belongs to classification (*b*).

(*a*) In case (1), *near* means "close to" and is therefore indefinite in its import. We do not know how close to the house the accident occurred. This signification is quite general. If Sergeant Smith says, "The bullet passed near me," we do not know exactly how close the bullet came to him, as no definite spot is specified.

In case (2), *near* takes on the meaning of "accessible" in its indefiniteness. This use is also common. If Mr. Brown says, "Go to any grocery store near the house and buy some cookies," he means go to a store that is accessible.

Case (4) shows *near* with the same meaning as in case (1), except that the meaning is extended. "Near the Massachusetts line," however, did not include a location two and three-quarter miles away. That distance, which could not be considered near the line, was about one-seventh of the whole distance. In ordinary life one does not consider such a large per cent *near*.

Case (5) presents another variation of the indefinite meaning of *near*. In this instance it takes on the signification of "capable of being seen." The notice may be in view from many places about the door. There is no definite spot for it. The indefiniteness is limited, however, in that the notice has to be in a place that can be seen.

In case (6), we again find that indefinite use of *near*, which does not tell the distance. The distance, which was measured and found to be three miles, was not considered *near* or "close by."

(*b*) Occasionally *near* has a definite meaning, as shown in case (3). The spine near the shoulders would have to be between the shoulders. This definite use, which is determined by the surrounding facts, is sometimes employed in everyday speech. There are two buildings adjoining each other—Philosophy Hall and Clinton Hall. One will often hear somebody say that the building near Philosophy Hall is Clinton Hall. Because of the fact that Clinton Hall is next to Philosophy Hall *near* has a definite meaning.

Of

The word *of* is defined according to: (1) Interpretation based on intent; (2) Interpretation suggested by fact; (3) Common meaning; (4) Dictionary meaning; (5) Historical development.

Case 1.—In Pennsylvania, in 1889, the Delaware Division Canal Company brought suit for tax on loans from a settlement of account by the auditor general and state treasurer. The court decided in favor of the company and the commonwealth brought a writ of error under the act of June 30, 1885, which required the treasurer of every private corporation, upon payment of interest, to assess the tax "three mills on every dollar of the interest paid as aforesaid." The commonwealth's claim was for taxes upon that portion of the bonded indebtedness held by resident owners, at the rate of three mills on the nominal value thereof for the year ending on the first Monday of November 1886. The Delaware Division Canal Company was a corporation of Pennsylvania, chartered in 1858, having authority to borrow money, issue bonds, and secure them by mortgage. During the year ending as aforesaid the defendant's bonds, secured by mortgage, were worth $800,000, $700,000 of which were held by residents of the state. The company denied the authority of the Legislature to require an assessment by the treasurer.

It was decided that the company was bound to make the assessment and deduct the tax from the interest paid, for by the word *of* in the phrase "three mills on every dollar of the interest paid," the Legislature meant "off." Thus the judgment was rendered in favor of the commonwealth for $940.50, with interest at 12 per cent a year from June 27, 1887, and costs.

The decision was based on the interpretation of the intent of *of* in the act. It was thought that the Legislature meant "off."[1]

Case 2.—In Texas, in 1901, Juan Rocha was convicted of murder and appealed. Motion was made to quash the second and third counts of the indictment, each of which alleged the act was done "of his malice aforethought" instead of "with malice aforethought," the phrasing used in the statute concerning murder in the first degree. Juan Rocha and Mrs. Grimsinger were in love with each other. They planned the murder of Mr. Grimsinger and Rocha executed it. He confessed.

The judgment was affirmed, for it was decided that if the appellant killed Grimsinger "of his malice aforethought" it was murder, as much so as if he had killed him "with malice aforethought." The court held that one phrase was the equivalent in meaning of the other and that the use of the phrase "of his malice aforethought" in an indictment for murder instead of "with malice aforethought" did not invalidate the indictment, though the latter was the statutory form.

The decision was based on the interpretation suggested by fact. The meaning of *of* became "with." Mr. Grimsinger was killed whether it was done "of malice aforethought" or "with malice aforethought." The two phrases were thus equivalent in meaning.[2]

Case 3.—In Indiana, in 1895, Louise Jordan was indicted as having unlawfully, willfully, and maliciously set fire to and burned a certain flour, grist, and corn mill house of Samuel Jordan, Aaron Jordan, and Winfield Lane. Louise Jordan contended that the indictment was insufficient, because it failed to charge the burning of a building, and failed to charge that such a building was the property of another.

She was convicted, for it was decided, according to ordinary use, that the word "house" meant building and that the phrase "millhouse of Samuel Jordan, etc.," sufficiently explained that the mill house was the property of those named.

The decision was based on the common meaning of *of:* "belonging to." To say "the house of Samuel Jordan" in ordinary speech means "the house belonging to Samuel Jordan."[3]

Case 4.—In 1902, in Frederick County, Maryland, James King was indicted for larceny. The indictment read: "He with force and arms, at the county aforesaid, $26.50 current money, . . . of the goods and chattels of one John Lipscomb stole." King demurred on the ground that money was not properly described as "goods and chattels." Judgment was rendered for King and the state appealed. The case was reversed as a result of the use of Webster's International Dictionary, which defined *of* as "belonging to" and "denoting possession or ownership." The court then decided that *of* showed that the money belonged to Lipscomb, that "of the goods and chattels," really surplusage, could be left out, and that the meaning would be clear anyway.

The decision was based on an appeal to the dictionary in which *of* meant "belonging to."[4]

Case 5.—A writ of entry was brought on May 12, 1871, by E. F. Hannum and another, administrators of the estate of W. S. Pomeroy, to recover a parcel of land in Northampton. The deed of land read, "all the land situate and lying north of the road aforesaid, bounded north of the heirs of Matthew Clark's land." Here *of* was construed in its obsolete, but perfectly grammatical meaning of "by," as in the familiar examples, "seen of men," and "tempted of the devil."

Judgment was therefore rendered in favor of the demandants.

The decision was based on an appeal to the history of the language, whereby the meaning of *of* was traced back to one of its former significations, no longer used: "by."[5]

The word *of* has come down to Modern English with the same form and meaning that it had in Anglo-Saxon times. In Anglo-Saxon it was *of*, meaning "of" in the possessive sense, "from," "among," and concerning." It is true that as the centuries have passed it has taken on other meanings that are slightly different. The word is usually employed either in the sense of separation, or in that of possession. The illustrative cases given here fall under the three linguistic classifications: (*a*) Separation; (*b*) Possession; (*c*) Juxtaposition. Case (1) belongs to classification (*a*); cases (2), (3), and (4) belong to classification (*b*); and (5) belongs to classification (*c*).

(*a*) Case (1) shows *of* with the meaning "off," distinctly an idea of separation. The tax assessed was to be deducted from the interest paid. This use is heard in connection with discounts. If a merchant says, "Mr. Brown, you will get 2 per cent discount on every dollar of the original payment," he means 2 per cent of the original payment will be taken off that amount.

(*b*) In the sense of possession, *of* is far more commonplace than *of* in the sense of separation. If a person hears the word alone, he immediately thinks of "belonging to." This use is shown in case (3), where the "mill house of Samuel Jordan" referred to the "mill house belonging to Samuel Jordan." This meaning is heard everyday. If John says, "Here is the bolt of the car," he means the bolt belonging to the car. The same sense of possession is illustrated in case (4).

Case (2), however, shows possession in a different sense. "Of malice aforethought" takes on the meaning of "with malice aforethought," because the person felt malice toward the man he killed. This use of *of* is heard often. In this sense, it indicates the cause, motive, or reason by which a person or thing is actuated or impelled. If Mr. Smith says, "Mrs. Brown died of tuberculosis," he means that tuberculosis caused the death.

(*c*) Case (5) shows *of* with an entirely different meaning—that of juxtaposition. "North of the road" means that the land borders the road on the north side. Thus *of* takes on the import of "by." One of the original meanings of *of* was "among." In the sense of "by," *of* comes out of the meaning of "among," which denotes that one thing is in the midst of many, and that one is therefore by another. But, this employment of *of* in the sense of "by" is rare in everyday speech, for the reason that this signification is archaic and obsolete.

Off

The word *off* is defined according to: (1) Interpretation based on intent.

Case 1.—In 1902, in Connecticut, the American Fisheries Company sought an injunction restraining Linnen and others for the period of twenty years from November 26, 1897, from becoming interested in or connected with any business other than that conducted by the complainant, its successors or assigns, in catching menhaden, herring or other fish used in the manufacture of oil or scrap, and restraining them from becoming either directly or indirectly interested in the business of manufacturing such fish, or any fish, into oil or guano, upon, along, or off the Atlantic Seaboard, according to the contract made between them on February 21, 1898. In 1900, the American Fisheries Company, after buying the interest of Linnen and others, went into the hands of the receivers, under the chancery laws of New Jersey. Then Linnen, as treasurer and general manager, and Allyn, as secretary, took part in the purchase of a fishing plant at Harburton, Virginia, and on April 11, 1900, assisted in the organization and management of the Menhaden Oil and Guano Company, which acquired, refurnished, equipped, managed, and carried on the plant and business of menhaden fishing and manufacturing at Harburton. The American Fisheries Company objected.

The case turned upon the meaning of the words "upon, along, and off the Atlantic Seaboard." The judge said that, according to the intent of the parties making the contract, "upon" and "along" referred to the waters adjacent to and easily reached from the coast line and that *off* added to and enlarged the meaning of the words "upon" and "along," carrying the prohibition out into the deep water more distant from the coast.

Judgment was therefore rendered in favor of the plaintiff. The prohibition extended from Maine to Florida, including all bays and indentations along the coast.

The decision was based on an interpretation of the intent of the parties using *off*.[1]

The word *off* is used in both a physical and figurative sense. The sentence "He stepped off the box" shows it in its physical sense, implying separation. To step off a box is to separate one's feet from the box and place them elsewhere. In the statement, "John is a little off the game," however, there is nothing physical about the use of *off*. It is employed in its figurative sense, implying that John is not up to the game, or is not in condition for the game; that is, John is not nearly so good as usual. The illustrative case given here falls under the linguistic classification: (*a*) Physical meaning. This case shows definitely *off* in the physical sense, conveying as usual the idea of separation. In the expression "upon, along, and off the Atlantic Seaboard" *off* only enlarges the meaning of the words "upon and along," which refer to the waters adjacent to the coast line; that is, *off* refers to the waters more distant from the coast than those considered as "upon and along," but adjoining those. Thus the waters *off* the coast are separated from the coast itself by the waters adjoining the coast. This employment of *off* designating separation in the physical sense is the usual one.

On

The word *on* is defined according to: (1) Literal interpretation; (2) Interpretation based on intent; (3) Common meaning; (4) Technical meaning; (5) Dictionary meaning; (6) Context; (7) Circumstances.

Case 1.—In Georgia, in 1911, E. Hutchinson was convicted for being intoxicated on a public highway. He brought a writ of error, for he was within fifteen to thirty feet of the road. The case was reversed, for the court said that *on* in the Laws of 1905, making it unlawful for a person to be in an intoxicated condition on any public street or highway, was not synonymous with "near" and that one could not be convicted under the act for being intoxicated on a porch or shed of a store within fifteen to thirty feet of a public road.

The literal interpretation of *on* was considered. Because Hutchinson was not actually *on* the highway, as the law required for the imposing of a penalty, the case was reversed and he was set free.[1]

Case 2.—Hoskins claimed title to a piece of land on validity of a tax deed. The Iowa Land Company contested the deed because no notice of the sale for taxes was posted on the courthouse door as was required by the statute. The notice had been posted upon a bulletin board at the door.

The court said that "on the door" did not necessarily mean on the swinging panel which filled the opening or entrance to the building, but that a conspicuous posting upon the building at the side of the opening, or upon a separate board or panel or bulletin kept there for that purpose was sufficient, to all reasonable intents and purposes, because the design of the law was to have the notice in a public place, easy of access.

It was decided that posting "on the courthouse door" was fairly and fully complied with by posting upon a bulletin board at the door. Judgment was therefore rendered in favor of the plaintiff.

The decision was based on the interpretation of the intent of *on*, as used in the law. The idea was to have a conspicuous notice for the public, whether actually on the door or near it.[2]

Case 3.—C. H. Hempstead, in 1879, brought action against Des Moines, Iowa, for injuries to real estate caused by changing of the grade and excavating of the streets upon which the property was situated. The city established the grade in 1857 and re-established it in 1861, but in 1876 changed it; thus decreasing the value of Hempstead's property. The statute under which the plaintiff claimed to recover provided: "When any city or town shall have established the grade of any street or alley, and any person shall have built or made any improvements on such street or alley, according to the established grade thereof, and such city or town shall alter said established grade in such a manner as to injure or diminish the value of said property, said city or town shall pay to the owner or owners of said property so injured the amount of such damage or injury."

The defendant contended that the improvement had to be made actually on the street in the way that the statute read before the plaintiff would be entitled to recover. The court, however, said the ordinary meaning of *on* when used to designate a place is "at," "near," "adjacent to," and that the statute evidently contemplated improvements upon lots situated *on* the street.

Judgment was therefore rendered in favor of the plaintiff, the decision being based on the common meaning of *on*, which is "at," "near," "adjacent to."[3]

Case 4.—On April 3, 1886, in Connecticut, a contract was made between Dwight Connell and George Richmond. Richmond agreed to let Connell have a farm on shares. Connell agreed not to sell any hay, corn, or fodder of any kind from the farm, to manage it for the best interests of both parties, and to pay Richmond on the first day of June, 1886, and every two months thereafter, up to the expiration of the year, one-half of the amount of all sales from the farm. Connell grew oats, a portion of which, not exceeding one-half, Richmond took and appropriated to his own use without Connell's consent. The latter brought suit for that liberty, which he claimed was illegal.

The court said that "letting land on shares" was a phrase well understood among farmers, meaning that both parties should share equally in the products of the land, to compensate the one for his labor, and the other for the use of his land, and that as a result after the crops were harvested before a division, each party was owner of an individual moiety of the same, and was a tenant in common with the other, unless the contract contained some special provision taking the case out of the general rule.

Judgment was therefore rendered in favor of the defendant.

The technical meaning of *on shares* was considered. *On shares* means "equal shares."[4]

Case 5.—The London Assurance Corporation was a foreign insurance firm and Thompson was one of several individual underwriters, who issued what are known as "Lloyd's policies" and did business under the name of the New Jersey State Fire Association.

The plaintiff issued to Patterson, Downing and Company a policy covering all the risks by railroad, etc., for rosin, turpentine, and other goods commonly known as "naval stores" in warehouses, yards, and elsewhere. The policy of the defendant agreed to "*reinsure the London Assurance Corporation* . . . against all direct loss or damage by fire . . . to the following described herein and not elsewhere, to wit, on the fire risk on naval stores, i.e., rosin turpentine, etc., in barrels while waiting shipment, in or on the warehouse, and/or sheds of Downing and Co. at Brunswick, Georgia, and insured under policies issued by the London Assurance Corporation marine branch." A fire occurred. The plaintiff contended that the original policy embraced "all risks by railroads and/or other inland conveyances, and in warehouses, yards, or elsewhere," but that the policy of reinsurance made no mention of property in yards, or in any place except warehouses and sheds and that unless the rosin destroyed was in or on the warehouses or sheds, it was not covered. The plaintiff thought that the defendant should have to pay for the rosin stored in the yard, his contention being that the defendant reinsured only such property as was stored within the warehouse or shed.

The judge said that to reinsure is to insure what has already been insured. He referred to the Worcester Dictionary which defined *on* as expressing the relation of nearness in place, contiguous to or abutting on, as for instance: "as their navy on your shores," "on each side," "the town on the lake," "the store on Main Street."

It was thus decided that the yard in which the rosin was stored surrounded the warehouse, and was abutting on or contiguous thereto and that the intention of the parties was that the rosin in the yard should be insured. Judgment was therefore rendered in favor of the defendant.

The decision was based on an appeal to the dictionary, which showed *on* as expressing the relation of nearness in place, contiguous to, or abutting on.[5]

Case 6.—In 1874, W. S. Niblett brought action against the mayor and city council of Nashville to recover damages for an injury received by stumbling into an excavation on the margin of an alley. The plaintiff originally declared that the pitfall was "in and on a public alley and common highway." An amendment in 1872 said that the excavation was adjacent and contiguous to the alley. The defendant objected to the original declaration.

The judge did not consider the description in the strictest sense, but considered the subject matter and the ordinary acceptance of the phraseology. He said that when one spoke of a town or city as situated on a lake or a river, everybody understood that the place was on the bank or the shore of the lake or stream, adjacent to it; thus, he said, Niblett's declaration, especially when taken in connection with other descriptive circumstances, meant that the excavation was along the side of and adjacent to the alley, just as a church would be referred to as situated on the alley, and would be understood to be adjacent to or along the side of the alley.

Judgment was therefore rendered in favor of the plaintiff.

In this case the context was considered.[6]

Case 7.—In Massachusetts, Horatio Slocomb conveyed to Alvira Smith land described in the deed as "beginning at an angle in the stone wall on the easterly side of the aforesaid road"; thence running around the rear of the lot granted "to a stake and stones at the aforesaid road; thence northerly on the line of said road to the first mentioned bound." She contended that her land extended to the middle of the road and brought in 1857 an action of tort against Slocomb for breaking and entering her close.

Judgment was rendered in favor of the defendant, because actual monuments on the road were mentioned. The court said that since the land began and ended at the side of the road, and extended thus "thence northerly on the line of said road to the first mentioned bound" the road was excluded.

The decision was based on circumstances: actual monuments on the road were mentioned.[7]

The illustrative cases given here that turn on the meaning of *on* fall under the following linguistic classifications: (*a*) Limited physical meaning; (*b*) Extended physical meaning; (*c*) Figurative meaning. Cases (1) and (7) belong to classification (*a*); cases (2), (3), (5), and (6) belong to classification (*b*); case (4) belongs to classification (*c*).

(*a*) In case (1), "on a public highway" means being in the public highway. There we have the limited physical meaning. Near the road was not considered on the road. In common parlance, if a person says, "Look on the table for my book," he does not mean look near the table; he means give attention only to the table.

In case (7), *on* also has a definite limited physical meaning, for it applies to the side of the road, and does not carry the grant to the middle of the road, because monuments which were situated on the side of the road were mentioned. This meaning of *on* is common, especially in speaking of land bordering highways, streams, or streets. If monuments placed at the side of the road are mentioned, a description "on the road" takes the land to the side of the road and not to the center.

(*b*) In case (2), the meaning of *on* extends to neighboring places. "On the door" meant in a conspicuous place near the door and not necessarily on the door itself. The same is true in case (3) in the statement "on the street." In case (5), the expression "rosin in or on the warehouses" includes rosin in the yard, adjoining the warehouse. In case (6), "on a public alley" means "along the side of the alley." This use of *on* is common in daily speech. If Mr. Brown says "My house is on the lake," he means his house is near the lake.

(*c*) Classifications (*a*) and (*b*) show physical relationship, but occasionally *on* is used in a sense that is figurative, as illustrated in case (4), where the expression "on shares" is used, and means that the man who owns the land takes half the crop and the one working for him takes the other half. It is a common expression among farmers and is well understood by them. A man often says, "I am working on shares." The phrase, probably, originated from the statement "on the condition that I receive a share and he a share," shortened and changed to "on shares."

Over

The word *over* is defined according to: (1) Literal interpretation; (2) Interpretation based on intent; (3) Interpretation suggested by fact; (4) Common meaning; (5) Dictionary meaning.

Case 1.—Commonwealth *ex rel.* Bell Telephone Company, Philadelphia, sought mandamus to compel Charles Warwick, mayor of Philadelphia, F. M. Riter, director of public safety, and D. R. Walker, chief of the electric bureau, to grant permits for the erection of terminal poles. The Bell Telephone Company was authorized by the ordinance of 1879 "to run and maintain its wires over and through the streets of the city of Philadelphia for the purpose of establishing telephone communication between its patrons and between its exchange office and the subscribers thereto." The company wanted to lay its wires under the streets and to erect such terminal poles as it deemed necessary, subject only to the regulation of the use of the streets by general ordinances of councils.

The court interpreted the ordinance literally and said that the authority to run and maintain wires "over and through" the streets did not include permission to lay them under, below, or beneath.

Judgment was therefore rendered in favor of the defendant, the decision being based on the literal interpretation of *over*: "higher than."[1]

Case 2.—In 1861, the Boston and Maine Railroad sought a writ of certiorari, representing that the mayor, aldermen, and common council of Lawrence, Massachusetts, laid out a highway in 1856, across the company's railroad track, on a level with it. The most important question raised was whether city officials had authority to lay out such a street. The statute provided that "if, after the laying out and making of any railroad already granted, or which may be hereafter granted, any turnpike road or other way shall be so laid out as to cross said railroad, the said turnpike road or way may be so made as to pass under or over said railroad, and said turnpike or way shall in all cases be so made as not to obstruct or injure such railroad."

The court said that the Legislature did not mean at the same level as the railroad, but at a higher level; thus it was decided that the city had no authority for laying out the highway. The writ of certiorari was granted.

The decision was based on the interpretation of the intent of the Legislature in its use of *over*.[2]

Case 3.—In Texas, in 1912, R. G. Milling was convicted of unlawfully practicing medicine. He appealed. The indictment alleged that the accused practiced medicine without a license, treating a patient by means of physical manipulations with his hands *over* the patient's body, for which he charged two dollars. Milling said he treated McFall as a masseur and not as a physician. It was proved that the accused placed his hands "upon" the patient and rubbed and manipulated his hands "upon" his body.

The court held that the indictment was sufficient and should not be quashed, as it was shown by fact that *over* and "upon" were synonymous.

Judgment was therefore affirmed.

The decision was based on an interpretation suggested by fact. Because it was proved that Milling had his hands upon the body of McFall, *over* took on the meaning of "upon."[3]

Case 4.—In Massachusetts, in 1839, the Newburyport Turnpike Corporation sought an injunction against the Eastern Railroad Company to prevent them from constructing a railroad over the turnpike road by raising the turnpike road a few feet to the same level. The question mainly turned upon the interpretation of the statutes, which provided that every railroad company might raise or lower any turnpike or way, for the purpose of having its railroad pass over and under it.

The complainants contended that it was not the intention of the Legislature to authorize the railroad to raise the turnpike road a few feet to bring it up to the level of the railroad, and thus let it pass over the railroad on the same level, but only to raise it so as to pass above the railroad, by a separate and independent bridge. They argued that the words "raise" and "lower," as applied to the turnpike road, were relative and opposite and that therefore the corresponding words "under" and *over* should be construed as applying to the railroad; and that as the railroad could not lower the turnpike road to pass under the railroad, by an independent passage, it was only intended that the company should raise the turnpike road to pass over the railroad at a higher grade and by an independent bridge.

The judge said that in the ordinary sense of the words, as applied to surface, *over* and "under" are not opposites, for a person passes over a road, if he crosses it on the surface, as well as when he crosses above it, on a bridge, but he cannot be said to pass under it unless he does so on another surface at a lower level. Thus, the judge added, it was as much within the words and intent of the statute to permit the railroad to pass over it at the same level as to raise it much higher to carry the travel over the railroad by an independent bridge.

Judgment was therefore rendered in favor of the defendants.

In this case the common, ordinary meaning of *over* was considered: "upon the surface of."

This case also illustrates the common meaning of "under."[4]

Case 5.—The Illinois Central Railroad Company brought several bills to enjoin Chicago from extending streets across its right of way. By the Act of 1872, the city was given the following authority: "The city council shall have power by condemnation or otherwise to extend any street, alley, or highway over or across, or to construct any sewer, under or through, any railroad track, right of way or land of any railroad company. . . ." The plaintiff contended that the streets across the tracks would be a nuisance of a serious and irreparable nature in the delay of business and increased danger to life.

The judge turned to Webster's Dictionary and found "across" defined as "from side to side; athwart; crosswise; quite over" and *over* as "above, or higher than, in place or position, with the idea of covering; across; from side to side of; upon the surface of." Thus, he said, that the words *over* and "across," having the same meaning, could be used interchangeably.

The bill was therefore dismissed, an appeal having been made to the dictionary.[5]

The word *over* is used in both a physical and a figurative sense. If a napkin is over some cakes, it is on top of the cakes, touching them. This meaning of *over* is physical. The physical meaning of *over* may convey the idea that one object is above another but that there is an intervening space. Such a statement as, "the ceiling is over the floor," indicates an intervening space.

The figurative meaning is shown in such sentences as, "He has advantage over me," implying superiority, as authority, power, dignity, or preference in some way. No material relationship is designated. The relationship shown in the preceding illustration is in the metaphorical sphere.

The illustrative cases given here fall under the classification: (*a*) The physical meaning. Under this classification another division may be made: (I) *Over* meaning "in contact with"; (II) *over* meaning that an intervening space separates the two objects that are placed one above the other. Cases (3), (4), and (5) belong to division (I); cases (1) and (2) to division (II).

(*a*) (I) In case (3), *over* took on the meaning of "upon," a use that is common in everyday speech. If Mary says, "Rub your hands over my head," she means that the hands are to be placed in contact with her head and passed across it. Cases (4) and (5) show the same application of *over* in regard to a street *over* a railroad, where it has the import of "upon the surface of," a use frequently heard. If Mr. Brown says, "John was killed by the train as he walked over the tracks," he means that John walked upon the tracks.

(*a*) (II) In case (1), we find *over* used in the sense of "higher than." Telephone wires never run on the surface of the street, but at some distance above the street. This use of *over* is common. If Mr. Smith says, "The wires over Fulton Street are sagging, he means the wires at a distance above. If they were on the surface, he would not know that they were sagging. In case (2), we find *over* in the expression "under or over said railroad" meaning at a higher level. In daily speech one might say, "The bridge over the railroad is a strong one," meaning the bridge which is at a higher level than the railroad.

Through

The word *through* is defined according to: (1) Literal interpretation; (2) Interpretation based on intent; (3) Common meaning; (4) Dictionary meaning.

Case 1.—In Rhode Island, in 1887, Fiske brought action against Wetmore for putting a drain from a certain portion of land to the sea beyond, though the indenture only granted a right of drainage in and through three private ways or avenues which did not extend to the sea. Wetmore contended that the avenues extended, by implication, to the sea, for the land, then owned by Fiske, belonged to the grantors at the date of the grant.

The court said that an indenture granting a right of drainage in and through three private ways or avenues named did not entitle a grantee, either by direct expression or by implication, to extend the drain to the sea beyond, across another person's land.

Judgment was rendered in favor of Fiske.

The decision was based on the literal interpretation of *through*: "from end to end."[1]

Case 2.—In Texas, in 1907, a controversy arose over property purchased by James McCulloch, on April 13, 1888, for cash. He married Mrs. M. J. Tullis on November 13, 1888. In 1899, he died intestate, in Harrison County, Texas, and left his wife, who died in 1904. James McCulloch left no children or descendants of any children, no parents or descendants of any parents, except Emily Berry, who was his illegitimate sister. Mrs. M. J. McCulloch left as her heir John Tullis, her only child, the issue of her former marriage. On January 1, 1903, Mrs. M. J. McCulloch and John Tullis and his wife sold the land to D. W. Powell for cash, and on February 1, 1903, D. W. Powell sold it to Charles Steples for $400 and three notes aggregating $1900. Steples defaulted in 1904, and Powell sued for foreclosure. Steples died in 1906, and his heirs were made parties, who also refused to pay the balance due on the notes. Emily Berry, being the sole survivor of Mrs. Elizabeth McCulloch (her mother and James' mother), and next of kin to James McCulloch, claimed the land.

The court had to consider the meaning of the statute adopted in 1848, which read: "Bastards shall be capable of inheriting from and through their mother and of transmitting estates, and shall also be entitled to distribute shares of the personal estates of any of their kindred, on the part of their mother, in like manner as if they had been lawfully begotten of such mother."

The judge said that the statute meant that the inheritance could be directly from the mother and indirectly from any one to whom or from whom kinship could be traced through her, either in ascending or descending line, inasmuch as he thought the intention of the Legislature in using "from" was to allow the child to inherit real property from the mother direct and that its intention in using *through*, which signifies "by means of," the channel by means of which, was to let any one to whom or from whom the blood of kinship could be traced through the mother inherit, either in ascending or descending line.

Thus it was decided that since James McCulloch died intestate without child or children or their descendants, his wife under the law of descent and distribution was entitled to all his personal estate and to one-half of his lands, and Emily Berry, his bastard sister, was entitled to the other half of his real estate.

The decision was based on the interpretation of the intent of the law concerning bastards, *through* having the meaning of "the channel by means of which."[2]

Case 3.—On May 15, 1886, the General Assembly of Kentucky passed "an act to authorize the county of Mercer to subscribe aid to the Louisville Southern Railroad Co." The bill provided that the bonds would not be binding until the railway should be so completed through such county that a train of cars should have passed over the same. The Provident Life and Trust Company purchased $100,000 of the bonds, and on default in payment of the coupons it began action against Mercer County. The county contended that the word *through* meant entirely traversing the county from one end to the other; and that the railway entered on the north line of the county and ran within the county limits a distance of nearly twenty miles, but did not touch the south county line, nor come within a nearer distance of it than two miles; and consequently did not run through the county and thus did not make the bonds binding.

The court showed that *through* does not always mean "from end to end," or "from side to side," but frequently means "within." The court said by way of illustration that if one spoke of a person's travelling *through* New England, no one would understand that the person had been from one side to the other or from one end to the other, but that it would be understood his travels had been within the limits of New England. The road was to begin at Louisville, the principal city on the northern border of the state. The court concluded that the purpose of the road was to connect the county with that city and to have trains moving over the track.

Judgment was therefore rendered in favor of the Provident Life and Trust Company, thereby making the bonds binding.

The decision was based on the common meaning of *through:* "within."[3]

Case 4.—In 1909, in Vermont, W. J. Blodgett, administrator of Flint, who was killed by a train of the Central Vermont Railway Company, sued the company. The statute provided: "If a person having control of a detached engine or an engine with a passenger train of cars attached runs such engine or such passenger train into or through a passenger depot at a speed exceeding four miles an hour, he shall be fined ten dollars." When the train killed Flint, it was running at forty-five miles an hour. The plaintiff considered that speed as negligence.

The judge said that according to Webster's International Dictionary the law could not apply in this case, for it could not apply to flag stations, but only to passenger depots which were so constructed in the state as to cover the main tracks of the railroad and through which trains, running on such tracks, had to pass. He could not see how "into or through" could apply to a depot of any other construction, for the dictionary defined "into" as "in the sense of inside of; within," and *through* as "from end to end, or from side to side; into or out of at the opposite end or at another point; between the sides or walls of; within; as to pass through a door, or to go through an avenue."

Judgment was rendered in favor of the defendant.

The decision was based on an appeal to the dictionary. The finding was that *through* meant "from end to end."[4]

The word *through* is used in both a physical and a figurative sense. The illustrative cases given here show both uses. The two linguistic classifications are: (*a*) Physical meaning; (*b*) Figurative meaning. Cases (1), (3), and (4) belong to classification (*a*); case (2) belongs to classification (*b*).

(*a*) In case (1), we find ***through*** with one of its usual physical meanings, to denote "from end to end of" or "into at one point and out at the opposite point." To go ***through*** the private avenues was to go from end to end of them. This idea is frequently employed in such statements as, "He bored through the board"; that is, he bored from one side of the board to the opposite side. Case (3) shows another variation of its physical import. In the expression "through such county," ***through*** took on the meaning of "in the midst of," or "within." The railroad did not have to extend from one end of the county to the other. If, in daily speech, John says, "Look at the fish swimming through the water," he does not mean that the fish are swimming from one end of the body of water to the other, but are in the midst of the water, or within it. Case (4) illustrates the same use that is found in case (1).

(*b*) At times, ***through*** takes on a figurative meaning as shown in case (2), in the statement "Bastards will be able to inherit through their mother." Here ***through*** indicates a channel, but not a material one, by which property can be inherited. If a bastard can trace blood relationship by means of the mother, or on the mother's side, he can always inherit property. In every day speech we often hear such statements as, "He got his money through his mother," meaning that he inherited it from his mother's side of the family.

Throughout

The word ***throughout*** is defined according to: (1) Literal interpretation; (2) Interpretation based on intent.

Case 1.—In Massachusetts, in 1889, the inhabitants of Quincy brought action to enjoin Boston from laying water pipes through Quincy to Long Island, a part of Boston. The statute of 1846 authorized the city to build aqueducts into and through the city and to distribute the water "throughout the city."

The court said that the phrase only carried with it a suggestion of continuity in distribution within the city and did not authorize a construction of the system beyond the city limits.

It was decided that the injunction should be issued.

The decision was based on the literal interpretation of *throughout:* in every part of."[1]

Case 2.—In Georgia, in 1898, Reuben Thomas sued out a petition for habeas corpus before the judge of Dekalb Superior Court, alleging that he was illegally deprived of his liberty by H. C. Austin, sheriff; that he was arrested by the sheriff upon a pretended warrant issued by H. L. Parry, judge of the City Court of Dekalb; that the warrant was based upon a pretended accusation purporting to be sworn out in the City Court; that Parry had no authority to issue the warrant; and that the document was a nullity, because the act of the Legislature approved December 13, 1893, establishing the City Court, was in violation of the Constitution of the state, which declared, "Laws of a general nature shall have uniform operation throughout the state."

The sole question was whether or not the local act establishing this City Court was legal, according to the state constitution. Thomas insisted that the Act of the Legislature for the establishment of a City Court upon the recommendation of the grand jury of any county having a population of 10,000 or more, where a City Court did not then exist, was a general law, and that, therefore, the Local Act of 1893, creating a City Court for Dekalb County was unconstitutional because provision for such court had been made by an existing general law.

The court said that the words *throughout the state*, as used in the constitution, necessarily implied generality; for a law to partake of generality, it should, by its terms, show that it was capable of being applied in any county in the state. He explained that it was not necessary for every county in the state at the time of the passage of the law to fall within its operation, but that it was necessary that none should be excepted in such a way that it would never fall within its provisions.

It was decided that the warrant was legal and the writ was therefore denied to Thomas.

The decision was based on the interpretation of the intent of the Legislature in using the word *throughout*.[2]

The word *throughout* is usually employed in a physical sense. If a person hears the word alone, he immediately thinks of "in all parts of." The illustrative cases given here fall under the linguistic classification: (*a*) The physical meaning.

(*a*) In case (1), *throughout the city* means in every part of the city; in case (2), *throughout the state* means in every county. This meaning of the word *throughout* is commonplace. If Mrs. Brown says, "I smell gas throughout the house," she means that she smells gas in every part of the house.

Till

The word *till* is defined according to: (1) Literal interpretation; (2) Dictionary meaning; (3) Circumstances.

Case 1.—In Indiana, in 1874, a petition for the partition of real estate was filed by John De Haven, Nancy De Haven, and others against Isaac De Haven, Jacob De Haven, and James De Haven. William De Haven had died in 1871, intestate, owner in fee simple of the real estate, without leaving any issue, or widow. Judgment was rendered in favor of the partition. The defendants objected. Time was given them "till next term" to file their bill of exceptions. It was not filed until the sixth day of the term.

It was decided that the sixth day of the term was too late, for "till next term" of the court did not include the time during the term, or any part of it.

The decision was based on the literal interpretation of *till:* "up to."[1]

Case 2.—In Alabama, in 1911, McNamara filed a quo warranto petition in the City Court of Mobile charging that Oberhaus was unlawfully usurping the office of jury commissioner of Mobile County, and was exercising the powers and duties of that office without warrant or authority of law. Oberhaus, in accordance with the prayer of the petition, was required to answer and show cause why he should not be ousted and excluded from office.

Under the Act of 1909, he had been on November 12, 1909, duly and legally appointed as jury commissioner of Mobile County by Governor B. B. Comer, his term of office being "till the first Monday after the second Tuesday in January, 1911." On January 9, 1911, while still serving under this appointment, he was again duly appointed as jury commissioner of Mobile County for a term of three years from the expiration of his first term, as his own successor in said office.

The Constitution of 1901 provided that the governor and other officers named should hold their offices "for the term of four years from the first Monday after the second Tuesday in January next succeeding their election and until their successors shall be elected and qualified."

Governor Comer was inaugurated and installed in office on Monday, January 15, 1907, and Governor O'Neal on Monday, January 16, 1911, at 2:15 p.m., each date being "the first Monday after the second Tuesday in January next succeeding their election."

Whether the term of each incoming governor included the "first Monday after the second Tuesday," or whether Monday was a part of, and the last day of, the term of the outgoing governor, depended, of course, on the meaning to be given the word "from" as used in the Constitution in the phrase "from the first Monday, etc." The court decided that Monday was the last day of the old term. Thus Governor Comer's term of office *de jure* expired at midnight on Monday, January 16, 1911; and consequently Governor O'Neal's term *de jure* began on and with the Tuesday following.

By the act, the term of Oberhaus, as jury commissioner under the appointment made by Governor Comer, ran "till the first Monday after the second Tuesday in January, 1911."

The dictionary was referred to. Webster's New International Dictionary defined *till* as meaning in relation to time "up or down to; as far as; until." The court said that *till* and "until" were synonymous and that in marking the end of a period of time *till* would have to be construed as *prima facie*, exclusive of the *terminus ad quem.*

Thus it was decided that the term of Oberhaus expired at midnight of Sunday, January 15. Therefore Governor Comer could, while he was serving as governor on January 16, 1911, appoint the successor of Oberhaus. It was also decided that Oberhaus was lawfully holding the office of jury commissioner of Mobile County.

The decision was based on the appeal to the dictionary, the meaning of *till* being "up or down to," and "until."[2]

Case 3.—In Nebraska, in 1924, the Lancaster Farmers' State Bank and others brought action against George Buckner. Judgment was rendered in favor of the plaintiffs and the defendant appealed.

George Buckner, acting for himself and for his banking associates, had sold to the Lancaster County Bank the capital stock and the assets of the Farmers' State Bank. In the transfer a note given by Bartley McHugh was guaranteed by Buckner.

The original debtor, McHugh, absconded without paying the note. The action was brought against Buckner as guarantor.

The question presented was the meaning of the term "till maturity," for Buckner, acting for himself and associates, made the transfer, guaranteed "all notes . . . till maturity now on books." Buckner contended that the date of the maturity of the note, March 1, 1919, was the end of the period covered by his guaranty, for *till* was used in the sense of "at."

The court said that the defendant, in transferring the note to the plaintiffs, represented McHugh to be a man of integrity and that the plaintiffs consequently trusted him as such, believing the proceeds of his farm would pass through their hands; that McHugh went to another bank to transfer the title to his farm; that he procured the remainder of the purchase price in currency without the knowledge of plaintiffs, and absconded, leaving the note guaranteed by the defendant unpaid.

Judgment for the plaintiffs was therefore affirmed.

The decision was based on circumstances: the notes transferred were guaranteed.[3]

When a person hears the word *till*, he usually thinks of it in a limited sense. If Mr. Brown says, "I shall be at the office till five o'clock," we expect him to leave at five o'clock. The illustrative cases given here fall under the two classifications: (*a*) Limited meaning; (*b*) Extended meaning. Cases (1) and (2) belong to classification (*a*); case (3) belongs to classification (*b*).

(*a*) In case (1), "till next term" means up to the beginning of the next term, thus showing a limited meaning. The same significance is seen in case (2) in the expression, "till the first Monday after the second Tuesday," where Monday is excluded. This use of the word *till* is common. If Mary says, "Wait till the clock strikes," the striking of the clock is the limit. The person does not have to wait any longer.

(*b*) Occasionally, however, the meaning of *till* is extended, as is seen in case (3) where circumstances extend the meaning of the word *till* in the expression "till maturity" several years beyond maturity. If, in everyday life, Mr. Smith asked Mr. Brown to wait *till* four o'clock for him and if at a few minutes before the appointed time Mr. Brown heard that a transaction took place shortly before which must have required Mr. Smoth's attention, Mr. Brown would extend the meaning of *till* and wait longer for Mr. Brown. (See *until*.)

To

The word *to* is defined according to: (1) Literal interpretation; (2) Interpretation based on intent; (3) Common meaning; (4) Specialized meaning; (5) Context.

Case 1.—In Maine, in 1878, George Keeley bought a railroad ticket with the words "Portland to Boston" printed on it. He was going from Boston to Portland and offered the ticket to the conductor, who refused to take it. He had to get off the train. Later he brought suit against the railroad. Another conductor had told him the ticket would be good and had allowed him to use such a ticket at former times.

It was decided, however, that a ticket with the words "Portland to Boston" on it did not entitle the holder to a ride from Boston to Portland, although the holder had been permitted to take such rides on similar tickets over the same railroad before and had been told by another conductor on the same road that the ticket was good for a passage either way.

The decision was based on the literal interpretation of *to*, indicating movement toward a place.[1]

Case 2.—In New Hampshire, James Scales, in 1901, brought action against the Masonic Protective Association. The benefit certificate issued by the association stipulated: "a disability, to constitute a claim for sickness, . . . shall require absolute, necessary, continuous confinement to the house for not less than fourteen days; . . . and no disability . . . shall constitute a claim for a longer period than the insured shall be totally disabled, and absolutely, necessarily, continuously confined to his house." The plaintiff was seriously ill and incapacitated for labor during a period of sixty-seven days. He remained in the house the first five days, and after that, being advised by his physician to keep in the open air all he could, and move around as much as his strength would allow, he was in his dooryard a portion of the time, sitting in a chair or lying in a hammock. The association contended that he had not been continuously confined to the house.

The judge said it was unreasonable to suppose that departure from the strictly literal words in the certificate would defeat the contract if the insured, although totally disabled from labor by sickness, should go from his house to an outbuilding for a necessary purpose, or should, by the advice of his physician and for the purpose of recovery, sit in a chair or lie in a hammock on the porch of his house or in his yard. The court also said that, strictly speaking, confinement to a house differed from confinement in a house, for *to* signified direction, connection with, while "in" denoted the quality of being interior. The judge added that it would not be presumed that an association of the character of the defendant association would give such an interpretation as that.

Judgment was rendered in favor of the plaintiff.

In this case the decision was based on the interpretation of the intent of the benefit certificate. The principal idea was that the man was sick and not that he had to stay inside the house.[2]

Case 3.—In Kansas, in 1899, Garden City, the plaintiff in error and the defendant in previous suit, brought a case before the court against a decision made for the Merchants' and Farmers' National Bank. The defendant in error contended that the case-made was not served upon it within the time fixed by the order of the court and that the second court could not consider the alleged errors complained of. The language of the court was: "The time to make and serve a case-made . . . is hereby extended to the 22nd day of March, 1897." If, under that order, March 22 were included in the additional time allowed for serving a "case," then the order made on March 22, extending the time for thirty days, was made in time, but, if the time expired at midnight on March 21, the order granting further time was made too late.

The court said that while it could not be maintained that *to* had any settled legal meaning, it was generally defined as a word of exclusion, unless, by necessary implication, it was regarded as being used in an inclusive sense.

It was decided that the "case" was not served in time and the petition in error was dismissed.

The decision was based on the common meaning of *to*, as a word of exclusion.[3]

Case 4.—In 1878, James Oxton, in Maine, brought an action of trespass against Daniel Groves for cutting and carrying away grass on ground that both claimed. The question, one of boundary, was whether the defendant's land extended to the center of a road or stopped at the side of it. The land was described as running "to said road; thence by said road to point begun at, containing twenty acres and no more."

The judgment was rendered for the defendant according to the legal construction, which provides that "to the road," as used in a deed of land, means to the center of the road, though the measurement of distances may extend only to the side of the road.

The decision was based on the specialized meaning of *to* as used in relation to boundaries, such as highways, and stream. "To the road" carries the owner to the center of the road.[4]

Case 5.—In Vermont, the Littleton Bridge Company put in a petition against Daniel and Robert Pike for the appointment of commissioners to determine the damages sustained by them for land taken according to the Acts of 1896. The commissioners determined the damages. Then an appeal was made by the land-owners from this decision. The petitioner moved to dismiss the appeal on the ground that the County Court had no jurisdiction, according to the Acts of 1896. The act provided that two judges of the Supreme Court, on being applied to by the corporation, should appoint such commissioners. It further provided: "The proceedings thereafter shall be the same as those provided for in sections 3815 to 3821 of the Vermont Statutes, and said sections shall govern all proceedings had by said commissioners and corporation and by the court and all concerned, to the final determination of the matter." The only provision for an appeal contained in the sections of the Vermont Statutes was in Section 3821. The petition, however, contended that that section was excluded by the language quoted above.

The court said from the context it was clear that the Legislature regarded Section 3821 as included, because the act provided that in all subsequent proceedings "the court" should be governed by the sections referred to and that thus it would be impossible to have any subsequent proceedings before any court unless Section 3821 should be included.

It was thus decided that Section 3821 was included in the expression Sections 3815 to 3821.

As a result of the decision the court appealed to could have no cognizance of the case, because the provision of the section was that the decision of the County Court should be final upon the report of the commissioners. Thus the petitioners had to stand upon the rights given them by the judgment of the County Court.

The decision was based on the context, the subject matter that followed the expression "sections 3815 to 3821," giving to it significance. If Section 3821 were not included there could be no further proceedings in court, as it is the section that provides for an appeal.[5]

The word *to* primarily denotes the relation of approach and arrival, making its governed word denote the terminus. That is, it usually, but not always, has a limited signification. The illustrative cases given here fall under the two linguistic classifications: (*a*) Limited meaning; (*b*) Extended meaning. Cases (1) and (3) belong to classification (*a*); cases (2), (4), and (5) to classification (*b*).

(*a*) Case (1) shows *to* with its ordinary signification. The question involved was the meaning of "Portland to Boston." Here *to* indicated that there was movement toward Boston, the word governed, and that there would be an arrival at Boston. In other words, *to* has a definite limitation—Boston. This limited meaning of the word is common. If I say, "I am going to the drug store," it is understood that I am going toward the drug store and that the drug store will be my destination.

Case (3) also shows the limited meaning of *to*, but not in its physical sense as in case (1). Here *to* has a figurative sense. The time extends *to* March 22 as a limit. It is used in its exclusive sense, March 22 itself being excluded. This limited meaning in the figurative sense is frequently heard, especially in relation to time.

(*b*) The extended meaning of *to* is also common. In case (2), the phrase "to the house" does not mean that the patient is to be kept in the house only. He can sit in a chair or lie in a hammock in the yard. The meaning of *to* extends to neighboring places. The idea is that the man is ill and cannot work. If a teacher goes into a school and the superintendent says, "Your work is limited to mathematics," he does not mean that the teacher will not have anything else to do in the school. She may, for example, be called on to take charge of and keep order in a study hall.

In case (4), the meaning of *to* is extended to take in one-half the road. Here it is a word of inclusion. The expression "to the road" does not have reference to the side of the road. This meaning is commonplace with reference to land that has for its boundary a road, a street or a stream. It is understood that the land extends to the center of the road, the street, or the stream unless words are included which indicate definitely that it does not.

Case (5) shows the meaning of *to* extended to take in the word it governs. "Sections 3815 to 3821" includes Section 3821. To take an example from daily life, if a teacher is assigning different sentences to different students and says, "Mary, take sentences one to four; John, five to eight," she includes four and eight respectively.

UNDER

The word *under* is defined according to: (1) Literal interpretation; (2) Interpretation based on intent; (3) Common meaning; (4) Technical meaning; (5) Dictionary meaning; (6) Context.

Case 1.—In Missouri, in 1901, Henry Ruckert brought suit against the Grand Avenue Railway Company to enjoin it from constructing a street railway, which he claimed would deprive him of the rights which he had hitherto enjoyed as owner of real estate upon Grand Avenue, along and adjoining the line of the route. An order denying the injunction was issued and the bill was dismissed. Then the plaintiff appealed.

The statute provided that before granting any franchise for constructing and operating any elevated, underground, or other street railroad, on, over, or under any street or alley or any incorporated town or city, the authorities of such town or city should, by ordinance duly enacted, establish the route and clearly define the terms and conditions of such franchise, and locate all depots, stations, turnouts, and switches.

It was decided that the words "over," *under* and "on" should be taken literally and that "over" meant "over" and applied only to elevated roads; *under* meant "beneath" and referred only to underground roads; and "on" meant "on" and referred only to surface roads on the street. Therefore the Grand Avenue Railway Company had a right to construct its railway and judgment was affirmed.

The decision was based on the literal interpretation of *under:* "beneath."[1]

Case 2.—In Iowa, in 1885, Bates sought to recover judgment against the Independent School District of Riverside upon interest coupons belonging to two series of bonds issued in June, 1880, and in July, 1881, by the defendant corporation. The first series, it was claimed, was issued by virtue of powers granted to independent school districts under the provisions of Sections 1821 to 1823 of the Code of Iowa and the Acts of the Eighteenth General Assembly. The second series, it was claimed, was issued under the provisions of the Acts of the Eighteenth General Assembly.

The plaintiff claimed that the clause in the bonds, which stated that they were "issued under the provisions of the sections named" was in effect a statement that the indebtedness of the district did not exceed the constitutional limitation, and that he could rely thereon in making the purchase, and thereby estop the defendant from showing that in fact the indebtedness of the district largely exceeded the constitutional limit.

The object of the court was to show the meaning of the phrase "under provisions of sections 1821, 1822, and 1823." The court said that *under* was not synonymous with the phrases "in pursuance of," "in conformity with," "by virtue of," and "by authority of," all of which implied a compliance with the provisions of the statute, but that it was primarily the correlative of "over," which signified being in a lower position, and that, secondarily, it indicated a relation of subordination to some superior power. Thus when the recital was that the bonds were issued under the provisions of a given statute, the court thought it simply asserted that the bonds were subject to or controlled by the provisions of the statute named; or that the purchaser was thereby informed where he should look in order to learn that the provisions of the statute were what conferred and limited the power to issue the bonds.

The conclusion reached upon the question was, that in none of the bonds owned by the plaintiff to which the coupons sued on were attached was there any recital touching the amount of the indebtedness owed by the school district when the bonds were issued, and that consequently the defendant was not estopped from showing that the bonds were void by reason of the fact that when they were issued the indebtedness of the district was then in excess of the constitutional limit.

Judgment was therefore entered for the defendant, the meaning of *under* being based on the interpretation of the intent of the word as it was used in the bonds. It was thought to mean "controlled by."[2]

Case 3.—This case, illustrating the common meaning of *under*, has already been discussed with "over." (See No. 4 under *Over*.)[3]

Case 4.—In Maine, in 1902, Robert Hewey signed in blank an application for a life insurance policy and delivered it to the agent of the defendant company, with the understanding that the agent should fill in the answers to the questions from information contained in a previous application, which had been made out in the applicant's presence and signed by him. The second application, as filled out by the agent, was forwarded to the company and the policy in suit was issued thereon. He died in 1905. The company then found fault with the policies and Annie Hewey, his wife, brought action.

In the first application Hewey had said that his usual medical attendant was Dr. H. H. Cleveland, who treated him nine months before for a cold, and that he had not consulted any other physician since childhood for any illness except on one occasion four years ago for grippe. In the second application he said that he had not been under the care of any physician within two years, unless as stated in previous answers, where it was stated that Dr. Cleveland was the physician who last attended him on February 9, 1902, for grippe.

It was decided that "consulting" a physician and being "under the care" of a physician, not only in the technical use of the terms but to the common mind, meant very different things. Judgment was therefore rendered in favor of the plaintiff and the defendant brought exceptions which were overruled.

The decision was based on the technical meaning of *under* in the expression of "under the care of a physician." It has the meaning of being looked after at all times by the physician—"subject to" the physician's orders and suggestions.[4]

Case 5.—In Texas, in 1896, action was brought by O. T. Bassett against Anson Mills, Charles Fruin, and others to enforce a mechanic's lien upon a building and the lots upon which it stood for material furnished and work done on the building. The lumber for which Bassett sued was furnished to Fruin, a subcontractor. The statute, which purported to fix and to provide for the enforcement of mechanics', laborers', and material men's liens, was passed in 1889 and read: "Any person or firm, lumber dealers, artisan, laborer, machine or subcontractor, who may labor or furnish material, machinery, fixtures or tools to erect any house or improvement, or to repair any building or improvement whatever, under or by virtue of contract with the owner or his agent, trustee, contractor or contractors, upon complying with the provisions of this act, shall have a lien on such house, building, fixtures or improvements, and shall also have a lien on the lot or lots of land necessarily connected therewith to secure payment for labor done, lumber, material, machinery or fixtures, and tools furnished for construction or repair."

The case turned on "under or by virtue of the contract with the owner, or his agent, trustee, contractor or contractors." The dictionaries were used to determine whether *under* and "by virtue of" meant the same thing. According to the Century Dictionary, the phrase meant "by or through the authority of" and *under* meant "in conformity with" and, according to the Worcester Dictionary, *under* meant "in subordination to."

It was decided that the word and phrase had the same signification and that when one furnished material to a subcontractor, to be used in fulfilling the original contract, it was furnished in conformity with and in subordination to that contract. It was also brought out that the statute never intended to give a lien upon property for labor or material applied to its improvement, without authority from the owner; and that hence it was proper to limit the lien to cases in which the owner had contracted for the improvements.

Judgment was therefore rendered in favor of the plaintiff, fixing a lien upon the lots and improvements.

The decision was based on an appeal to the dictionary. It was found that *under* meant "in conformity with."[5]

Case 6.—In West Virginia, in 1910, Philip Osborne sought a writ of mandamus from the County Court of Kanawha County and others to compel registration as a voter. He was indicted for bribery in an election, and in 1909 pleaded guilty, was convicted, and paid the fine and costs. The County Court refused to put his name upon the registration list of voters because he had been convicted of bribery.

The Constitution read: "The male citizens of the state shall be entitled to vote at all elections held within the counties in which they respectively reside; but no person who is a minor, or of unsound mind, or a pauper, or who is under conviction of treason, felony, or bribery in an election, or who has not been a resident of the state for one year, and of the county in which he offers to vote, for sixty days next preceding such offer, shall be permitted to vote while such disability continues."

According to the context of the Constitution, the court said Osborne was a citizen, for there were several things that caused disability to vote, a disability which was not permanent as disfranchisement lasted only "while such disability continued." Then the court said that while the sentence stood unexecuted, the party was "under conviction"; that he stood ***under*** it and that it rested upon his head; but that as soon as he had suffered the penalty, he had paid the debt, the sentence had spent its force and no longer hovered over him. Therefore the court ruled that the word ***under*** in connection with the words "while such disability continues" indicated that when the sentence had been executed the party was no longer ***under*** conviction.

The mandamus was therefore awarded, the decision being based on the context of the law concerning voters. The expression "While such disability continues" indicated that the words "under conviction" did not mean a permanent disfranchisement.[6]

The word ***under*** is employed in both a physical and a figurative sense. If one object is below another, the one on the bottom is under the one on top. The relationship of the objects is physical. If, however, a person speaks of one man's being under another, he is using the word in a figurative sense. In this meaning it applies to authority or power. The man with more authority is over the man with less authority. The illustrative cases given here fall under the two linguistic classifications: (*a*) Physical meaning; (*b*) Fgurative meaning. Cases (1) and (3) belong to classification (*a*); cases (2), (4), (5), and (6) to classification (*b*).

(*a*) In case (1), "under any street" means "beneath any street." The employment of ***under*** in this sense shows physical relationship.

The railroad was to be actually beneath the street or another surface at a lower level. This meaning of *under* is common. If Mr. Brown says, "Put a box under the table," he means put the box beneath the table. The same use of *under* is shown in case (3), which was discussed under "over."*

(*b*) In case (2), we find *under* used in a figurative sense, meaning "subject to"; that is, the bonds issued were subject to the provisions of the statute. This employment of *under* is common. If a teacher says of a student, "He is under the regulations of this school while he is here," she means that he is subject to all the regulations of the school and controlled by them.

In case (4), we find *under* in its figurative sense with a meaning which is slightly different from that found in case (3). It still has the idea of "subject to" but not subject to in so strict a manner. If a man is under the care of a physician, the latter suggests to him what he should do for his health and the patient is supposed to carry out the instructions. This use of *under* is employed often in speaking of persons in ill health.

In case (5), *under* means "in conformity with," a signification commonly employed. If Mr. Brown says, "I did that under the laws of Iowa," he means that he acted in conformity with the laws of Iowa. This meaning is practically the same as the meaning in case (2).

Case (6) shows *under* including a time element. A person is "under conviction" until he finishes suffering the penalty. In this sense *under* means "beneath, simply as sustaining, or receiving." This use of the word is also common. If Mr. Smith says, "John is going under an operation," he means that John will undergo an operation as treatment.

UNTIL

The word *until* is defined according to: (1) Literal interpretation; (2) Interpretation based on intent; (3) Common meaning; (4) Dictionary meaning; (5) Context; (6) Circumstances.

* See case 4.

Case 1.—In Georgia, in 1910, Homer Davis was convicted of crime and brought a writ of error, filing a motion for a new trial. The court provided that the movement should have "until the hearing of said motion in which to prepare for filing and approved a brief of the evidence." The hearing was set for December 4. Upon that day the judge continued the hearing until January 10. On that day he dismissed the motion since no brief of evidence had been filed as required by law.

It appeared, however, that the brief was filed on January 10, prior to the signing of the order dismissing the motion for a new trial, but after the court had stated that it would dismiss the motion. The judge gave the movant until the hearing to prepare and present a brief of evidence. Though the hearing was continued, the movant had not complied with the order at the time that the motion was called for a hearing and the judge dismissed the motion.

It was decided that the judge had a right to dismiss the motion, as the movant had not presented the brief at the arrival of the time set for hearing.

The decision was based on the literal interpretation of until: "up to."[1]

Case 2.—In Maryland, Walter Abell died January 3, 1891, leaving a will dated July 3, 1889, in which he directed that a trust he had created was to continue until the expiration of the period of twenty years after his death and that of his wife. The will also declared that the trustee should apply the rents and profits from two-thirds of the real estate during the life of his wife, and from the whole of the estate after her death, as might be necessary, for the maintenance and education of his children and their respective issue. He left a widow and three children by a former marriage. In 1905, Sallie Robinson, Marie Edwards and Walter Abell brought suit against Charles Bonaparte, substituted trustee under the will.

It was decided that the intent of the testator was to have the trust continue twenty years after the death of his widow, as well as twenty years after his own death.

The decision was based on the interpretation of the intent of the testator, who wanted his children and their respective issue educated. Thus it is evident that he wanted the trust to continue twenty years after the death of his widow as well as twenty years after his own death.[2]

Case 3.—In New York, in 1899, a writ of certiorari was sought by the people, on the relation of the Cornell Steamboat Company, against Emzey Hornbeck and others, as assessors of Rochester. The assessors had made an assessment for the year 1899 against the Cornell Steamboat Company of $75,000. They met to review the assessments on the third Tuesday of August, pursuant to notice. The company appeared before them, and applied for a reduction of the levy. The assessors reduced the amount to $25,000. They completed their roll on the third Tuesday of August and on that day verified, and filed it with the town clerk of Rochester, and posted notices stating that the roll had been finally completed and that it had been filed. After more than fifteen days had elapsed from the filing of the roll and the posting of the notices, the motion was made by the company for a writ of certiorari to review the assessment of $25,000. The company claimed that the fifteen days within which a petition must be presented to obtain a writ of certiorari to review such assessment had not been entered upon, for the reason that the roll and the notices could not be legally posted until the Wednesday following the third Tuesday of August. The Tax Law provided that a copy of the assessment roll should be left with one of the assessors at a specified place, where it might be seen and examined by any person "until the third Tuesday of August."

The court said that, according to the ordinary meaning of *until*, the time did not include the third Tuesday of August and that the assessors were justified in filing the notices on that day instead of on the Wednesday following.

The writ was therefore denied.

The decision was based on the common meaning of *until*, in its exclusive sense.[3]

Case 4.—In Kansas, in 1903, a case was brought by H. J. Hille against W. H. Croco. On May 9, Croco was allowed until June 20 to make and serve a case for the court. It was served on June

20. The court decided that the time granted had expired. Then Croco brought a writ of error against Hille. The question was whether the word *until* used in the order of the court meant "to" or "up to" June 20, so as to exclude that date, or whether service on the day named was in time.

The court turned to the dictionaries and found in Webster that in contracts and like documents *until* was construed as exclusive of the date mentioned unless it was the manifest intent of the parties to include it, and found in the Century Dictionary also that the exclusive signification to the word was given.

The proceedings in error were therefore dismissed.

In this case an appeal to the dictionary was made. It was found that *until* was construed as exclusive of the date mentioned.[4]

Case 5.—In New Jersey, an act of the Legislature, approved March 2, 1891, read: "Be it enacted, etc., that the judges of all district courts in cities of this state now in office shall continue in office until the first day of April, one thousand eight hundred and ninety-one, on which day their term of office shall end. The successor of the judges of said courts now in office shall be appointed by the governor, by and with the advice and consent of the senate, and shall continue in office for five years from the first day of April, one thousand, eight hundred and ninety-one. Their successors shall be appointed by the governor, by and with the advice of the senate."

At the time of the passage of the act, John Miller, Esq., was a judge of the First District Court of Newark and on April 1, 1891, rendered in that court a judgment for which Elizabeth Fulton brought a certiorari action against Corydon Woodward to review the judgment. Elizabeth Fulton contended that, by the force of the language of the act cited above, Miller's term of office ended on March 31, 1891, and that *until* usually excluded the day.

The court, considering the controlling words of the act, "on," *until*, and "from," said that where language is employed with respect to an existing and continuing power, which is to end on a future day and not *until* that day, the function of the preposition is not to limit, but to extend; that in the act an existing state of things was directed to continue *until* a day, upon which day something was to happen to it; and that as nothing can happen to a thing which does not exist, it was clear that a termination cannot happen to an office which had already ceased to be. The court added that all doubt of the correctness of that interpretation was removed by the word "from," which in the context excluded the day of departure; a meaning not resting upon authority, but upon the inherent force of the word itself.

It was therefore decided that the judge in office at the time of the passage of the act was to continue to exercise his function until his term ended, on April 1, from and after which day his successor was to take up the judicial duties. Thus the judgment of the District Court, rendered on April 1, 1891, was affirmed, with costs.

The decision was based on the context. The force of "on" and "from" in connection with *until* served to extend the meaning. The act said, "until the first day of April . . . on which day their term of office shall end." "On" designates a particular day, the one named. Later in the act, the word "from" in the expression "five years from the first day of April" is a word of exclusion, excluding the first day of April, as the beginning of the term of the new judge. If the first day is excluded from the new term, it must be included in the old term, for the District Court must have a judge at all times.[5]

Case 6.—In September 24, 1863, in New Jersey, an agreement was made between A. Boisaubin and E. V. Houghwont. It read: "Mr. Boisaubin also agrees to sell to Mr. Houghwont the plot of land of about twenty-two acres, called the Spencer woods, for the sum of $200 per acre, and Mr. Houghwont has until the first day of March, 1864, to accept of the proposition." A few days after March 1, 1864, Boisaubin notified the attorneys of Houghwont that he would not convey the tract to Houghwont. On August 31, 1865, this bill was filed to compel such conveyance.

Boisaubin said that such acceptance could not be made after February 29, 1864. On February 29, the lawyer of Houghwont went to Madison to get the deed from Boisaubin and to settle with him for the prices to be paid, but the two missed each other. The lawyer understood that Boisaubin had been talking of coming to deliver the conveyance and intended to come. He waited for him the next day in his office. In the afternoon of March 1, as Mr. Boisaubin had not appeared, the lawyer wrote him a letter, which implied that a previous acceptance had been made and that they had been waiting and expecting to close the business of the purchase that day. The lawyer also requested him to name a day convenient to himself when the business might be closed.

It was decided that *until*, as used in a stipulation reciting that a certain party shall have *until* a certain day to accept a proposition, includes that day, if the offer be still open, as it was in this case.

The decision was based on circumstances. Houghwont had *until* March 1, to close the trade. The fact that his lawyer, on February 29, tried to get the deed and failed because of Boisaubin's absence from his home, showed that he wanted the land and would have accepted the proposition if it had been possible. Understanding that Boisaubin was coming to deliver the conveyance, the lawyer went home. After Mr. Boisaubin failed to arrive on the next morning, the lawyer wrote a letter to him stating that Mr. Houghwont wanted to close the business of the purchase. The fact that the trade was not closed was not Houghwont's fault. He did everything he could. It was only fair that the time should be extended.[6]

The word *until* is synonymous with "till." It, too, is usually thought of in a limited sense. At times, however, the meaning is extended by circumstances. The illustrative cases given here then fall under the two linguistic classifications: (*a*) Limited meaning; (*b*) Extended meaning. Cases (1), (2), (3), and (4) belong to classification (*a*); cases (5) and (6) to classification (*b*).

(*a*) In case (1), "until the hearing of said motion" means up to the time of the hearing and not any longer. In this case we find the limited signification of *until*. In case (2), the clause "until the expiration of the period of twenty years after his death and the death of his wife" extends the period of the trust for twenty years after her death as well as twenty years after his own. The time had a definite limitation—the end of twenty years after the death of the testator and his wife. In case (3), the expression "until the third Tuesday of August" does not include the third Tuesday but extends the time to that limit. The same meaning is found in case (4). "Until June 20" does not include June 20. This limited meaning of *until* is the one most often used and universally understood. If Mr. Brown says, "Wait until the gong strikes," the period of waiting is to be ended when the gong strikes.

(*b*) Frequently *until* is used in the inclusive sense, as in case (5), where "until the first day of April" includes the first day of April. The same signification is found in case (6), where "until the first day of March" includes the first day. This meaning is not one unheard of in everyday speech. We occasionally find the extended meaning of *until*. If a teacher says to her class, "I shall give you until Monday to bring in your paper," she includes Monday. That inclusive meaning is understood by all the students. (See *till*.)

Unto

The word *unto* is defined according to: (1) Literal interpretation.

Case 1.—In Michigan, in 1895, Edwin Rathbun was convicted of unlawfully conveying to a jail an instrument adapted to aid the escape of a prisoner. Rathbun brought a writ of error.

Howell's Annotated Statutes provided that "every person who shall convey into any jail, prison, or other like place of confinement, any disguise, or any instrument, tool, weapon or other thing, adapted or useful to aid any prisoner in making his escape, with intent to facilitate the escape of any prisoner there lawfully committed or detained . . . shall be punished." The information in the case charged that Rathbun, on October 26, 1893, "did feloniously and unlawfully convey unto the jail aforesaid, to wit, four keys being adapted and useful to aid any prisoner in making his escape, with intent to facilitate the escape of said George N. Duell from said jail, he being such prisoner as aforesaid." Rathbun insisted that the word *unto* had a different meaning from "into," and that, therefore, no offense was charged.

The judgment was reversed and Rathbun was discharged.

The decision was based on the literal interpretation of ***unto***. ***Unto*** never means "into," the word used in the statute. Since Rathbun was not accused of conveying keys to the inside of the jail, he could not be convicted of the charge.[1]

Ordinarily ***unto*** denotes "until." If Mr. Brown says, "Unto this day, John has not taken a drink," he means until this day. Its obsolete meaning is "to." Many illustrations of this meaning are found in the Bible, such as "Give unto the Lord," signifying "to the Lord." The latter meaning was used in the illustrative case given here. This case falls under the following linguistic classification: (*a*) Limited meaning. It is used as a word of exclusion. The phrase ***unto the jail*** did not mean "into the jail," or "within the jail." The jail is excluded.

Up

The word ***up*** is defined according to: (1) Literal interpretation; (2) Interpretation based on intent; (3) Common meaning; (4) Technical meaning.

Case 1.—Wharton, in 1887, brought an action of trespass in New Jersey against Brick and others for digging up and carrying away a large quantity of cranberry vines. The plaintiff put in evidence two surveys, the "George West 110-acre Survey" and the "West and Shreve 600-acre Survey." The latter included the former. The question was whether the West and Shreve 600-acre survey covered the *locus in quo*. The description after fixing the beginning was: "Thence (1) north, 39 deg. 15 min. east, 141 chains and 60 links, to the main branch of the Mechescatuxen; thence (2) north, 72 deg. 30 min. West, up the said Mechescatuxen, 211 chains and 70 links, to the mouth of O'Neil's branch," etc.

The court considered the phrase "up the said Mechescatuxen" from a fixed monument on the edge of a branch to another fixed monument on said branch literally and decided that a straight line should be followed and not the windings of the branch, for the words "the several courses thereof" or "the general course being" were not used. Thus the decision was that the survey did not embrace the *locus*. The verdict was for the defendants.

The decision was based on the literal interpretation of *up*, denoting a straight line measured toward the source of the river.[1]

Case 2.—In Iowa, in 1879, John Murphy owned a tract which was described in the deed as beginning where Pine Creek crossed a certain section line. The third call carried the line "east to Pine Creek; thence north-easterly up the west bank of Pine Creek, to the point of beginning, containing 19½ acres, more or less." R. H. Copeland was the owner of the north half of the quarter section, excepting the 19½ acres owned by Murphy. Having occasion to erect a fence between his land and Murphy's, Copeland erected it upon the west bank of the creek, claiming that line to be the right one. The plaintiff claimed to own to the middle of the creek.

The court said that the parties would not have used the words "west bank" if it had been intended to convey the land to the middle of the stream. Although the first line commenced and the third line ended in the middle of the stream, according to the technical meaning, the court decided that the introduction of the words "up the west bank" showed that the intention of the parties was not to convey the land to the middle of the stream. The decision was therefore rendered in favor of the defendants.

The decision was based on the intent of the party that used *up* in the deed.[2]

Case 3.—In Ohio, in 1841, an action of ejectment was brought by the lessee of Buckley against Blackwell's heirs. The defendants were in possession of all the land on the west side of Darby Creek. The plaintiff's survey and patent was bounded on the east line of the defendants' two patents, so that when the defendants' line should be found the question would be settled. The description of the defendants' patent began at a corner, which was described by its timber as being the upper corner of Parker's survey, on Darby Creek. From the corner it was described as running "up the creek" many stations, described by course and distance only, to another corner, described by timber. The other patent calls were similar, beginning at the last named corner, thence up the creek, by course and distance to a third timber corner. The corners were all identified and stood on the bank of the creek. The case then hinged on a single point: whether a call "up the creek," by course and distance, meant with the creek and bounded on the creek, or whether the notice of the creek was intended to indicate the general direction of the line.

The court decided that since all the corners were on the creek, it could hardly be supposed that a tract of land, lying for miles on a stream and described by a line running parallel with its meanders and within a few poles or yards, was not intended to be bound by the water. Thus judgment was rendered in favor of the defendants.

The decision was based on the common meaning of *up*, used in speaking of land bordering a stream.[3]

Case 4.—In New York, in 1814, Jackson brought an action of ejectment against Louw.

The court said that the description "up the same," as used in the deed which provided that the boundary should continue to a certain creek and thence up the same to the corner of a certain lot could not be satisfied by running a straight line to the corner of the lot but implied that the line was to follow the creek according to its windings and turnings, and that it would have to be in the middle or center of it, according to the well settled rule, that when a creek which is not navigable and which is beyond the ebb and flow of the tide forms a boundary, the line must be run in the middle or center of the creek.

Judgment was therefore rendered in favor of Jackson, the decision being based on the technical meaning of *up* when used in relation to streams. The line was described as running in the middle of the creek toward the source of the stream.[4]

The word *up*, like "down," is used almost entirely to represent place relationship. It is used in a physical sense. The illustrative cases all fall under the following linguistic classification: (*a*) Physical meaning.

In case (1), we find a use of *up* commonly employed in connection with rivers or streams. "Up the said Mechescatuxen" has the meaning of "from the direction of the mouth of the river toward the source." As fixed monuments were given, the measurement was in a straight line up the said Mechescatuxen. If Mr. Brown says, "Measure up the river the distance from the cedar tree to the poplar tree," he means measure the distance in a straight line from the cedar tree, nearer the mouth of the river, to the poplar tree, nearer the source of the river than the cedar.

In case (2), "up the west bank" signifies that the line should follow the west bank of the stream in the same direction given in case (1), from the mouth towards the source of the river. In this case, however, the measurement should follow the bank of the stream and should not be measured in a straight line. This use of *up* is also a common one. "Up the bank of a stream" always refers to a line along the windings of the bank.

Case (3) was concerned with the phrase "up the creek," which also signifies that the line should follow the meanderings of the stream, as in case (2). The same meaning is also found in case (4).

With

The word *with* is defined according to: (1) Literal interpretation; (2) Interpretation based on intent; (3) Interpretation suggested by fact; (4) Common meaning; (5) Technical meaning; (6) Dictionary meaning; (7) Context; (8) Circumstance.

Case 1.—In England, in 1737, Sir John Leeke, by a Codicil, said, "I give to my niece *Elizabeth Martin*, during the time of her natural life, my house on *Maze-Hill* in *Greenwich*, *with* all the household goods that shall be found therein at the time of my decease."

The case turned on the construction of *with*. The question was whether Elizabeth Martin, then Bennett, was supposed to have the household goods forever or for just her life time.

The court held that the word *with* so conjoined the devise of the house and household goods, that the devisee could have no larger interest in the letter than was expressly limited as to the former. Elizabeth Martin therefore received the household goods for her life time only.

The decision was based on the literal interpretation of *with*, meaning association in the way of possession. The household goods were to be given in addition to the house. Both thus fell under the same restriction.[1]

Case 2.—In Vermont, in 1882, the question arose as to whether the exemption from attachment of forage in the statute of exemptions was conditional upon the debtor's having the exempt animals specified to consume such forage. Kimball owned only an exempt cow and horse. Woodruff, the sheriff, left him barely hay enough to keep them through the winter, and sold a quantity of hay needed to keep all the stock exempted by statute. Kimball brought action of trespass. The statute exempted one cow, ten sheep, and also, "one yoke of oxen or steers, as the debtor may select, two horses kept and used for team work, and such as the debtor may select in lieu of oxen or steers, but not exceeding in value the sum of $200 with sufficient forage for the keeping of the same through the winter."

At the time of the attachment, the debtor had two cows and one horse, and had no other exempt animals. He claimed, however, forage sufficient to keep exempt animals through the winter, although he did not own such animals.

The judge said that the preposition *with*, as used in "two horses . . . *with* sufficient forage for the keeping of the same," was to be construed as connecting two independent subjects rather than as joining a dependent or qualifying clause to one subject, the meaning being the same as if written, "a yoke of oxen, and, *in addition thereto*, forage," etc.

Considering the intent of the Legislature, the court gave judgment to the plaintiff. The forage was to be given in addition to the two horses.[2]

Case 3.—In 1842, in Edgefield, South Carolina, Wiley Freeman was convicted by an indictment which alleged that he "with a certain rifle gun charged with gunpowder and two leaden bullets, which in his hands he had and held at and against the said Mary Freeman, then and there feloniously &c., did shoot off and discharge."

The prisoner moved the Court of Appeals to arrest the judgment against him, contending that there was no sufficient averment that the gun was shot off or that the contents were discharged. The court held that the contention was of no merit, since the expression "with a gun did shoot off and discharge" might be unusual but it could not be termed inaccurate, especially as it was stated that he did shoot off and discharge with a gun charged with gunpowder and leaden bullets.

In this case *with* took on the meaning "by means of," for it was a known fact that Freeman killed his wife, by discharging a gun. The interpretation was suggested by fact.[3]

Case 4.—In 1891, A. C. La Bounty, of Franklin, Vermont, was indicted for feloniously, unlawfully, and maliciously killing "with and by means of poison," in 1890, a cow owned by H. Record and valued at forty dollars. La Bounty brought exceptions. The indictment charged offenses under the statute, which, in accordance with the form given in Bishop's Directions and Forms for an indictment under the English "Black Act," created a felony under the words "unlawfully and maliciously kill, maim or wound any cattle."

In accordance with the ordinary meaning of "with and by means of poison," the court decided that the phrase sufficiently charged in the indictment the mode for the felonious, willful, and malicious killing of an animal. The judgment was therefore affirmed.

The decision was based on the common meaning of *with*; "by means of."[4]

Case 5.—In New York, in 1881, Christina Eckhardt was charged with using an instrument upon the body and womb of Minnie Pape (she being then a woman with child), with intent thereby to produce a miscarriage. The statute under which the indictment was framed provided for the punishment of every person who should administer to any pregnant woman any medicine, etc., or should use or employ any instrument or other means whatever with intent thereby to produce the miscarriage of any such woman. Christina Eckhardt was convicted and brought a writ of error. She contended that the patient should not have been described as a *woman then with child* instead of a "pregnant woman," the words of the statute.

Judgment was affirmed.

The decision was based on the technical meaning of *woman with child*, which is the equivalent of "a pregnant woman."[5]

Case 6.—In Montana, in 1909, Arthur Pemberton was convicted of robbery. He appealed, saying that it was not alleged that the taking of the property had been accomplished by force or fear, according to the definition of robbery in the statute: "Robbery is the felonious taking of personal property in the possession of another, from his person or immediate presence, and against his will, accomplished by means of force or fear." The indictment stated that he "willfully, unlawfully, and feloniously, and with force and fear, commit the crime of robbery upon one John Mathison by willfully, unlawfully, and feloniously, and with force and intimidation, and putting in fear of great bodily harm, him, said John Mathison, and taking from the person and immediate presence of said John Mathison, with force against his will, money, watch, etc."

The Century and International Dictionaries were cited to show that the primary meaning of *with* denotes accompaniment, association, proximity, but that it likewise denotes the means or instrumentality by which an end or purpose is accomplished and that in this case it is synonymous with "by."

The evidence on the part of the prosecution showed that Pemberton and another, Ellison, assaulted Mathison, and, after choking and beating him into insensibility, took the articles from his person.

Judgment was therefore affirmed.

The decision was based on the appeal to the dictionary. It was found that *with* denoted the means by which an end or purpose was accomplished.[6]

Case 7.—In North Carolina, in 1850, a deed, after reciting a sale of land by execution, proceeded thus: "In consideration, &c., the said P. R. Sheriff, &c., doth hereby bargain and sell, alien, enfeoff, convey and confirm *with* the said Jas. Brooks, &c., their heirs and assigns all, &c. to have and to hold the same to the said, &c., their heirs and assigns." Ratcliff contended that the deed was void on account of the use of *with*.

The court held that *with* did not affect the sense or operation of the instrument; as, upon the context, it was evident, between or with whom the contract was, and by and to whom the estate was conveyed.

Judgment was therefore rendered in favor of the plaintiff.

The decision was based on the context. A series of verbs was used with the one preposition. The preposition was correctly used with some of the verbs, such as "bargain." It was correctly used with the last mentioned "confirmed." Thus it was evident to whom the land was conveyed.[7]

Case 8.—In New York, in 1903, an action was brought by the town of Southold against Francis Parks and others to determine title to land under bays eastward from Riverhead.

The action involved the determination of the ownership of land under the waters of Peconic and Gardiners Bays at the eastern end of Long Island. In 1884, the Legislature, assuming the title to that land to be in the state of New York, passed an act which ceded to Suffolk County all the right, title, and interest which the people of the state of New York had in and to the waters of Gardiners and Peconic Bays for the purpose of oyster culture only, to be managed and controlled by the board of supervisors. The defendants, by virtue of conveyances made under the provisions of the act, claimed title for the purposes of oyster culture to a tract under that portion of Peconic Bay locally known as "Southold Bay."

Southold brought this action to eject the defendants from the premises under the claim that the town had title to the premises by virtue of a colonial patent granted to it by the colonial governor, Andross, dated 1676. The colonial patent described the southern boundary as "on the south with an arm of the Sea or River which runneth up between Southampton land and the aforesaid tract of land unto a Certaine Creek which fresh water runneth into called in English the red Creek." The claim of the town was that *with* should be construed as synonymous with the word "including." The defendants, however, contended that *with*, as used in defining the bounds of a grant, was synonymous with "by." They referred to Webster's Dictionary, which stated in a note under *with:* "*with* and 'by' are closely allied in many of their uses and it is not easy to lay down a rule by which to distinguish their uses."

The northern boundary was described as *with* or by the sound. The court said that if the south boundary were held to be inclusive of "south arme of the Sea or River," then the north boundary must be held to be inclusive of the sound, an interpretation that was incredible. The judge added that if the arm of the sea ran up between the land granted by the patent and the Southampton land it could not possibly be a part of Southampton or Southold.

The court also showed that the evidence of usage of the bays in question tended to establish the conclusion that the town did not own any portion of either bay, and that, for over two centuries after the patent was granted, the inhabitants had made no claim of any such ownership, inasmuch as the inhabitants of the town and of other towns had fished in the bays with the same freedom that they would enjoy in the ocean without any regulations from the town.

It was shown also that in 1733, the colonial governor, by a separate patent, granted Robins Island, in Peconic Bay, to Charles Williams and Frederick Morris; a transaction indicating that the sovereign power did not construe the term patent to include Peconic Bay.

It was shown, too, that since the organization of the state government, the state authorities in numerous instances had made grants of land under the water of the bays in question to adjoining landowners and that the power had not been questioned until just before this case. The town had always exercised control over the creeks and inland waters, admittedly within the limits of the patent, but had not attempted before to make any grants of land under the waters of these bays. The court also showed that no part of the bays was included in the patents to the towns of Easthampton, Southampton, or Shelter Island, and said that there was no good reason why the sovereign power should exclude all those towns which border on the bay and give exclusive ownership to Southold.

All the circumstances being considered, it was decided that the patent to the town did not include the land under water occupied by the defendants and that the defendants were entitled to judgment with costs.[8]

The word *with*, in general, denotes a relation of contact or association, which relationship may or may not be physical. If one says, "The man with a hoe cut the weeds down," *with* expresses a physical relationship. If, however, one says, "Such arguments had influence with the people," the relationship expressed by *with* is figurative and not physical. The illustrative cases fall under the following linguistic classifications: (*a*) Inclusive meaning; (*b*) Exclusive meaning; (*c*) Instrumental meaning. Cases (1), (2), (5), and (7) belong to classifiction (*a*); case (8) belongs to classification (*b*); cases (3), (4), and (6) belong to classification (*c*).

(*a*) In case (1), we find *with* used in an inclusive sense. It denotes association in the way of possession. Sir John Lake bequeathed to Elizabeth Martin his house with all the household goods in it. The household goods were to be added to the gift of the house. This use, inclusive in its connotation, is a very common one. If Mr. Brown says, "Take the pears with the apples," he means take the pears in addition to the apples. The pears are to be included. The same use is exhibited in case (2)—"two horses, . . . with sufficient forage for the keeping of the same."

In case (5), we also find *with* in its inclusive sense. "A woman with child" means that the child is included. The child is in addition to the woman. This employment of *with* is common. Often one hears the statement, "She is a woman with child," meaning the woman is pregnant.

In case (7), *with* is used as a word of inclusion, but in a different sense from that of the preceding cases. It is used here in the place of two words, "to" and *with*, owing to the fact that a series of verbs is employed, some of which require "to" and some of which require *with*. Among the verbs are sell and convey, which require "to," and bargain and confirm, which require *with*. Therefore the word *with* has the meaning of "to," plus the meaning of association in respect of interaction, as in the sentence, "He is talking with her." The word, however, is used in its inclusive sense, for the land is to be added to the possessions of James Brooks.

(*b*) Case (8) shows *with* in its exclusive sense. The boundary is described as "on the south with an arm of the sea or river which runneth up between Southampton land and the aforesaid tract of land unto a Certaine Creek." Here *with* has the meaning of "by." The land was bounded on the south by an arm of the sea. The arm of the sea was excluded. This use of *with* is commonly heard. If Mrs. Brown says, "The dress is fringed with tan," she means the dress is fringed by tan. The dress is thought of independently of the tan fringe on the edge.

(*c*) One of the most common meanings of *with* is the instrumental one—"by means of." This use is illustrated in case (3), the case of a man who kills his wife *with* a gun; that is, by means of a gun. The gun was the instrument used. In everyday English a farmer will say, "Kill the hog with an axe," meaning by means of an axe. Case (4) shows *with* used in the same way. A cow was killed *with* poison; that is, by means of poison. The poison was the cause of death. Also in case (6) "with force and fear" means "by means of force and fear."

Within

The word *within* is defined according to: (1) Literal interpretation; (2) Interpretation based on intent; (3) Interpretation suggested by fact; (4) Common meaning; (5) Specialized meaning; (6) Technical meaning; (7) Dictionary meaning; (8) Circumstances.

Case 1.—An act was passed in 1815 to protect New Haven, Connecticut, from damage or fire. The statute prohibited the erection of a wooden building, or of any addition to a wooden building, having a chimney within it. Mr. Daggett erected, within such limits, an addition to an old building and placed a chimney and fireplace entirely *without* such addition, but looking into it and fitted solely for its accommodation.

The court, interpreting the statute literally, decided that the act constituted no violation of the law, for the chimney was not on the inside of the house.

Judgment was therefore rendered in favor of Daggett.[1]

Case 2.—In Pennsylvania, Mrs. Sinnickson was having a house erected. Stacy Reeves and Sons had the contract to undertake the whole work. They in turn had subcontractors, among whom were W. H. Harrison and Bros., who were engaged on July 11, 1890, to do the work for the house for $1,763. The contract concerning the tiles read: "The new tiles for fire place fronts and hearths to be estimated at $40 each, each fireplace set complete, and the grates or backs and jambs are to be included also in this proposal at $40 each. The owner is to have the privilege of selecting these articles within the above figures." The thirteen fireplaces, according to the original estimates, were to cost eighty dollars each, or $1,040 in all. Mrs. Sinnickson's selections, however, amounted to $572—a difference of $468. The plaintiffs claimed that they should have the $1,040. The Court of Common Pleas decided in favor of the plaintiffs, whereupon the defendants appealed.

The court held that *within* meant "lower," for "within the above figures" meant "at lower figures." The judgment was therefore reversed.

The interpretation of *within* was based on the intention of the contract, which stated that the selection of the owner was to be "within the above figures," meaning "at lower figures."[2]

Case 3.—In England, in 1847, an action of debt was brought by Baddeley as clerk to the commissioners to recover money, which Gingel refused to pay. According to the statute, "for better paving High Street, Whitechapel, and removing obstructions and annoyances therein," commissioners appointed under that act were empowered to rate "all and every person and persons who do or shall inhabit, hold, occupy, possess, or enjoy any house, shop, warehouse, cellar, vault, or other tenement, *within the said street.*"

The problem was to determine the meaning of the term "within the street." The court said that it was clear, strictly speaking, that no house was "within the street" and that the intention of the Legislature, in using the words, which was to impose a rate on all persons whose access to their houses was improved by the paving and repairing of the street, should be considered.

It was thus decided that the words "every inhabitant within the street" meant every person whose sole access to his premises was from the street and that "within the said street" meant "abutting on said street."

The interpretation of *within* to mean "abutting" was based on the fact that houses are never within the street, but by the side of it. The interpretation was thus suggested by fact.[3]

Case 4.—In New York, Jeremiah Hakes sold to John Peck a tract of land for $1,500 and received in payment another lot. John Peck at the time of the sale, October 21, 1854, signed an agreement by which he stipulated that the lot should sell within one year at that price or over, and in case of its not selling for that amount that he would make up the deficiency in cash to Hakes, within sixty days, with interest after the sale. Hakes held the lot until June 15, 1855, when he sold it at a public auction in Troy, after advertising it well, for $1,250. Then Peck contended that the sale before the year expired put it out of his power to fulfill his agreement.

The court held that *within* included any time during the subsequent year, so that Hakes had been at liberty to sell the lot at a public auction, at any time during the year, and that if it had not brought the price stipulated, Peck was liable for the deficiency.

The decision was based on the common meaning of *within*: "on or before" a certain date.[4]

Case 5.—In New York, in 1908, Veryl Preston brought action against the Ætna Insurance Company to recover for the damage caused to an automobile by fire. The policy contained the following provision: "It is understood and agreed that this policy does not cover loss or damage caused by fire originating 'within the vehicle.'" The automobile ran off into a ditch filled with water to the depth of a man's knees. Three men left to get assistance. Immediately afterward they heard an explosion and rushed back. The automobile was in flames and the chauffeur was lying on the ground across the ditch with his clothes torn. He died before the trial. Two kerosene lamps on the dashboard of the vehicle were lighted. Both parties assumed that on account of the slanting position in which the vehicle stood the gasoline ran out of the tank, covering the surface of the water, and that its vapor coming in contact with the lighted lamp took fire and caused the explosion. Therefore the question was whether such a fire fell within the exception of the policy as a "fire originating within the vehicle."

From a judgment of the Appellate Division, reversing a judgment for the Ætna Insurance Company, the company appealed.

The judge said that what the policy intended to except was fire developed by or originating in the use of the automobile as distinguished from fire occasioned by external causes, and that *within* was used as the antithesis of "extrinsic" or "without," not as the synonym of "interior."

The court therefore held that the policy did not cover loss by fire resulting from the explosion of gasoline, which, after an accident to an automobile, flowed from its gasoline tank and covered the surface of certain water in a ditch, and was thereafter ignited from fire burning in an oil lamp on the automobile.

The decision was based on the specialized meaning of *within* as used in a policy regarding the destruction of automobiles by fire. *Within* was used as the antithesis of "without."[5]

Case 6.—John Robinson, a resident of Ohio, in July, 1882, was, and for a long time prior thereto, had been the owner of a circus and menagerie on which he paid taxes in Ohio. In July he was traveling and exhibiting his shows, transporting them on the cars of the Union Pacific and Central Pacific Railway from Omaha, Nebraska, to Reno, Nevada, where he remained and exhibited his possessions one day. He also exhibited them in other towns in the state, not remaining in any place longer than was necessary for the performances. He intended to go to the principal cities and towns in California.

While this circus property was in Washoe County, A. A. Longley, as assessor, assessed it and threatened to seize and sell it, unless the tax of $275 was paid. To prevent such proceedings, Robinson paid the tax under protest and brought action to recover it.

The plaintiff contended that the property was not assessable in Nevada and that in the sense of the statute, for the purpose of taxation, it was not within the state, for it was only passing through the state at the time of the assessment and was there only temporarily.

Judgment was therefore rendered in favor of Robinson.

The decision was not based on the literal interpretation of

within, for the animals were actually within Nevada, but upon the technical meaning of the word as used in tax laws. To be considered *within* a state, there must be permanence.[6]

Case 7.—In Alabama, Francis Levert on September 18, 1866, filed and registered in the probate judge's office a duly verified claim against the insolvent estate of John Read, deceased. The filing was after the report, but before the declaration of insolvency. Mrs. Levert, in filing the claim verified, thought she was complying with the requirements of the statute concerning insolvent estates, which required claims against an insolvent estate to be filed within nine months.

Webster's Dictionary was referred to. The first definition was: "In the inner part"; the second was: "In the limit or compass of, *not beyond*, used of place and time"; the fifth was: "Not later than."

The court decided that the first definition would make no sense in the statute, but that the other two defined the intent of the lawmakers, which was to fix a time after which claims could not be filed. Judgment was therefore rendered in favor of Mrs. Levert.

The decision was based on an appeal to the dictionary, *within* being interpreted to mean that the claim could be filed within a time not "beyond the time fixed."[7]

Case 8.—The charter of St. Louis gave the city authority to tax all property "within the city." The authorities laid a tax on the value of all ferry boats used by the Wiggins Ferry to carry passengers and cargo on the Mississippi River, between St. Louis, Missouri, and East St. Louis, Illinois, on the opposite shore. The company refused to pay the tax on the ground that the boats were not property *within* the city.

The company was incorporated by the laws of Illinois, but had its principal office in St. Louis, Missouri. It was manifest that all the practical, life-giving, and fiscal operations of the corporation were performed within St. Louis, for its head and the center of its operations were there. In the jurisprudence of the United States a corporation is regarded as in effect a citizen of the state which created it. The company had an office in Illinois. Such minor officers, as engineers and pilots, lived in Illinois, where its real estate, including a warehouse, was situated. The company also had an office in St. Louis. Its president, vice-president, and other principal officers lived in that city, and there the ordinary business meetings of the directors were held and the corporate seal was kept. The court found that the boats, when not in actual use, were laid up by the Illinois shore, and were forbidden, by a general ordinance of St. Louis regulating ferries and ferry-boats, to remain at the St. Louis wharf or landing longer than ten minutes at a time. A tax was paid upon the boats in Illinois. Their relation to St. Louis was merely one of contact, that city having one of the termini of their transit across the river in the prosecution of their business.

The court decided that the boats were not property *within* the city. Judgment therefore was rendered in favor of the company.

The decision was based on the circumstances that determined whether the boats constituted taxable property in St. Louis or not.[8]

The word *within* is used in both a physical and a figurative sense. In the sentence "John is within the house," meaning John is on the inside of the house, the *within* denotes a physical relationship. In the expression "Come within an hour," however, the relationship expressed is figurative. Mr. Smith means that the person should come before the hour has ended, at some time during that hour. The illustrative cases here fall under the two following linguistic classifications: (*a*) Physical meaning; (*b*) Figurative meaning. Cases (1), (3), (5) and (8) belong to classification (*a*); cases (2), (4), (6), and (7) to classification (*b*).

(*a*) Case (1) shows *within* in its physical relationship. The chimney was by the side of the house, but not inside it. It was therefore not within the house. This use of *within* is the most common. If a person says "Happiness lies within man," he means that happiness is on the inside of man and comes from the inside.

In case (3), the phrase "within the said street" also illustrates the use of *within* in a physical sense, but in a physical sense with an extended meaning. The houses described as being "within the said street" actually were abutting on the street; that is, the houses were not actually *within* the street but on the side of it. This use is not frequently heard.

In case (5), *within*, used as the antithesis of "without," expresses a physical relationship. Fire "within the car" refers to fire developed by, or originating in the use of the automobile, or in the operation of its parts, an interpretation limiting the meaning of *within* to the inside of the automobile. This signification of *within* is frequently heard. If Mr. Brown says, "The fire originated within the lamp," he means that the fire began on the inside of the lamp, caused by a defect in some part of it.

Case (8) shows *within* meaning "not beyond." St. Louis claimed that the ferry boats were property on the inside of the city and that it had the power to tax them. It was decided that the boats were outside of the city, and not within it, for they were allowed to stay on the St. Louis shore only ten minutes at a time and had to remain on the Illinois shore when not in use. The boats were not actually in the inner part of the city, but were beyond the city limits and city authorities. Thus they were not considered as property *within* the city. Likewise, steamships from other countries, docking in New York at regular times, are not considered as property *within* the city, although they, in docking, do touch and make use of other property which is *within* the city.

(*b*) Case (2) shows *within* used in a figurative sense. The price was *within* "the above figures" and was not to exceed in quantity the figures given; an interpretation which gave a person the privilege of selecting materials at lower figures than the highest quoted. This use of *within* is common. If Mr. Brown says, "The man's expenses should be kept within his income," he means that the man's expenses should not exceed his income.

Case (4) illustrates the same idea in relation to time. "Within one year" means at any time during the year, but not beyond the limit of the year. In case (7), the expression "within nine months" has the same meaning. This use is a common one. If Mr. Brown says, "Do this within the next week," he means do it at any time during the next week, but do not take longer than the week.

In case (6), we find an entirely different interpretation of *within*. The circus and menagerie were literally and physically within, on the inside of, the state borders, but they were not considered legally inside the state; that is, settled inside the state, for they were only passing through. They would have been considered as inside the limits if they had been stopping for a year, or some long period. This use of *within* is common. If the dean of a college requires that every one *within* the institution attend chapel, a guest of one of the students, though actually *within* the college walls, would not have to attend, for the visitor could not be regarded as a resident of the college. One from the outside would not be considered an important part and would therefore not be considered *within*.

Without

The word *without* is defined according to: (1) Literal interpretation; (2) Interpretation based on intent; (3) Common meaning; (4) Technical meaning; (5) Dictionary meaning.

Case 1.—In Pennsylvania, in 1896, A. D. Wood brought an action of libel against P. C. Boyle for having published the statement that Wood without a following in politics had set up as a political boss "without brains, credit, or capital." He had appeared at the head of a gigantic business enterprise, requiring liberal bank balances and a large mental endowment.

The court said that the statements impugned one's business capacity, business standing, and character in the community.

P. C. Boyle was found guilty and the plaintiff recovered a verdit of $600.

The decision was based on the literal interpretation of *without*, meaning "lacking."[1]

Case 2.—The General Statutes of Rhode Island opened "all the public schools in the state to the children of officers and soldiers," etc., "without any cost or expense for taxes, or other charges imposed for purposes of public education." Under this statute George Carpenter, on March 25, 1878, wrote a letter to the commissioner of public schools, citing his Civil War record and claiming exemption from a tax of $2,000 in ratable property imposed upon him by joint school districts No. 2 and 4 of Hopkinton and 8 of Westerly.

The school trustees in Hopkinton thought that he should pay taxes. Carpenter had children in school. The levy on the property was an extra tax imposed for school purposes.

The court said that the intention of the Legislature was merely to relieve the children of the classes of persons named from the payment of rate bills, which, under the provisions of the law, existing at the time of the enactment of the provision, were liable to be, and were, in fact, assessed on pupils attending public schools.

It was decided that Carpenter was not entitled to the exemption. The decision was based on the intent of the statute.[2]

Case 3.—Antole, owner of the Italian bark Padre, a boat of 608 tons, chartered it, on September 29, 1879, through his agent in Baltimore, to Gill and Fisher, two merchants of Baltimore.

The vessel was then at Genoa, having arrived on September 23, with a cargo of 987 tons of coal. The charter-party represented the vessel as "now at Genoa, and to proceed without delay to Baltimore to enter upon this charter, vessel having permission to take cargo of coals as ballast out." She began discharging the cargo at Genoa on September 25, and finished on October 30, thirty-one days after the date of the charter-party. She then took in sand ballast, sailed for Baltimore on November 7, and arrived on January 14, 1880. The merchants had chartered another vessel in the meantime and refused to take the Padre when it arrived. Antole chartered it to someone else at a lower price and brought action to recover the difference.

It was shown in court that the vessel, while in Genoa, had been engaged in operations of which the charterers did not know, and that it could not leave Genoa for thirty days, after which the ship had to be made ready for sea.

The judge said that "proceed without delay to Baltimore to enter upon this charter-party, the vessel having permission to take cargo of coals as ballast out" meant without such delay as would arise from taking cargo on board.

Judgment was therefore rendered in favor of defendants.

The decision was based on the common meaning of *without*. If a person charters a vessel at a particular time, he does not want to wait four months for it. *Without delay* in common conversation means "shortly."[3]

Case 4.—In Connecticut, Sage, Birge and Company, in 1844, brought an action of assumpsit to recover moneys owed by Hawley and omitted by mistake in a settlement between them.

Hawley was a citizen of Connecticut, resided there with his family, and had property of greater value than the amount of the plaintiff's demand. He publicly left his family and property and went at different times in two successive years to one of the southern states, where he remained, each time, for about eight months, to take charge of a store of goods and to attend to the business thereof. He intended that these visits should constitute a temporary absence only, with a return to his residence in Connecticut, each time without abandoning, or intending to abandon, his domicile there.

The law gave the creditor six years within which to bring suit. A proviso in the statute read: "In computing the time limited . . . the term during which the party against whom there may be any such clauses of action shall be without this state, shall be excluded from the computations."

Over six years of actual time had passed when Sage brought action but he claimed that the time Hawley was away should be excluded. Hawley claimed that he was not actually "without the state," according to the meaning of the statute.

The court held that Hawley, during his absence, was not "without the state" within the meaning of the statute of limitations, and that therefore the time of such absence was not to be excluded from the computation of the time limited for bringing action.

The decision was based on the technical meaning of *without*. Hawley was literally without the state, but according to law he was not, for his domicile was in Connecticut.[4]

Case 5.—In West Plains, Missouri, in 1900, the board of aldermen decided to issue bonds to the amount of $27,500, to erect water works and an electric light plant. The ordinance was voted on and passed. For 1900 and for several years prior thereto, the board of aldermen had levied for city purposes fifty cents on the $100 valuation upon all property. In addition to this levy for the year 1900 the board on November 5, 1900, levied twenty-five cents on the $100 valuation to pay interest on the bonded indebtedness.

The plaintiffs, or taxpayers of the city, claimed that the additional twenty-five cents on the $100 valuation was invalid, and not authorized under the constitution or the statutes by the election voting the bonds. The defendants claimed that the levy was valid and that they would sell the property of the plaintiffs. On the first hearing, the decision was rendered in favor of the plaintiff. The defendants then appealed.

The Statute of 1899 provided that the alderman should have power to borrow money and issue bonds for the payment thereof, within the limits prescribed by the constitution, to erect waterworks, electric light works, a city hall, and other public buildings and improvements, and to equip them, without increasing the annual rate of taxation.

The appellant contended that in the phrase "without increasing the annual rate of taxation," the word *without* should not be judicially interpreted as meaning "unless" or "except," but "independently of," "excluding," "with the exclusion of," "outside of," "unconnected with," thus making the whole phrase the equivalent of "independently of increasing the annual rate of taxation" or something of like significance.

The judge said that good usage, according to Webster's International Dictionary and Anderson's Law Dictionary, permitted the meaning of *without* to be, when employed in a correct prepositional sense, "independently of," "otherwise than with."

The case was therefore reversed and the tax was sustained.

The decision was based on an appeal to the dictionary. It was found that *without* had the meaning "independently of."[5]

The word *without* has a physical meaning as well as a figurative one. If Mr. Smith says, "John stood without the gate," he means that John was on the outside of the gate. The five illustrative cases given here fall under the linguistic classification: (*a*) Figurative meaning.

Case (1) shows *without* as "lacking," a very common signification. If Mary says, "I am without an evening dress," she means that she lacks an evening dress.

Case (2) shows a variation of the meaning in case (1). "Without any cost" means "not having any cost." This signification too is heard often. If John says, "I did that without any trouble," he means that he did not have any trouble. In case (3), *without* has the same import. "Without delay" means "not having delay."

In case (4), *without* has an entirely different meaning. Mr. Hawley was literally outside of Connecticut, but his domicile was still there and so he was not regarded as being without the state. This meaning applies to all organized bodies. A person may not be within a hundred miles of a meeting of a particular organization of which he is a member, but he is not considered as being *without* the organization.

Case (6) shows *without* meaning "exclusive of," or "independently of," a rather frequent meaning. If Mr. Brown says, "There were 500 spectators, without those in the gallery," he means exclusive of those in the gallery, who were not counted.

Thus it is seen that *without* is often used in a figurative sense with a variation of meanings.

Chapter V

CONJUNCTIONS

CONJUNCTIONS also give the law courts difficulty. Though they are connecting words, they do not always make clearly defined connections.

Pursuing the method used in the discussion of the articles and prepositions, I have formulated for conjunctions classifications based on judicial decisions, and then have cited, in consecutive order, illustrative cases. Thirty-one conjunctions have been studied as form-words, and this study has also been presented in alphabetical order, beginning with *after*.

After

The word *after* is defined according to: (1) Literal interpretation; (2) Interpretation based on intent; (3) Context; (4) Circumstances.

Case 1.—In New York, in 1850, suit was brought against Fulton by Judd to recover for the escape of Eli Hubbard from the jail limits. Hubbard had been committed on August 25, 1847. On September 25, Hubbard made the affidavit required by the statute, and verified it on that day. The plaintiff contended that as the affidavit had been sworn to on September 25, it had been verified, or sworn to before the expiration of the thirty days after commitment. The statute provided that a party may be discharged from imprisonment, on making the requisite affidavit, "after he shall have remained in prison thirty days." September 25 was the thirtieth day of his imprisonment, excluding the day of his committment. According to law the rule is well settled that in computing time the first day, or the day when the time begins to run, is to be excluded. Thus the thirty days had not expired according to the statute.

The court held that a person committed to prison on August 25 could not be discharged on September 25, in view of the statute which stated: "after he shall have remained in prison thirty days."

The report was therefore set aside as the plaintiff desired.

The decision was based on the literal interpretation of *after* as "later than." September 25 was not thirty days later than August 25.[1]

Case 2.—In New York, in January, 1887, the will of Isaac Smith, of Yonkers, stipulated that, *after* all his just debts were paid, all the real property should be distributed among designated persons.

The court held that the real property was "devised, expressly charged with the payment of debts."

The decision was based on the intention of the testator. The debts were to be paid first; and then the remaining property was to be given to the designated persons.[2]

Case 3.—In Missouri, in 1920, a suit arose to determine the title to a tract of land. M. Joachimi, its owner, had died in 1911, leaving a will which read:

"To my daughter, Carrie Walter, and to Lillie Joachimi, and my dear wife, Mollie G. Joachimi, shall share alike in money and property left, after my debts are paid, except my homestead in Spurlock's addition, shall be left intact as long as my wife lives. After she leaves the homestead Lillie shall have this as a home, and at her death it shall go to Carrie Walter, if both survive and neither occupy the property, said property may be sold and proceeds divided among the two, and in case of Carrie Walter's death before Lillie Joachimi's death, said property shall go to Lillie Joachimi or her heirs."

The two daughters were children by his first wife. His wife Mollie moved to another town and while there married one Hecht. After her marriage she still paid the taxes on the homestead and improved it in many ways.

Lillie Wetzel and Carrie Walters contended that since Mollie left the homestead, and the will read "after she leaves the homestead Lillie shall have this as a home," etc., the homestead belonged to Lillie.

The court held that M. Joachimi did not say "if she leaves, but *after* she leaves"; and stated also in the previous sentence it (the homestead) "shall be left intact as long as my wife lives."

It was therefore decided that the wife should have the property during her lifetime.

The decision was based on the context of the will. The statement that the homestead should be left intact as long as his wife lived made it definite that she was to have it until her death. *After* was therefore construed as referring to a time subsequent to the death of the wife.[3]

Case 4.—In New York, in 1905, Eva Conklin brought action against Edwin Clarke, executor, to determine the amount of her legacy under a will, which read:

"First. After all my lawful debts are paid and discharged, I give, devise and bequeath to Eva Conklin, the interest on $5,000, and after her death the said $5,000 to be put out on interest until her son Glen shall be twenty-four years old; then he and Roy Conklin to have one-half of said $5,000 and their sister Mary Conklin to have the other half of said $5,000."

At the time of the testator's death, the personal estate was appraised at $43,000. The amount of the debts and legacies, inclusive of the $5,000 trust fund, amounted to $38,000. A large portion of the estate had been invested in securities yielding 6 per cent interest.

The court held that since the debts of the estate were small and the estate had the benefit of plaintiff's annual legacies, less what had been paid her, and since the executor had unnecessarily used the money devised to her for the payment of debts and legacies, and since the securities were yielding 6 per cent interest and the income was more than sufficient to pay all debts and legacies, the bequest would have to be construed as giving the legatee a title to the income from the date of the testator's demise.

Judgment was therefore rendered in favor of the plaintiff and the clause "after all my lawful debts are paid and discharged" could not be interpreted as authorizing the executor to withhold all payments of income until he had liquidated the last debt against testator, since there was more than enough personal property to pay all debts and all the legacies.

The decision was based on circumstances. It was a known fact that there was enough money to pay all debts and legacies. Therefore the widow should have the payments of income, even before the last debt was paid.[4]

The word *after*, as a conjunction, may have a limited or an extended meaning. The illustrative cases given here therefore fall under the two linguistic classifications: (*a*) Limited meaning; (*b*) Extended meaning. Cases (1), (2), and (3) belong to classification (*a*); case (4) belongs to classification (*b*).

(*a*) Case (1) presents *after* with a definite, limited meaning. It has the import of "later than." In this case it means later than thirty days. Not until Hubbard had stayed in jail for thirty days was he to be released. This definite meaning is often illustrated in everyday speech. One may say, for example, "After I have bought six gifts, I shall stop," using the word *after* in a limiting sense.

The same definite, limited meaning is shown in case (2). Just as soon as the debts are paid, the remaining property can be divided for the devisees. The limit is the paying of the debts. Here *after* has the signification of "subsequent in time," or "later than," as in case (1).

Case (3) also shows the definite, limited meaning of *after*. The limit is the death of the testator's widow.

(*b*) Case (4) shows *after* with an extension of meaning. It has in it the meaning of "while," for the income was to be paid to the widow while all the debts were being paid. The signification extended forward to take in time previous thereto. In everyday speech *after* in its extended meaning is rare.

Also

The word *also* is defined according to: (1) Literal interpretation; (2) Interpretation based on intent; (3) Common meaning; (4) Dictionary meaning; (5) Context; (6) Circumstances.

Case 1.—In 1858, in North Carolina, Thomas Williamson bequeathed to his daughter Tempy Fulgham, "one negro girl named Mary, now in her possession, and her increase, if any, also one negro girl named Bethany, to her heirs forever." There was no gift of Bethany's increase, and the only argument for including her children in the bequest of their mother was derived from the use of the word *also*, which, it was insisted, connected with her whatever of a like kind was intended to pass with the girl Mary. The testator did not in any other way manifest in his will that such was his intention.

The court held that the children of the girl, Bethany, did not pass with their mother, but were included in the residue to be sold.

The literal interpretation was given to the will in which the term *also* was taken to mean that only some other subject of gift besides what had been already mentioned was to be included—that which was specified by name or description.[1]

Case 2.—In Maine, in 1894, Betsy Loring brought a bill in equity against Jacob Hayes and others to obtain a construction of the will of Perez Loring, deceased.

The clauses involved in the question were as follows:

"Second, I give, bequeath and devise to my wife, Betsy Loring, my house with all the furniture and housekeeping articles contained in my dwelling house in said Yarmouth to have and to hold the same for her use during her natural life, also my horse, carriage, sleigh, harness, farming tools, also my watch and jewelry, Pen No. 9 first Parish Church. I also give and bequeath to my said wife, Betsy Loring, $4,500 to be paid to her in cash or in such personal securities as she may select from my estate.

"Fifth, and upon the decease of my said wife I give, bequeath, and devise all that may remain unexpended of the real and personal or mixed estate given to my said wife in the second clause of this will, to Jacob L. Hayes and others [naming them] to be divided equally between them to share and share alike, to have and to hold to them, and each of them in severalty, their heirs and assigns forever."

The question was whether the last portion of the second clause, taken in connection with the fifth clause, gave the widow $4,500 absolutely, or only the use of that sum for her life, with or without the right to expend it.

Hayes and others said that the use of the word *also* in "I also give and bequeath" showed that the testator had intended to limit that bequest as he had the other devises and bequests in that clause; that the word meant "in like manner" and that the testator's intention was to bequeath the sum of money in like manner with the rest of the devises and bequests in the clause; that is, "for her use during her natural life."

The court held that one meaning of the word *also* was "in like manner," but that another meaning and one quite as common was "in addition," "besides."

The court further held that by the language of the testator he made an absolute gift to his wife of the $4,500, and that the meaning of the word *also* in this connection was "in addition" rather than "in like manner."

The decision was based on the intent of the testator, who wanted his wife to have $4,500 to use as she liked.[2]

Case 3.—In Maine, in 1901, Albert Mace, as executor of the will of Isaac Mace, brought a bill of interpleader against George Mace and others to construe the will.

The following clauses gave trouble:

"Thirteenth. I give, devise, and bequeath to my beloved wife, Melinda Mace, so long as she is my widow, and my son George H. Mace, who is to live on said homestead, my homestead situate in Aurora, with the buildings thereon, containing about eighty acres; also all my farming tools and utensils, carts, carriages, sleds, sleighs, farm stock, houses, harnesses, carriage and sleigh robes, household furniture, and household goods; also one thousand dollars.

"Fourteenth. I give and bequeath to my daughters Helen C. Rowe and Maria Stover, equally, whatever there may be found and disposed by my executor hereinafter named, the residue, remainder, not otherwise disposed of."

One theory was that Melinda Mace was to have one half of the estate during her life, provided that she did not remarry, and that George Mace was to have a fee simple in the other half. In the event of Melinda Mace's death or remarriage, her share of the estate was to pass to the residuary devisees under the fourteenth clause; another interpretation was that the widow took a life estate, determinable upon her remarrying, in the whole homestead, with remainder over to George.

The judge thought the second theory was the right one, because to the same devisees were *also* given all farming tools and utensils, carts, carriages, etc. The judge believed that there was nothing to show that the qualification as to the wife's interest in the real estate was to be carried forward and applied to the personalty, and that therefore *also* should take its most ordinary meaning, that of "in addition thereto."

The court held that the devisees named took the testator's entire interest in the homestead, the widow an estate for life in the whole homestead determinable upon her remarrying, and the son the remainder, and that they each took an absolute title to one-half the personal property.

The decision was based on the common meaning of *also:* "in addition thereto."[3]

Case 4.—In Dakota, in 1884–85, an act for the creation of a new county provided "that a portion of Kidder County and a portion of Stutsman County, hereby proposed to be segregated, shall not be cut off unless the question of segregation shall be first submitted to the vote of the people of Kidder County, and also to the voters of that part of Range 69 proposed to be detached from Stutsman County, at a special election called for that purpose. . . . In case a majority of the legal voters of said Kidder County, and of said Range 69, voting, shall vote in favor of said segregation, then this act shall be in full force and effect."

In 1889, Van Dusen and others brought an action against Fridley, the treasurer of Kidder County, to restrain him from selling their property for taxes alleged to be illegal and void. They contended that the property was in the new county, Stanton, created from portions of Kidder and Stutsman. At the election in Kidder County there were 244 for the division and 173 against it; at the election in Stutsman there were five for the division and six against it. Fridley claimed that the act required that a majority of each district named in the act must have voted affirmatively before the new county could become created; that is, the act required a majority in each district affected thereby, and not a majority of all votes in both districts.

The court held that *also*, according to Webster, means: "In like manner; further; in addition"; etc.; therefore the act required that the question should be submitted to the voters of Kidder County, and in like manner, or in addition, to the voters of Range 69.

The court further held that a majority of the aggregate vote cast in both counties was insufficient, and that a majority of each was necessary to the creation of the proposed county.

The decision was based on an appeal to the dictionary. It was found that *also* meant "in like manner."[4]

Case 5.—In New Jersey, John Morgan's will, after providing for his funeral expenses and payment of his debts, read:

"Second. I give, devise and bequeath unto my beloved wife Caroline Morgan all of my household goods and furniture, also one-third of the income or interest of my estate during her widowhood in lieu of dower."

The plaintiff contended that the entire gift was intended to be limited to the period of Mrs. Morgan's widowhood.

The court held that the testator gave the goods and the interest of his estate, and added "during her widowhood," thus signifying that the word *also* meant "in like manner."

The court further held that the widow took only an interest in the goods and furniture during her widowhood.

The decision was based on the context. It is a matter of syntax. Both gifts are mentioned in the same sentence, at the end of which is added "during her widowhood in lieu of dower," thus showing that the same statement applies to both devises.[5]

Case 6—In North Carolina, in 1846, two parties claimed ownership of a negro named David, under Alexander Sherrill's will, which made a general gift to Mrs. Sherrill of everything, real and personal during her life or widowhood. Then the will continued: "At the decease of my wife I give, to my son Gabriel, my man Stephen, and to Lawson my man Charles. Also I give to my son Logan W. all my land, except that given to Lawson; *and also* my two boys Dick and David."

The judge said that the grammatical construction established the fact that the son Logan W. could not take until the decease (or, at all events, the marriage) of the wife, for after the clause beginning with "at the decease of my wife" followed the other clauses beginning with *also*, meaning "in like manner." He showed that that position was rendered more certain by the two gifts to Logan W. himself, the one of two horses and the other of the land, which was unquestionably left after the death or marriage of the mother, for in a previous part of the will Logan W. was directed to live on the farm with his mother and manage it for her, and to receive compensation in part of the annual productions, when they exceeded the consumption of the family. The judge also said that if the mother had not taken that land there would have been none left.

The court held that Logan W. should take the land at the mother's death or marriage and thus the other gifts, by the words "and also," were likewise to be received at the mother's death or marriage.

The decision was based on the circumstances of the case. Logan W. was to live with his mother and other gifts were devised to him in another part of the will. Thus *also* meant "in like manner."[6]

The connecting word *also* is frequently employed. It usually denotes addition, but not always. The illustrative cases given here fall under the two linguistic classifications: (*a*) *Also* denoting addition; (*b*) *Also* denoting instrumentality. Cases (1), (2), and (3) belong to classification (*a*); cases (4), (5), and (6) to classification (*b*).

(*a*) Cases (1), (2), and (3) show *also* meaning definitely, "in addition thereto." One thing has been given and another one is to be added. This use is common in everyday speech. If Mary says, "I shall give my sister a dress; also a coat," she means that she is going to give to her sister a coat and a dress too.

(*b*) In case (4), we find *also* meaning "in like manner," to denote instrumentality, the manner of doing a thing. A question was to be submitted to the voters of Kidder County, and in the same way to the voters of Range 69. This use of *also* is common. A professor wanting to give a test to boys and girls separately would say, "I am giving this test to the boys; also to the girls," meaning that he would give the test to the girls in the same manner that he had given it to the boys. Cases (5) and (6) illustrate the same use of also.

Although

The word *although* is defined according to: (1) Common meaning.

Case 1.—In Wisconsin, Hogan, quarreling with his brother over a boundary of land, hit him on the forehead with an axe, the injuries resulting in death. Convicted in 1874 of murder in the second degree, Hogan brought a writ of error. He did not deny the crime or try to extenuate it, but he said the verdict should be changed from the second degree murder to manslaughter and in support of that view cited the fact that he had given uncontradicted evidence of good character. It became necessary, therefore, for the court to examine the definitions of murder in the first, second, and third degree, and of manslaughter.

There was no proof by the defendant that the killing had been done in the heat of passion, a circumstance which would have classified it as manslaughter. The court said that good character had nothing to do with heat of passion, and that heat of passion would have to be proved as good character had been.

On all the definitions of murder in the third degree, and of manslaughter in the first, second, and third degrees were found the words "without design to effect death." The definition of murder in the second degree did not use the same words, but read: "although without any premeditated design to effect the death of any particular individual." This clause, the court said, implied a doubt and a concession of something not positively determined. The court further said that it was not the circumstances of the homicide, but the actual or constructive intent, which determined the distinction between the first and second degree of murder.

At the first trial the court instructed the jury, in substance, that if they did not find that Hogan intended to kill his brother, but found that the motive which caused death evinced a depraved mind in Hogan, and that he had no regard for human life, they might find him guilty of murder in the second degree. On this instruction the jury found Hogan guilty of murder in the second degree.

The Supreme Court, considering the circumstances and the definitions, found no error. Judgement was affirmed.

The decision was based on the common meaning of *although*, which always denotes concession and has the signification of "grant all this."[1]

The conjunction *although*, which was originally more emphatic than "though," is now used interchangeably with the latter in the sense of concession. As in the case of "a" and "an," the indefinite articles, euphony determines the choice. The illustrative case given here falls under the linguistic classification: (*a*) The use of *although* as a word of doubt. In this case it takes on the meaning of "supposing that," which implies doubt. If there were no doubt, the wording "knowing" would be substituted for "supposing." It was not a certainty that the murder was not premeditated. This employment of *although* is quite common in everyday speech. If Mr. Smith says, "Although Mr. Brown may be angry, I am not," he implies doubt. Mr. Smith is not sure that Mr. Brown is angry; he only puts in the supposition.

And

The word *and* is defined according to: (1) Literal interpretation; (2) Interpretation based on intent; (3) Common meaning; (4) Context; (5) Circumstances.

Case 1.—In Massachusetts, in 1815, an action of assumpsit was brought on a policy of insurance upon the brig Eliza and cargo, in which the plaintiff declared for a total loss. A policy had been written for $3,000 on the ship and $1,000 on her cargo, from the United States to Ireland. At the foot of the policy was the memorandum, "Should this *vessel and cargo* be insured in *England*, this policy is to be cancelled." Insurance was made in England by the plaintiff's agent there, on the vessel only. The vessel was lost. The insurance company contended that the whole policy was void, since the vessel was insured in London. They considered the meaning of *and* as "or." The plaintiff, however, contended that, by the terms of the memorandum, the policy was to be void only in case the vessel *and* cargo were insured in England.

The court held that the plaintiff was entitled to recover for a total loss on the cargo.

The decision was based on the literal interpretation of *and*, as a particle expressing the general relation of addition. Both cargo and vessel were not insured in London; therefore the plaintiff could not recover on the one not insured—on the cargo.[1]

Case 2.—In Indiana, in 1855, Smith brought action to recover money alleged to have been unlawfully exacted from him by the city authorities. In 1850, the city had passed an ordinance taxing bowling saloons fifty dollars a year, and prescribing a penalty of not over fifty dollars a week against any person keeping one, in violation of the ordinance. Smith said that he was compelled to pay a tax of $116.50. He contended that the ordinance by virtue of which the tax was levied was not authorized by the city charter and that he should recover his money. The charter read: "the common council is authorized for and within the city, to make and establish ordinances to suppress and restrain disorderly houses and groceries, houses of ill fame, billiard tables, nine or ten pin alley or tables, and ball alleys, and to authorize the demolition and destruction of all instruments of gaming."

Smith argued that the grant of a power to suppress and restrain did not by direct statement or by implication confer the power to tax and license.

The court held that the word *and* was obviously used disjunctively and that the common council might, in their discretion, restrain and regulate such places, or they might suppress them, and as a result the council deemed it proper to permit bowling saloons to exist in the city, and by way of restraint, imposed a tax of fifty dollars per annum.

The court further held that the tax was properly levied and that Smith had no right of action.

The decision was based on the intent of the ordinance. In this case *and* took on the meaning of "or."[2]

Case 3.—In Illinois, in 1901, Hyacinth Kostka brought action against the city of La Salle to recover damages for injuries sustained by him in consequence of the caving in of the banks of a sewer in which he was working under the direction of the city's street superintendent. Judgment was rendered in favor of the plaintiff, and the city appealed.

The declaration alleged that the city disregarded its duty by failing to keep "the earth, sand, and other substances" of the walls or sides of the sewer "firmly in place," by wrongfully, carelessly, and negligently suffering the excavation for the sewer to remain in an unsafe condition, "by suffering the earth, sand, and other substances forming the sides or walls of said excavation to remain in a loose, water-soaked, and dangerous condition."

The contention of the city was that the allegations of the declaration were merely to the effect that the side or sides of the ditch were in a loose or water-soaked condition, and not in a dangerous condition.

The court said that the conjunction *and* in the declaration was a coördinate conjunction, not explanatory but signifying and expressing the relation of addition, and that the declaration meant that the earth, sand, and other substance of the walls or sides of the ditch were in a condition beyond, or in addition to, that of "a loose and water-soaked" condition; they were also in a dangerous condition.

Testimony showed that the braces to prevent the sides of the ditch from collapsing had been put in under the direct supervision and express orders of the foreman for the city.

Thus it was decided that the city was responsible; that the foreman of the city was chargeable with the specific duty of exercising reasonable care to see that the place where he sent Kostka to work was reasonably safe. The judgment was therefore affirmed. The decision was based on the common meaning of *and:* "in addition to."[3]

Case 4.—In Oklahoma, in 1927, Bill Baker was convicted of selling narcotics. He appealed.

The statute read as follows:

"Any person who violates any of the requirements of the provisions of this act, shall, upon conviction, be deemed guilty of a felony, and be fined not less than $500 nor more than $5,000, and shall be imprisoned not less than one year nor more than seven years, or both."

Baker appealed from the court's instruction, given over his objection. This instruction was:

"Should you find the defendant guilty of the crime charged against him, it will be your duty to fix the punishment therefor, which shall be a fine of not less than $500 nor more than $5,000, and by imprisonment in the state penitentiary for not less than seven years."

He was tried, and the jury returned a verdict finding him guilty and assessing his punishment at a fine of $500 and imprisonment in the state penitentiary for a term of one year.

In his appeal Baker contended that to give effect to the phrase "or both" the punishment would have to be fine or imprisonment or both fine and imprisonment, and that the conjunction *and* meant "or."

The higher court reversed the judgment.

The decision was based on the context, the fact that "or both" was included. If that phrase had not been added *and* would have been considered in its ordinary sense.[4]

Case 5.—In Illinois, in 1895, William Tipton was convicted for selling intoxicating liquors contrary to the statute, making it a criminal offense to sell intoxicating liquors outside of cities, towns, and villages "in any less quantity than five gallons, and in the original package as put up by the manufacturer."

Tipton contended that the statute did not without qualification prohibit sales of less than five gallons; it only prohibited sales in the original packages as put up by the manufacturer.

The judge said that it was against reason to think that the Legislature intended to permit the sale of any intoxicating drink outside of the incorporated limits of any city, town, or village, by the gill, half pint, or in any other quantity less than five gallons, provided only such sales were not made in original packages, notwithstanding a statute then in force absolutely prohibiting all sales of intoxicating liquors in the state, without a license, in less quantities than one gallon, or in any quantity to be drunk upon the premises. He also said that the word *and* commonly meant "in addition to" and should be so construed in the statute so that sales of less than five gallons should be prohibited except when contained in an original package.

The judgment was therefore affirmed.

The decision was based on an appeal to circumstances. At that time there was in force a statute prohibiting all sales of intoxicating liquors, without a license, in quantities less than one gallon, or in any quantity to be drunk on the premises.[5]

When a person hears the word *and*, he immediately thinks of one thing joined to another—an addition. The word, however, does not always have the conjunctive meaning, but is at times disjunctive. The illustrative cases given here fall under the two linguistic classifications: (*a*) The conjunctive meaning; (*b*) The disjunctive meaning. Cases (1), (3), and (5) belong to classification (*a*); cases (2) and (4) belong to classification (*b*).

(*a*) In case (1), "the vessel and cargo" means the cargo in addition to the vessel, the most usual meaning of *and*. It is generally used to show connection and to conjoin word with word, clause with clause, or sentence with sentence. If John says, "Mary and Helen have gone," he means that Mary has gone and that in addition to Mary, Helen has gone. Case (3) illustrates the same meaning. The walls were in a loose and water-soaked condition, and in addition were dangerous. The same meaning is found in case (5).

(*b*) At times, *and*, strange as it may seem, is used in a disjunctive sense. Case (2) illustrates that use. One cannot suppress and restrain at the same time. If a disorderly house is suppressed there is nothing to restrain. Thus *and* takes on the meaning of "or." The same disjunctive use is shown in case (4). This meaning of "or" given to *and* is also used in everyday speech. If a woman is given the privilege of teaching cooking and sewing and then is asked which she prefers, she knows that one of the two is to be chosen and that she is not to teach sewing in addition to cooking.

As

The word *as* is defined according to: (1) Literal interpretation; (2) Interpretation based on intent; (3) Common meaning; (4) Dictionary meaning.

Case 1.—In 1899, in Texas, Dr. William McQuery was convicted on an indictment alleging that he "as a regular practicing physician" gave, without examination, to Walter Caldwell, who was not sick, a prescription for intoxicating liquors to be used as a stimulant. The first clause of the statute prohibited any one but a regular physician from giving a prescription; the second clause denounced and punished any physician giving a prescription if he were interested in the sale of the intoxicant; the third clause prescribed a punishment for any physician giving a prescription, without making a personal examination, to anyone who was not actually sick.

Dr. McQuery appealed. The higher court held that the allegation was not sufficient to convict him and ruled that the word *as* did not signify that Dr. McQuery was a regular practicing physician or was a physician at all.

The decision was based on the literal interpretation of *as*, used in the allegation. Because he had not been clearly called a regular physician in the indictment, he was not convicted.[1]

Case 2.—In Connecticut, in 1866, Christopher Colt, a legatee of Samuel Colt, brought action against Hubbard, the executor of the will, to recover several dividends declared on the stock bequeathed to him before he became of age.

The will read: "To each of the other children, &c., *I give and bequeath, as they shall respectively arrive at the age of twenty-one years*, 100 shares of stock in Colt's Patent Fire-arms Manufacturing Company."

The judge said that the clause "as they shall respectively arrive at the age of twenty-one years" meant "when they shall have arrived at the age of twenty-one years."

It was decided that the dividends accruing on the shares before Christopher Colt was twenty-one should not go to him as the stock did not become his until he was of age.

In this case *as* took on the meaning of "when," determined by the intent of the testator.[2]

Case 3.—In New Jersey, in 1833, Joseph Rogers made his will. In accordance with Section 13 he directed his executor, Wills, to sell all the rest and residue of his estate, and after paying all his debts and legacies, to divide the proceeds equally among his six grandsons, J. Rogers, T. W. Rogers, R. Roberts, J. E. Roberts and N. S. Roberts and Allen Rogers, subject, nevertheless, to the guardianship and trust as hereinafterwards directed.

In Section 14 he appointed his nephew Allen Rogers, guardian of all the estate, real and personal, of his grandsons devised and bequeathed as aforesaid, with an expression of great confidence in his integrity and faithfulness. In Section 17 he directed Allen Rogers, the guardian, to do certain things with the money in educating the grandsons, etc. In 1840, codicils were added revoking certain devises to certain of his grandsons on account of their disrespectful attitude to him.

In litigation, in 1846, it was decided that "as aforesaid," which was used in the will relating to the property devised and bequeathed, could only apply to previous clauses of the will, and could not be extended to subsequent provisions in a codicil. Rogers thus revoked only Sections 5 and 6 of the will, part of Sections 13 and 14 concerning the bequests, in which was also contained the appointment of the guardian. In the revocation nothing was said about the guardian. The will and codicil were construed together and no revocation of the trust was found in the will. It was decided that the guardian was not deprived of his rights and powers.

The decision was based on the common use of *as* in the expression "as aforesaid: "in the same manner with which" or "in accordance with."[3]

Case 4.—In 1864, in California, Hooper sued the Wells, Fargo and Company to recover $10,755, the value of a package of gold bullion delivered to the defendants, at Los Angeles, to be transported to San Franciso. The package was lost in consequence of the explosion of the boiler on the steam tug, "Ada Hancock," while being carried by the defendant's messenger, Ritchie, from the shore, at San Pedro, to the anchorage of the steamer, "Senator."

The receipt given to Hooper contained this stipulation: "It is further agreed, and is part of the consideration of this contract, that Wells, Fargo and Company are not to be responsible except as forwarders, nor for any loss of damage arising from the dangers of railroad, ocean or river navigation, fire, etc., unless specially insured by them and so specified on this receipt."

The case turned upon the meaning of "except as forwarders." The court said that the word *as* was defined in the last edition of Webster's Dictionary in the following way: "Like; similar to; of the same kind; or in the same manner; in the manner in which" and that obviously the defendant's liability was "similar to" that of forwarders—"of the same kind"—that is, they were to be liable "in the same manner"—"in the manner in which" forwarders are liable. The court also said the fact that defendants made use of various public conveyances, their messenger with the treasure traveling a part of the way by stage, a part by steam tug and lighters, and a part by ocean steamer, made no difference as to their liability, for Ritchie, the messenger of the defendants, had actual custody over the treasure during the transit.

The judgment was rendered in favor of the plaintiff, for it was decided that forwarders were responsible for all injuries to property while in their charge, resulting from negligence or misfeasance of themselves, their agents or employees. The boiler had exploded because of negligence and had killed Ritchie.

In this case *as* is used as a conjunction, the meaning of which was decided upon by consultation of the dictionary.[4]

The word *as* is usually limited in its meaning. The four illustrative cases given here fall under the linguistic classification: (*a*) The limited meaning.

In case (1), Dr. McQuery is referred to "as a regular practicing physician," showing him in the character of a regular practicing physician, but not stating definitely that he is one. There are definite limits in the idea, for Dr. McQuery can have only the attributes that belong to a regular practicing physician. This employment of *as* is common. If a man says, "Hampden will appear as Hamlet," he means that Hampden will appear in the character of Hamlet, and not that Hampden will actually become Hamlet.

Case (2) shows another variation of the limited meaning. "As they arrive at the age of twenty-one" means "when they arrive at the age of twenty-one," thus designating a very definite limit—the age of twenty-one. Here *as* takes on the meaning of "when," another signification that is frequently employed. If Mr. Brown says, "John trembles as he speaks," he means that John trembles when he speaks.

In case (3), in the expression "as aforesaid," *as* takes on the meaning of "in accordance with." The devises are to be made in accordance with what was said before. What was said before limits the meaning. In everyday speech, if Mr. Brown says, "John, do as you are told," Mr. Brown intends for John to act in accordance with the orders given to him.

Case (4) shows *as* meaning "in the manner in which." Wells, Fargo and Company were responsible in the manner in which forwarders were responsible. The signification was limited to that of a forwarder. *As* in this sense is often heard. If students are being trained to be teachers and the supervisor wants each one to take the place of a teacher, she will say, "You must act as teachers," meaning in the manner in which teachers act.

But

The word *but* is defined according to: (1) Literal interpretation; (2) Interpretation based on intent; (3) Common meaning; (4) Dictionary meaning.

Case 1.—In West Virginia, in 1882, the Chesapeake and Ohio Railway Company sought to restrain Joseph Miller, auditor of West Virginia, from adding to the amount of taxes alleged to have been assessed upon their property or from doing anything toward the collection of these taxes. The bill of injunction was presented to Judge Joseph Smith of the Seventh Judicial Circuit and the injunction was granted by him under the act of the Legislature of West Virginia, dated March 1, 1866, declaring that "no taxation upon the property of the said company should be imposed by the State, until the profits of said company shall amount to ten per cent. on the capital of the company."

The Constitution, however, read as follows: "Taxation shall

be equal and uniform throughout the State, and all property, both real and personal, shall be taxed in proportion to its value, to be ascertained as directed by law. No one species of property, from which a tax may be collected, shall be taxed higher than any other species of property of equal value, but property used for educational, literary, scientific, religious or charitable purposes, and public property may by law be exempted from taxation."

It was decided that the act of the Legislature was unconstitutional, according to the literal meaning of *but*.

The injunction was therefore wholly dissolved and the complainant's bill was dismissed at costs. The decree was thus reversed.

The decision was based on the literal interpretation of *but*. Since the railroad property did not fall under the head of property used for educational, literary, scientific, religious or charitable purposes, the injunction was dissolved and the company's bill was dismissed. The word *but* indicated that only the property mentioned was excepted.[1]

Case 2.—In Pennsylvania, in 1897, Abraham Cox died, leaving a will, which directed: "Upon decease of my wife, if my son . . . survive her, then to pay the whole of such net income to my said son for life, but, in case my son should die, leaving my wife surviving, then, during the life of my said wife, the widow of my son is to receive one-third of my son's share of said income, and the issue of my son two-thirds, and, upon the decease of my wife, then the widow of my said son is to receive one-third of the principal of the trust fund, and the issue two-thirds."

The court said that argument was unnecessary because the intention of the testator was obvious, and fully expressed in the will, his only fault being that his expression was ungrammatical in that the disjunctive "or" should have been used between the two members of the clause instead of *but* to show that his meaning was to dispose of the income of his estate during the joint and several lives of his wife and son, and at the death of the survivor to give the corpus to the son's widow and children.

The son survived the testator's wife and left, at his death, a widow and two children. The fund was awarded to the widow and children of the deceased son, the decision being based on the intent of the testator. Thus *but* took on the meaning of "or."[2]

Case 3.—Richard Foster brought action against the First National Bank of Rock Springs, Wyoming, upon a lost certificate of deposit. Judgment was rendered in favor of the plaintiff, the verdict being signed by ten of the jurors, the other two refusing to concur. The Bank objected to the verdict's being received, for the reason that it was not unanimous. The objection was overruled, and the verdict was entered. The bank took exception.

The Constitution provided: "The right of trial by jury shall remain inviolate in criminal cases, but a jury in civil cases in all courts, not of record, may consist of less than twelve men, as may be prescribed by law. Hereafter a grand jury may consist of twelve men, any nine of whom concurring may find an indictment, but the legislature may change, regulate or abolish the grand jury system." The Statute of 1899 provided: "In all civil cases in any of the courts of the state of Wyoming, which shall be tried by a jury, three-fourths of the number of the jurors sitting in any such case may concur in and return a verdict in said case, and such verdict shall have the same force and effect as though found and returned by all the jurors sitting in said case." The bank insisted that the statute was in violation of the section of the constitution quoted above.

The judge said that the intention of the framers of the constitution was that in all criminal cases the right of trial by jury should remain as heretofore, but that in civil cases, it should remain as heretofore except that the Legislature might provide for a number less than twelve to constitute a jury, the word *but* being used in its very customary meaning of "except." He also said that the verdict was intended to be unanimous, even though there were fewer than twelve men.

Judgment was therefore reversed.

The decision was based on the common meaning of *but*: "except."[3]

Case 4.—In Illinois, in 1911, a bill was brought by Antoinette Winter, against Sarah Dibble and another concerning a will. Judgment was for the complainant and the defendants appealed.

Antoinette Winter claimed as the widow and sole devisee of Samuel Winter, who died in December 1908, leaving no descendant, but leaving the appellants, his sisters, surviving him. Shortly before he died, he had made a will devising all his property to his widow. The appellants filed a bill to have the will set aside. They contended that Winter was not lawfully married to Antoinette Winter. It was proved, however, that they had been married in 1907.

The testator devised all his real estate to his widow so long as she should remain such, and then provided that certain of his real estate should not be sold or encumbered, and, on the death of the widow, should be owned and used by his children as equal co-owners, "but in case of the death of any one leaving heirs, then the share of such deceased child," in equal portions, should descend to his or her heirs, and, on the death of the children or any of them, the property should descend to their respective heirs in fee simple absolute.

The court held that since the word *but*, following the creation of the life estate in the testator's children, marked the beginning of an exception, and was used in the sense of "except," "unless," "save," "yet," "still," "however," "nevertheless," according to Webster's New International Dictionary, the clause relating to the death of any of the children referred to their death during the lifetime of the widow, and that, as to children surviving her, a contingency no longer existed, the word "heirs" in the last clause not being limited to heirs of the body but referring to the testator's heirs generally.

The decision was based on an appeal to the dictionary.[4]

The word *but* is usually employed in an antithetical sense. The two linguistic classifications under which the illustrative cases given here fall are: (*a*) The exclusive meaning; (*b*) The disjunctive meaning. Cases (1), (3), and (4) belong to classification (*a*); case (2) belongs to classification (*b*).

(*a*) In case (1), we find *but* used in its exclusive sense. The property used for educational, literary, scientific, religious or charitable purposes could be excluded from taxation. This use of *but* is common. A superintendent of a school may say, "All students must report at two o'clock, but the boys on the team may get permission to stay later," signifying that the boys on the team may be excluded. Case (3) shows *but* in the same sense.

In case (4), *but* introduces an exception in "but in case of the death of any one leaving heirs, then the share of such deceased child," etc. The share belonging to the deceased child who has heirs is to be excluded from the other shares and divided among his or her heirs.

(*b*) Occasionally, we have *but* used in the disjunctive sense, as in case (2). The testator tells what he wants done at the death of his wife, if his son is living. Then he tells what he wants done if his son should die before his wife. Here *but* has the meaning of "or," introducing alternative conditions. This employment of *but* is heard at times in everyday speech. If Mr. Brown says to his son, "John, if Mary is here, go to school, but if Mary has not returned, go to the store for the groceries," Mr. Brown introduces an alternative condition, one or the other of which will be true. Thus *but* takes on the meaning of "or."

But Also

There is one case that turns on the compound conjunction *but also*. It is defined according to: (1) Common meaning.

Case 1.—In Missouri, in 1907, Henry Julian sued the Kansas City Star Company for libel.

Bouvier's Law Dictionary defined libel thus: "Everything written or printed which reflects on the character of another and is published without lawful justification or excuse is a libel, whatever the intention may have been."

The *Kansas City Star* published the following: "Julian is remembered here as a member of the Legislature, who did well in a legislative way, but also as Stone's chief of police, of whom a Democratic Senate committee said: 'He (meaning the plaintiff) is not a proper man for the position.' A Democratic Senate removed him (meaning the plaintiff) and the commissioners who appointed him (meaning the plaintiff)."

The point to be determined was the meaning of the disjunctive conjunction *but also*, interposed between the clauses of the sentence that the newspaper insisted was laudatory. The paper said that the whole sentence meant that while Julian was remembered there as the one who performed his duties well as a member of the Legislature, on the other hand, he was also remembered "as Stone's chief of police, of whom," etc.

The court said that when the term *but also* connected two parts of a sentence, it usually implied that what followed it was in addition to what preceded it, thereby carrying the idea of one thing as well as another. The court ruled that the paper had given the public the idea that Julian had made dishonest use of his office for his private gain.

Judgment was rendered in favor of the plaintiff.

The decision was based on the common meaning of *but also*, as "in addition to." This compound is a correlative conjunction, joined with "not only."[1]

The correlative conjunction *but also* is always joined with "not only," either expressed or implied. The illustrative case given here falls under the linguistic classification: (*a*) *But also* denoting addition.

In the case, the assertion "a member of the Legislature, who did well in a legislative way, but also as Stone's chief of police," meant that he did well not only as a member of the Legislature, *but also* as Stone's chief of police. The second idea is an addition to the first. This use of *but also* is common. If Mr. Brown says, "John is brave, but also selfish," he means that in addition to John's being brave, he is selfish.

Either

The word *either* is defined according to: (1) Literal interpretation; (2) Interpretation based on fact; (3) Common meaning; (4) Circumstances.

Case 1.—In New York, in 1907, G. E. Jones brought action against Harriet Sabin upon contract, obtained a warrant of attachment, and levied upon moneys of hers in a bank. She desired a release of the moneys, but instead of obtaining an order releasing the levy her attorneys presented an order which not only discharged the levy but also vacated the attachment itself. Shortly afterward she saw the mistake and made a motion to be relieved from that part of the order vacating the attachment. This action was granted and the attachment was restored with the levy discharged. Then the defendant moved that the plaintiff be compelled to give additional security on his attachment. The motion was granted and the plaintiff was required to give an additional undertaking of $3,000. This undertaking he failed to provide. Then under Section 3277 of the Code of Civil Procedure the defendant moved for judgment, dismissing the complaint with costs. This motion was granted and such judgment was entered. The plaintiff appealed from this judgment, which was not rendered upon a trial. Then his right of appeal was questioned.

The judge said that a judgment of dismissal of this kind rendered pursuant to the Code of Civil Procedure, Section 3277, authorizing a dismissal of the complaint on plaintiff's failing to comply with an order requiring him to give an additional undertaking, was not appealable, within Section 1346, which authorized appeals from judgments rendered on a trial by referee or court, or on verdict of a jury.

Section 1209 of Code of Civil Procedure provided that a final judgment dismissing the complaint either before or after a trial did not prevent a new action, for the same cause, unless it expressly declares, or it appears by the judgment roll that it is rendered upon the merits, does not help the situation. The plaintiff's motion of appeal was not a direct appeal from the various orders, but as the appeal was unauthorized a review of the orders was necessary.

The appeal was therefore dismissed.

The decision was based on the literal interpretation of the Code in which *either* was used as a correlative conjunction in connection with "or"—"either before or after a trial."[1]

Case 2.—In Michigan, in 1903, action was brought by the Detroit Electric Light and Power Company, under the receivership of Hoyt Post, against Applebaum *et al.*, for the value of 7,728 pounds of copper wire alleged to have been stolen from the power company by Robert Tress, line foreman, and sold by him through D. A. Casey, as manager, to the defendants, I. Applebaum and Company, who had a separate scrap-iron business. The defendants contended that they bought the wire in good faith through Casey, as manager, and Tress, as line foreman. The plaintiffs, however, contended that Applebaum bought it from Tress, individually, who had no title and was therefore liable. Judgment was for the defendants and the plaintiffs appealed.

Complaint was made of part of the charge: "The law presumes that parties, in their dealings, intend to conduct them honestly; and, where a transaction which is challenged will admit either of an honest or a dishonest construction, it is the duty of the jury to accept the former—that is, to accept the honest construction." The counsel for the appellees suggested that a typographical error had crept in, and that the word *either* was used where the word equally was intended.

The judge said that if the word "equally" had been used, the charge would not have been objectionable; but that unfortunately it was not used, and that by the charge a burden was put upon the plaintiffs which did not exist even in cases of fraud.

The case was therefore reversed.

The decision was based on an interpretation based on fact. The fact was that there could not be both an honest and a dishonest construction to choose from, if the transaction admitted of either one or the other. The phrase "either one or the other" means that there will be only one. Therefore in order to have two constructions of opposite significance, *either* must take on the meaning of "equally."[2]

Case 3.—In Oklahoma, in 1919, the First National Bank of Lawton obtained an act of replevin against J. D. Lankford, Bank Commissioner of the State. Judgment was rendered in favor of the plaintiff and Lankford appealed.

On January 4, 1913, one Garrett executed a chattel mortgage on certain personal property to the Bank of Lawton to secure an indebtedness to the bank. The mortgage was not acknowledged, but had two witnesses. Thereafter, on April 25 and 28, 1913, respectively, Garrett executed two chattel mortgages to the First

National Bank of Lawton, with a black horse as security. This security was included in the mortgage to the Bank of Lawton. The Bank of Lawton was not paid and therefore took the horse, whereupon the First National Bank instituted a replevin action to recover possession of the animal by virtue of its mortgage. Thereafter the affairs of the Bank of Lawton passed into the hands and control of the bank commissioner of the state and the latter was substituted as a party defendant in the proceedings.

It was necessary to determine whether the mortgage was valid or not. It had been witnessed by two stockholders, or interested persons. The Statute of 1910 read:

"A mortgage of personal property must be signed by the mortgagor. Such signature may either be attested by acknowledgment before any person authorized to take acknowledgments of deeds, or it may be signed and validated by the signature of two persons not interested therein. Mortgages signed in the presence of two witnesses or acknowledged before an officer, as herein provided, shall be duly admitted of record."

It did not appear from the face of the instrument that the witnesses were interested in the estate or property mortgaged.

It was decided that the chattel mortgage of the Bank of Lawton was valid as between the parties and that since the mortgage was witnessed by two persons who were interested in the subject-matter, (even though such disqualification did not appear upon the face of the instrument), it was entitled to be recorded and that having been recorded, it was constructive notice to subsequent purchasers and mortgagees.

Thus the judgment was reversed with directions to restore property to the Bank of Lawton, and in case the property could not be restored, judgment was to be rendered for its value, which it was agreed, amounted to $100.

The decision was based on the common meaning of the correlative conjunctions *either . . . or*. Either one or the other could be a witness.[3]

Case 4.—In Massachusetts, in 1903, Aldrich and Allen had street railway ties for sale. The Bay State Construction Company's purchasing agent offered them a price less than they asked and also offered to pay in stock of either of two railway companies. The defendant admitted that the offer in payment in stock was an offer to allow plaintiffs the choice as to the company whose stock they should take. After a few days the plaintiffs wrote on April 20, 1903: "Mr. Allen and I have decided to let you have the electric ties you saw the other morning, at 22 c. each down to 4 in. face, loaded on the cars at So. Vernon. Will take stock in either the Greenfield and Turner Falls or Deerfield roads. Please let me hear at once if this is all right." In the reply the defendant accepted the agreement, but did not mention the stock. The ties were delivered. On July 6, the plaintiff went to the defendant's office and sold more ties at the same rate and told the purchasing agent they wanted Greenfield and Turner Falls Stock, to which he replied, "All right." The defendant sent by mail to the plaintiffs four shares of stock in the Greenfield and Deerfield Railway Company, and a check for $38.02. They, in turn, returned both and brought action.

The judge said that according to the letter and interview the company was to be selected by the plaintiffs and not by the defendant. He also said that the plaintiffs made known their selection before the payment and that the purchasing agent consented to it.

Considering the circumstances, the court decided in favor of the plaintiffs. The defendant then brought exceptions, which were overruled.

The decision was based on the circumstances that surrounded the case: a letter stating the choice and also an interview in which the choice was made known. The plaintiffs chose one of the two mentioned.[4]

The correlative conjunction, *either*, is always joined with "or." It is always used in a disjunctive sense, as is shown in the illustrative cases given here. Therefore the linguistic classification is: (*a*) Disjunctive meaning.

In case (1), "either before or after a trial" shows that a particular act must happen at one time and not at two different times. It may be before the trial; or it may be after the trial. This use of *either* is commonplace. If Mary says to Jane, "Choose either the green dress or the red," she means that Jane should choose one of the dresses.

Case (2) illustrates the same disjunctive meaning, even though *either* takes on the meaning of "equally." It is the duty of the jury to select the honest construction from the two possible constructions.

Cases (3) and (4) also show the ordinary disjunctive signification in that one of two things is to be chosen. In case (3), the mortgagor's signature could be witnessed by a person authorized to acknowledge deeds or by two uninterested persons. In case (4), the Bay State Construction Company could choose the Greenfield and Turner Falls stock or the Greenfield and Deerfield stock.

If

The word *if* is defined according to: (1) Literal interpretation; (2) Interpretation based on intent; (3) Common meaning; (4) Technical meaning.

Case 1.—In Oregon, in 1898, J. H. Baum met Thomason who had just discovered copper. Thomason said to J. H. Baum, "If you will place this before capital, I will give you a one-third interest in the two claims." He continued, "I have got one, and Cantile has got the other." To make the prospect appear to better advantage, Baum gave him twenty dollars to help in developing the work. Later he sent more money for the same purpose. He also sent a written statement to Thomason stating that if he placed the mine before capital, one-third interest in the mine was his. The statement was returned with the signature of Thomason and Cantile. Baum was sure of Thomason's signature, but not of Cantile's.

The court held that the word *if*, which was employed in Thomason's statement, always expressed a condition, and that Baum did not fulfill the condition.

The court therefore decided in favor of the defendant.

The literal meaning of *if* was considered. If the condition had been fulfilled, then Baum would have had one-third interest in the mine according to the agreement.[1]

Case 2.—The Firemen's Fund Insurance Company insured a

church in Illinois. The policy contained the clause, "If a building shall fall, except as the result of fire, all insurance by this company shall immediately cease and determine." Not long before the church had been burned to the ground, the edifice had been greatly damaged by a storm and had become unfit for occupancy. All the movable furniture had been taken out before the fire.

In 1875, the question arose whether the insurance company should pay the insurance or not.

The court said that the clause should be understood in the ordinary meaning, and hence, so long as the building remained standing, no matter how much it might have been depreciated by the action of winds or other causes, the liability of the insurer continued.

Judgment was therefore rendered in favor of the congregation.

The court considered the intent of the policy. The word *if* took on the meaning of "when." Thus the clause should have read, "when a building shall fall," etc.[3]

Case 3.—On April 6, 1893, Alonzo Barney and Sarah Cunyes were married at Northampton, Massachusetts. In November, Barney discovered that she was the lawful wife of another man, who was still living. They at that time lived in Vermont. Barney wanted the marriage to be treated as void without a decree, according to the Statute of Vermont which read: "Marriages prohibited by law on account of consanguinity or affinity between the parties, or on account of either of them having a former wife or husband living, shall, if solemnized within the state, be void without a decree of divorce or other legal process."

The only question was whether the court of Vermont had jurisdiction in the matter, the marriage having been solemnized in another state.

The judge said that the words "if solemnized within the state" did not relate to the causes, but that they fixed the condition, upon which the marrige might be treated as void. He also said that it could not be assumed that the Legislature intended to restrict its jurisdiction to marriages solemnized in the state, without words clearly indicating it.

The marriage was declared null and void.

The decision was based on the common meaning of *if*, as introducing a condition.[3]

Case 4.—Civil Code, Section 1336, provided that words in a will referring to death or survivorship related to the time of the testator's death, unless possession was actually postponed. In California, a will of Emilie Alexander, dated June 5, 1904, provided that if Gussie Alexander, one of her children, remained unmarried she should have all that belonged to her and if she married, the house that the testatrix had bought and conveyed to Gussie prior to the making of the will should belong to her and that "the rest" should be divided among the three sons and other daughter who were married. The estate having been duly administered, a decree was made, distributing the entire estate to Gussie Alexander absolutely. From this decree the other children appealed.

The judge said that the gift was not a gift to Gussie "while she remained unmarried," or "so long as she remained unmarried," or "until she married," but it was hers "if she remained unmarried." He said that *if* in legal phraseology, as in ordinary speech, imported a condition and that the time would apply to the death of the testatrix and not to the rest of Gussie's life, for the mother wanted to protect the daughter unprovided for.

The court held that the estate was a gift to the daughter in fee in the event of her being unmarried at the time of the testatrix's death, and not an estate limited in its creation to the period during which she might remain unmarried, with a remainder to the other children to take effect on her death, or, if she should marry, on her marriage.

The decision was based on the technical meaning of *if* as used in the laws concerning deaths and wills.[4]

The conjuncton *if*, being a word of supposition and condition, gives a great deal of trouble. The illustrative cases given here fall under the two linguistic classifications: (*a*) *If* denoting doubt; (*b*) *If* with a definite meaning. Cases (1), (3), and (4) belong to classification (*a*); case (2) belongs to classification (*b*).

(*a*) In cases (1), (3), and (4), we have *if* employed in its usual way, introducing a condition, which denotes doubt. In case (1), "if you will place this before capital" is a condition. There is no certainty about the mine's being placed before capital. In everyday English, if Mr. Brown says, "If Mary writes, I shall not go," he is not certain that Mary will write. There is doubt in his mind. The same uncertainty is found in "if solemnized within the state" in case (3) and in "if she remains unmarried" in case (4).

(*b*) In case (2), we find *if* taking on the meaning of "when," which gives to it a definite meaning. The insurance was to cease when the building fell. The time of the falling of the building was a definite limit. Occasionally, in common parlance, *if* has this signification. When the superintendent of a school says to one of his teachers, "If the fire bell rings, march down the back stairway with the students," his meaning is "when the fire bell rings."

Likewise

The word *likewise* is defined according to: (1) Interpretation based on intent; (2) Common meaning; (3) Context.

Case 1.—In Tennessee, John King bequeathed to his wife his horses and cattle, with the household furniture, to be wholly and solely at her disposal and added, "and likewise Sam, Nan and Cuff to be at her disposal for the use and purpose of working and raising the children or so long as she continues a widow, or until the children come of age, then Nan to be hers, during her natural life; then they to be equally divided among my children."

Mrs. King married Abel Morgan, who died leaving her a widow. Nan had a number of children, one of whom was Amy, the subject of the suit. Mrs. Morgan kept Amy until 1832, Amy being then mother of two children, Philip and Betsy. At that time Mrs. Morgan sold her and her two children to Mr. Sharp for $600. He in turn sold the slaves outside the state so that no one could find them. He also asked before he bought them concerning the will of King and was informed that Mrs. Morgan had only a life estate in them.

Mrs. Morgan died in 1840 and action was brought against Sharp for the slaves. The judge said that by *likewise* the testator had not meant that the disposition to be made of the negroes was to be exactly like that of the horses and cattle, but that having devised the stock and furniture to his wife, he had also devised the negroes to her to be employed in accordance with the terms of the will.

The court decided that he should either deliver the slaves or make just compensation for them.

The decision was based on the interpretation of the intent of the testator in using *likewise* in his will. The word here takes on the meaning of "in addition."[1]

Case 2.—In Kentucky, in 1916, Mary Doyle brought action against the Maryland Casualty Company to determine the construction of an accident insurance policy issued to Dr. Howard Doyle by the company, wherein Mary Doyle was named as beneficiary.

The latter part of Section 6 of the policy read as follows: "Likewise this policy covers the assured in event of death or disability from septicaemia or blood poisoning due directly to a bodily injury sustained while this policy is in force."

Mary Doyle contended that Section 6 should be construed separate and apart from Section 1. The Maryland Causalty Company contended, however, that Section 6 was meant to be read and to be construed as though written thus: "Likewise subject to its term, limits and conditions this policy covers the assured in event of death or disability from septicaemia * * * *"

The whole of Section 6 read:

"6. Subject to its terms, limits and conditions this policy covers the assured in the event of death or disability due to freezing, hydrophobia, gas or poison (suicide, sane or insane, or any attempt thereat, not included); likewise in event of death or disability from septicaemia, or blood poisoning due directly to a bodily injury sustained while this policy is in force."

The court called attention to the fact that Section 6 was in one entire sentence and that the latter portion referring to blood poisoning began with the word *likewise*, separated from the preceding part of the sentence by a semi-colon, thereby showing that *likewise* must be a conjunction. The court added that to give the word meaning as a conjunction made the policy cover death or disability from blood poisoning resulting from a bodily injury in the same manner that it covered death or disability due to freezing, etc., which was "subject to its terms, limits, and conditions." The judge said that the clause was manifestly a statement of an agreed construction rather than a separate and additional promise as contended by Mary Doyle.

Judgment was therefore rendered in favor of the Maryland Casualty Company.

The decision was based on the common meaning and use of *likewise:* "in the same manner."[3]

Case 3.—An action was brought in Indiana, in 1861, by Esther Ewing against the State Bank of Indiana "to recover certain dividends on bank stock," to which, it was alleged, she was entitled under the will of her husband, W. G. Ewing, who had died in 1854.

The will provided that the testator's funeral expenses should be paid, and *likewise* all his just debts, and that certain land was to be set apart as dower for his wife, and *likewise* half of his share of any dividends he might be entitled to on bank stock and that certain persons "in likewise manner" were to have certain tracts of land. The will then reserved certain property from general distribution, part of which was bequeathed to a son, *likewise* certain land, and *likewise* a farm, etc.

In determining the meaning of *likewise* the whole will was considered, for the word was used in several cases.

There is a rule in common law that a widow cannot take a provision made by the will, expressly in lieu of dower, and at the same time take her dower. She must elect to take one or the other. The court, however, said that according to the will it was apparent that the testator intended to give his wife the provision in addition to the dower. Since the testator used "in likewise manner" to convey a different meaning from the one that the word "also" would convey, the court held that words occurring more than once in a will must be presumed to be used always in the same sense, unless a contrary intention appear by the context, or unless the words be applied to different subjects; and that as the word *likewise* was often used in the will in the sense of "also," that would have to be taken to be its meaning in the clause introducing the bequest of the dividends to the widow.

Judgment was therefore rendered in favor of Esther Ewing.

The decision was based on the context. Since *likewise* was used in the will several times in the sense of "also," it was decided that it had the same meaning in the case under dispute.[3]

The illustrative cases which turn on the word *likewise* fall under the two linguistic classifications: (*a*) *Likewise* denoting addition; (*b*) *Likewise* denoting manner. Cases (1) and (3) belong to classification (*a*); case (2) belongs to classification (*b*).

(*a*) In case (1), *likewise* means "in addition." In addition to what had already been given, the testator devises Sam, etc., to his widow during her natural life. In case (3), we find the same meaning given to *likewise*. Certain dividends were to be given to the widow in addition to the dower. This meaning of *likewise* is a common one. If Mr. Brown says, "I gave Mary my horse; likewise, I gave her my saddle," he means that he gave Mary the saddle in addition to the horse.

(*b*) The word *likewise* does not always mean "in addition," but at times takes on the signification, "in like manner," as is illustrated in case (2). The policy covered death or disability from blood poisoning resulting from a bodily injury in the same manner that it covered death or disability due to freezing, etc. This use of *likewise*, though not common in daily parlance, is found often in formal writings. A college catalogue, for example, may state: "These regulations apply to students majoring in English; likewise, to students majoring in history." Here the *likewise* indicates that the students majoring in history must conform to the regulations "in the same manner" as those majoring in English.

Moreover

The word *moreover* is defined according to: (1) Interpretation based on intent; (2) Common meaning; (3) Dictionary meaning.

Case 1. Mrs. Dermott leased a hotel to Dexter for three years from October 1, 1855, the lease to be extended to five years at the option of the tenant. The rent was $3,000 a year, payable in monthly sums of $250. It was expressly stipulated between the parties and made a condition that, if the tenant should assign or underlet the premises without the written consent of the landlord, or should remove or attempt to remove any of his goods or chattels from the premises without a like consent, then, at the option and election of the landlord, the term should cease, and, moreover, in either of said cases one whole year's rent, over and above all such rents as had already accrued, should accrue and immediately become due and owing.

Dexter took possession and afterwards executed two deeds of trust of the goods and chattels in the hotel to the defendant, Wallach, to secure certain promissory notes. One of the notes not being paid at maturity, Wallach advertised the goods and chattels for sale, and was proceeding with the sale when Mrs. Dermott levied a distress upon them for $3,000. This action was taken on May 18, 1857, a year and five months before the lease expired. The ordinary rent had all been punctually paid. She said that an attempt was being made to remove the goods from the premises and that therefore one year's rent accrued.

The question was whether the $3,000 was rent, or was a penalty, that is to say, whether the clause meant that in the event of a removal, or attempted removal, Mrs. Dermott might get a year's rent in advance, or whether it meant that she should have a sum of money equivalent to a year's rent "over and above" all rents, by way of penalty.

The court said that the use of *moreover* did not necessarily indicate that Dexter must pay a year's rent in advance, in addition to the rent he had previously paid, but that the year's rent in advance was an alternative remedy.

The court held—in a case where a removal and consequent levy had been made while the lease had yet more than a year to run—that, although the clause in the lease was obscure, the $3,000 was rent intended to be secured in advance and in a gross sum instead of in the monthly shape, and was not a penalty above and independent of the other and usual rents.

The decision was based on the interpretation of the intent of the agreement between the parties.[1]

Case 2.—In California, in 1917, Lyell Aldersley brought action against Julia McLeod and others to obtain land in their hands. The appeal arose over an objection to an order settling the first and final account of Ellen Williams, the administratix of the estate of James Aldersley, deceased. It involved the question of the scope and effect of certain deeds of trust which were proved to have a power of sale. In addition to the trustee's sale James Aldersley gave his personal or individual deed to Julia McLeod. The order objected to was:

"But even if the provision be merely regarded as a power of sale, the validity of the sale cannot be questioned. Moreover, as has been stated, James, for a valuable consideration, personally gave his deed to Julia McLeod," etc.

The judge said that the word *moreover* meant "beyond this," or "besides this"; so that the meaning of the opinion was that the sale by the trustees was not only valid and conveyed full title to Julia McLeod, but that all possible doubt of James' interest in the three tracts that had been conveyed to her was wholly removed by the personal deed of James himself, which for a valuable consideration conveyed to her whatever interest he possessed in the property described in the trust deeds.

The judgment for the defendants in the first trial was therefore affirmed.

The decision was based on the common meaning of *moreover*: "besides."[2]

Case 3.—In Ohio, in 1913, Vincenzo Basile, an Italian subject, died intestate. He left no heirs in the United States, but did leave a widow and two minor children, all at that time residents of Italy and subjects of that nation. The estate consisted solely of an unliquidated claim for damages for his wrongful death. Dr. Nicola Cerri, an Italian subject, was the consular officer for Italy in Ohio. The Probate Court appointed Giovanni Pagano administrator of the estate. Shortly thereafter, Dr. Cerri filed a motion seeking the removal of this administrator on the ground that the appointment had been made in contravention of the general law of nations.

The case in 1919 related wholly to the administration of the estates of aliens dying intestate in Ohio. Dr. Cerri asserted that, by virtue of his office as consular agent for Italy, he was invested with the sole, exclusive, and permanent right to be appointed as administrator of the estates of all subjects of Italy dying intestate in Northern Ohio. The General Code of Ohio, however, gave preference, first, to the husband or widow; second, to the next of kin; third, to creditors; and, fourth, to such persons as the court deemed fit, in the discretion of the Probate Court having jurisdiction.

Cerri based his arguments upon Article 17 of the treaty between Italy and the United States and Article 14 of the treaty between Sweden and the United States. Article 17, known as the most favored nation clause, appeared in all modern treaties between the United States and the other great powers, and was as follows:

"Article 17. The respective consuls-general, consuls, vice consuls and consular agents, as likewise the consular chancellors, secretaries, clerks or attachés, shall enjoy in both countries all the rights, prerogatives, immunities, and privileges which are or may hereafter be granted to the officers of the same grade, of the most favored nation."

Article 14 of the Swedish treaty provided:

"In the event of any citizen of either of the two contracting parties dying without will or testament, in the territory of the other contracting party, the consul-general, consul, vice consul-general, or vice consul of the nation to which the deceased may belong, or, in his absence, the representative of such consul-general, consul, vice consul-general, or vice consul, shall, so far as the laws of each country will permit and pending the appointment of an administrator and until letters of administration have been granted, take charge of the property left by the deceased for the benefit of his lawful heirs and creditors, and, moreover, have the right to be appointed as administrator of such estate."

The provisions of Article 14 of the Swedish treaty were not incorporated in the Italian treaty of 1878, but Cerri vigorously claimed that by the terms of Article 17 of the Italian treaty the consuls of that country were entitled to the same rights, privileges, and prerogatives granted the Swedish consuls, just as fully as if Article 14 had been inserted in the Italian treaty.

The judge said that the claim of Dr. Cerri that these superior and paramount rights had been accorded foreign consuls rested wholly on the last clause of Article 14 of the Swedish treaty, reading, "and, moreover, have the right to be appointed as administrator of such estate." He also said that the clause should be modified by the qualifying phrase, "so far as the laws of each country will permit"; that "counsul-general, consul, vice consul-general or vice consul" was the compound subject of the sentence and directly the subject of both "shall take" and "shall have" and that thus it was intended these officers "shall take charge of the decedent's effects" and "shall have the right to administer."

Cerri insisted that the word *moreover* indicated an independent grant of power, entirely dissociated from all that had gone before. The judge said that *moreover* was defined as meaning "in addition thereto," "also," "furthermore," "likewise," and that with the reasonable construction the treaty should read, "and, likewise, have the right to be appointed as administrator of such estate." He also added that that construction was in harmony with the high officials' established and well-settled policy of more than a century.

The court held that the provisions of Article 17 and the treaty between the United States and Italy were to be construed as investing the consuls of Italy with the same rights, privileges, and prerogatives as those of Sweden, and that they were made eligible thereby to act as administrators when no competent person having rights under subdivisions 1, 2, and 3 of Section 1067, General Code, applied, but that these provisions were not to be construed as conferring prior and paramount rights to such consuls as to permanent administration upon the estates of their fellow countrymen dying intestate in Ohio, thereby superseding and supplanting the provisions of Section 1067, General Code of Ohio.

The decision was based on an appeal to the dictionary, the definition of *moreover*, being "likewise," "in addition to."[3]

The illustrative cases given here turning upon *moreover* fall under the linguistic classification (*a*) *Moreover* denoting addition: (*b*) *Moreover* with the disjunctive meaning. Cases (2) and (3) belong to classification (*a*); case (1) belongs to classification (*b*).

(*a*) In case (2), *moreover* has the meaning of "in addition to" or "besides," a very commonplace meaning. If Mr. Brown says that he gave Mr. Smith twenty dollars and adds, "Moreover, I sent him a letter concerning the matter," he means that in addition to giving Mr. Smith twenty dollars he wrote a letter. The same meaning is found in case (3) in the statement "and, moreover, have the right to be appointed as administrator of such estate."

(*b*) In case (1), we do not find *moreover* with its usual signification. Instead, it introduces an alternative condition. It therefore has a disjunctive meaning in that one thing is not done and therefore another must be done. This signification is seldom employed. If Mr. Brown says to his son, "If you do not stop gambling, I shall stop giving you money, and moreover, I shall disinherit you," he introduces an alternative condition. The son has to choose.

Nevertheless

The word *nevertheless* is defined according to: (1) Interpretation based on intent.

Case 1.—In Kentucky, in 1902, Edwin Rowe, the commonwealth's attorney for the Sixth Judicial Circuit, was indicted for malfeasance in office. The court sustained a demurrer because under the constitution a commonwealth's attorney could not be indicted for malfeasance in office until impeachment and conviction thereon. Section 68 of the constitution was as follows: "The governor and all civil officers shall be liable to impeachment for any misdemeanors in office; but judgment in such cases shall not extend further than removal from office and disqualification to hold any office of honor, trust or profit under this commonwealth; but the party convicted shall nevertheless be subject and liable to indictment, trial and punishment by law."

When the commonwealth appealed, the attorney said that by the terms of the constitution the only person who was subject and liable to indictment, trial, and punishment by law was the party convicted.

The judge said that if that were true, the higher officers of the state could only be punished for malfeasance in office after impeachment, a condition which did not hold true in the case of other offenders against the criminal law. He cited Section 3749, Kentucky Statute, which said that any officer of the State who was in a state of intoxication while in the discharge of his official duties, or was disqualified to discharge them by the use of spirituous, vinous, or malt liquors, should be fined not less than $100 nor more than $1,000, and also cited Section 1360, which provided that if a commonwealth's attorney received or agreed to receive any money or other things from any person prosecuted, or supposed to be guilty of violating any of the penal laws, in consideration that he was not to prosecute such offender, or was to dismiss an indictment, he should be fined not less than the amount imposed upon the offense compounded, or imprisoned ninety days, or both. The judge referred likewise to Section 1366 in which provision was made for the punishment of legislative and executive officers guilty of bribery, and to Section 1371, which stated that any judge of a court should be fined not less than $100 nor more than $1,000 if he refused to give place to a special judge, or if he used or borrowed any money under the control of the court of which he was judge or of any officer of the court. The judge also pointed out that Section 68 was taken verbatim from the constitution of the state, adopted in 1792, showing that it was clear that the provision was not to protect state officers from criminal punishment until impeachment and removal from office. He also showed that the constitution provided that one could not be twice put in jeopardy for the same offense. He concluded by saying that after Section 68 provided for impeachment of officers, to prevent the impeachment proceedings from protecting the offender from criminal punishment, the concluding words were added: "But the party convicted shall nevertheless be subject and liable to indictment, trial and punishment by law." Here *nevertheless* was regarded as equivalent to "notwithstanding," a meaning which made the clause read: "Nothwithstanding the impeachment proceedings, the party convicted should be liable to indictment and punishment by law."

Judgment was therefore reversed.

The decision was based on the interpretation of the intent of the law.[1]

The word *nevertheless* denotes a certain amount of determination Certain things are done in spite of prevailing conditions. The illustrative case falls under the linguistic classification: (a) *Nevertheless* denoting certitude. In the case cited here, it is made clear that if a person occupying a high office violates the law, notwithstanding the impeachment proceedings, he is liable to indictment and punishment by law. The indictment and punishment should take place regardless of the impeachment. In daily speech if Mary says, "He will go; nevertheless, I shall go, too," there is certainty and determination in what she says. In spite of the fact that he is going, Mary is going too.

Nor

The word *nor* is defined according to: (1) Interpretation based on intent.

Case 1.—In New Jersey, in 1906, Charles Reed, executor and trustee under the will of William Conover, deceased, sought the direction of the court in the performance of his duties. One of the points in question, was: What were his powers in respect to a sale of the farm?

By the will, the testator empowered the trustee, if a mortgage which encumbered the farm was called in, to mortgage the farm to an amount not exceeding the encumbrance. He also empowered him to sell all his real estate, but with a proviso that no sale of the farm should be made during the lifetime of either of the two daughters [to whom everything was left] without their consent, *nor* unless it was necessary to pay debts.

The question was whether he had power to sell the farm even with the consent of the testator's daughters, unless the sale was also necessary to pay the testator's debts.

The judge said that it was apparent that the testator thought he would barely have enough property to pay his debts other than the mortgage and that it was his purpose to provide for a sale if necessary to pay debts other than the mortgage debt. He also said that after reading the whole will, it seemed clear that the testator used the conjunction *nor* in the fourteenth clause in the sense of "or."

The court held that a comparison of the provisions of the will sufficiently indicated that the testator used the word *nor* in the proviso to the grant of power to sell, in the sense of "or."

The decision was based on the interpretation of the intent.[1]

The word *nor* is a negative connective or particle, introducing the second member or clause of a negative proposition to continue the force of "not," "no," or the like in the first member or clause. It is also used as a correlative following "neither." In the illustrative case given here *nor* is misused. It is used instead of "or, which was intended. Therefore it is used in the disjunctive sense. The testator meant to say that no sale of the farm should be made during the lifetime of either of the two daughters without their consent, or unless it was necessary to pay debts. The word "no" is negative; so are *nor* and "unless"; therefore "or" should have been used, for two negatives make a positive. If Mr. Brown says, "Nobody is not going," he really implies that "Somebody is going."

Or

The word *or* is defined according to: (1) Literal interpretation; (2) Interpretation based on intent; (3) Common meaning; (4) Interpretation suggested by technical terms; (5) Dictionary meaning; (6) Context.

Case 1.—A bond given by Dumont at the port of New York, when certain goods were imported, was conditioned that the importer should pay $425—that being the estimated duty based on the invoice—or the amount which should be subsequently ascertained to be due, *or* that he should within three years withdraw and export them, *or* transport them to a Pacific port. About a month after importation the goods were withdrawn by the importer, upon payment of the sum named in the bond; but the duties were not regularly liquidated until about a month later. The liquidation showed that the duties payable were $676.75 instead of the $425 which had been paid. Suit was brought to recover the balance. Dumont pleaded payment of the sum named in the bond, as a fulfillment of one of the alternate conditions. The counsel for the government contended that the condition ought to be construed not alternatively, but as intended to secure the payment at all events of the true amount of duties, unless the goods should be exported or sent to the Pacific coast within three years.

The judge said that the word *or* was frequently construed to mean "and," in order to carry out the evident intent of the parties; but that if *or* were made to read "and" the condition would require the importer to pay the actual duties in addition to $425. He also said that there were, besides, two other alternate conditions dependent upon the same word. These conditions, he added, showed that *or* was intended to be taken in its ordinary sense, and not to mean what the counsel for the government said it meant. The government's interpretation would require, in place of the word *or*, the addition of several words, so as to make it read, "$425, and any additional amount of duties to be ascertained to be due and owing on the goods."

The court held that Dumont was not liable.

The decision was based on the literal interpretation of *or* in the condition—a coördinating particle that marks an alternative.[1]

Case 2.—In Mississippi, in 1902, R. V. Booth, an attorney, was employed by the board of supervisors of Warren County to defend four civil suits. At that time, the board had appointed an attorney as general advisory counsel, to attend all its meetings at a salary of $300 per annum, under the Code of 1892, which provided that the board of supervisors should have power, in its discretion, to employ counsel by the year, at an unusual salary not to exceed $300, or to employ counsel in all civil cases in which the county was interested.

After Booth had rendered his services, he presented his claim for the fees. The claim was rejected by the board on the advice of their attorney, and Booth brought suit. The board contended that, according to the Code of 1892, they did not have power to pay him.

The judge said that if the statute were interpreted literally and that if *or* meant *or*, then if a board employed general advisory counsel, it never could during that year employ counsel in any civil or criminal case, no matter how vast the interest involved, and no matter how great the damage entailed upon the county by such inability to employ counsel in a civil or criminal case. He thought it was absurd to think that the Legislature intended such an interpretation of the statute.

The court held that *or* meant "and" and that the employment of an attorney to defend civil suits was authorized, though there might be at the time an attorney employed by the year.

Thus Booth recovered his fees.

The decision was based on the interpretation of the intent of the Code of 1892.[2]

Case 3.—In Illinois, there was a statute which authorized cities and villages to make "local improvements by special assessment, or by special taxation, or both, of contiguous property, or by general taxation, or otherwise," as they should by ordinance prescribe. Section 2 of the statute required the ordinance providing for such an improvement to prescribe whether it should be made "by special assessment, or by special taxation of contiguous property, or general taxation, or both."

In 1892, the question arose as to whether Freeport could combine in making a single improvement, special taxation and special assessment. As the assessment was confirmed over the objections of Darius Kuehner and others, the latter appealed.

The judge said that the provision giving cities, towns, and villages the power to make local improvements by special assessment or special taxation—being an exception to the general rule and policy of the state and dominant principle of the constitution in respect of taxation—ought not to be extended beyond the clear import of the language employed and that the word *or* should be used in its ordinary and disjunctive sense, and correspond to "either"; meaning "one or the other of two, but not both." Thus he thought that corporate authorities of towns, cities, and villages might be clothed with power to make local improvements in both ways, either by special assessment of benefits or by special taxation of contiguous property, thereby preserving the principle of equality in bearing the public burden, in respect of all persons and property affected by the exercise of the power. In regard to "both" he also said that "general taxation" was intended to be included by the word, for "both," according to the dictionary, was never used as inclusive of or as referring to three or more and since it could only apply to two, the Legislature did not intend the combination of special assessment and special taxation.

The court held that a city could not combine general taxation, special taxation, and special assessment in making a single improvement.

The decision was based on the common, disjunctive meaning of *or*.[3]

Case 4.—Cumming *et al.* claimed that they were the importers of certain burlaps, upon which the duty chargeable by law was 30 per cent *ad valorem.* The collector, Arthur, insisted the goods were "oil-cloth foundation," upon which the duty was 40 per cent *ad valorem*, and compelled them to pay accordingly. They paid under protest and brought suit to recover the alleged excess of 10 per cent. A verdict and a judgment were rendered in their favor. The collector thereupon sued out a writ of error.

The Law of June 6, 1872, declared that after August 1, 1872, in lieu of the duties theretofore levied upon the articles mentioned in the section, the following duties should be paid upon those articles imported from foreign countries:

"*On all burlaps* and like manufacturers of flax, jute, or hemp, . . . except such as may be suitable for bagging for cotton, thirty per centum *ad valorem.* *On all oil-cloth foundations* or *floor-cloth canvas*, made of flax, hemp, or jute . . . forty per cent *ad valorem.*"

The mercantile testimony showed that the articles in question were "burlaps," that they were a "manufacture of jute," and that they were not suitable for bagging for cotton. The court said the fact that the burlaps were suitable, and could be used and were used for oil-cloth foundations or for any other purpose except bagging for cotton was immaterial.

The counsel for the United States insisted that the question was answered by the statement in the law. The mercantile testimony stated that "floor-cloth canvas" was used exclusively for the manufacture of "floor oil-cloth" and that a merchant, in speaking of "foundations for oil-cloth," would be supposed to refer to "floor-cloth canvas," which had a harder twist and was more expensive than burlap and was never confused with burlaps.

The court said that the testimony established two things: first, that the terms "oil-cloth foundations" and "floor cloth canvas," as used in the statute, meant in commerce the same thing; and, second, that the thing so understood was not burlap, but a thing entirely distinct and different from that article.

Thus the judgment of the circuit court was affirmed in the Supreme Court.

In this case *or* took on the meaning of "that is," the interpretation being suggested by technical terms.[4]

Case 5.—A codicil in William Austin's will directed: "On the death of my said wife the share of my estate to go to our son James and our grandson Charles shall be held by my executors in trust for them during their lives; . . . and at their respective deaths the principal shall go to their issue, if any; if none, then the same shall fall into my general estate, or as my wife shall by will direct."

In the court the intention of the testator, as to the disposition of the share of the grandson Charles, in case of his death before the wife's, without issue, was to be determined.

The judge turned to the lexicographers to find the definition of *or*. In Worcester he found it to be a disjunctive particle that marked an alternative, generally corresponding to either, as "either this or that," and in Webster he found it to be a connective that marked an alternative, as "you may read or may write; that is, you may do one of the things, at your pleasure, but not both."

The court held that as to the two shares, the wife had the power, in case of the death of either before her without issue, to give the share of such deceased by will to any person whom she might select, and that she was not confined, in such appointment, to the class named in her husband's will.

The decision was based on an appeal to the dictionary.[5]

Case 6.—In Kansas, in 1903, Margaret Kennedy brought an action in ejectment for the recovery of an undivided one-half interest in a tract of land. Prior to 1881 she became the wife of John Kennedy and in that year she settled with him upon the land in question and it became their homestead. They continued to reside upon it until 1883, when, on account of a disagreement between them, she abandoned her residence and returned to her former home in the East, where she remained. She took her children with her. Her husband continued to live upon the land until 1887. In 1888, he sold it to one who did not know he had a wife living who had resided in Kansas. Kennedy described himself in the conveyance as an unmarried man. Mrs. Kennedy had no knowledge prior to the death of her husband that he had conveyed or encumbered the land. He died intestate in 1897. Then the case arose.

The General Statutes of 1901, relative to descents and distributions, gave to the wife one-half a deceased husband's real estate which had not been sold on execution or other judicial sale, and was not necessary for the payment of debts: "Provided, that the wife shall not be entitled to any interest, . . . in any land to which the husband had made a conveyance, when the wife, at the time of the conveyance, is not or never has been a resident of this state." The trouble arose over the interpretation of *or* in the clause: "When the wife, at the time of conveyance, is not or never has been a resident of this state." The contention of the plaintiff was that the word *or* should be read "and," which would mean that if the wife had ever been a resident of the state, she would be entitled to the rights given under the law.

The judge said that if the word *or* were used and given a disjunctive signification, then the words following "never has been" were pleonastic and would have no sense or meaning whatever, for, if the wife were not a resident at the time of conveyance, she would be deprived of her right of heirship, regardless of whether she had or had not been formerly a resident of the state. He said that if "and" were substituted for *or*, all the words would have meaning—the purpose of the Legislature.

The court held that the word *or* in the clause should be read "and," an interpretation of which would give to the clause under discussion the meaning that a wife who had even been a resident of the state was entitled to the benefits of the act.

The decision was based on the context. The meaning of "and" was given to *or*, to give value to all the words in the statute.[6]

Usually, but not always, *or* is employed as a coördinating particle that marks an alternative. The illustrative cases given here fall under the linguistic classifications: (*a*) The disjunctive meaning; (*b*) The conjunctive meaning: (*c*) The explanatory meaning. Cases (1), (3), and (5) belong to classification (*a*); cases (2) and (6) belong to classification (*b*); case (4) belongs to classification (*c*).

(*a*) In case (1), we find *or* in its disjunctive sense. A series of propositions is presented and the importer can select one of them. In daily speech, if Mr. Smith says, "My son may study law or medicine or banking," he is naming a series of professions out of which his son may choose one.

Case (3) presents *or* in its usual disjunctive sense. One of two things is to be chosen. This employment of the word is the most common in everyday speech. If Mrs. Brown says, "Mary, you may have a red or a green dress," she means that Mary may have her choice of one of the two dresses, but not both. The same use is shown in case (5).

(*b*) At times *or* is used in a conjunctive sense, meaning "and." In case (2), in which the board of supervisors were given power to employ counsel at an annual salary or to employ counsel in all civil cases in which the county was interested, *or* has the import of "and." The board of supervisors were given the power to do both. In common parlance, if a seamstress says, "I can make a dress or a coat," she means that she is capable of doing both. She is able to make a dress and a coat. In case (6), in the statement "when the wife, at the time of conveyance, is not or never has been a resident of this state," *or* again has the meaning of "and" in order to give value to the last part of the statement.

(*c*) Occasionally *or* is used to connect an explanatory statement as is shown in case (4), where "oil-cloth foundations" and "floor-cloth canvas" refer to one and the same thing, but are connected by *or*. In this case it takes on the meaning of "that is." This use is also common in everyday speech. If Mr. Brown, in talking to his little son, has dirt in his hand, he may say, "This is earth, or dirt," to indicate that both names identify the substance. "Dirt" is purely explanatory in its meaning; it is only another name for earth. If a teacher says, "These elements may be combined, or put together in this way," she is using *or* again in its explanatory sense of "that is," for "put together" is only another way of saying "combined."

Provided

The word *provided* is defined according to: (1) Literal interpretation; (2) Interpretation based on intent; (3) Common meaning; (4) Dictionary meaning; (5) Context.

Case 1.—On July 31, 1883, in Wisconsin, an agreement was made between George Flanders and Ione Flanders and Lewis Royce and Mary Royce in which Mr. and Mrs. Flanders, the daughter and son-in-law, agreed to support and maintain Mr. and Mrs. Royce, during their natural lives, if the latter did not collect or ask for any further interest on a certain mortgage, executed to Mary Royce. She agreed to discount the mortgage, provided the mortgagors performed the contract on their part. She also agreed in case the mortgagors should perform their contract, according to its true spirit and meaning, to declare the mortgage fully paid and satisfied.

In July, 1884, Lewis Royce died. Until that time George and Ione Flanders kept their contract. In September, 1885, Mary Royce left the house of her daughter because of ill-treatment. Then she brought suit against Mr. and Mrs. Flanders for the mortgage. The defendants said that she could have returned. She died and her executor, Stoel, continued the suit in 1887.

The judge said that *provided* meant "so long as they shall perform."

The court held that the maintenance and support of the mortgagee and her husband during their natural lives was a condition precedent to the satisfaction and discharge of the mortgage. Since Mrs. Royce did not remain with them, they were held responsible for the mortgage.

The decision was based on the literal interpretation of *provided* in the agreement: "on condition."[1]

Case 2.—In New Jersey, when George Woodruff died in 1846 he had a farm near Trenton, called "Oaklands." He devised the possession and use of the farm to his wife, Jean Woodruff, for the mutual benefit of herself and his son, Patrick Woodruff, during the wife's life, and, after her death, to his four sons, Patrick, Robert, Thomas, and Dickinson, in fee, as tenants in common. After the death of Jean Woodruff, in 1851, Robert and Thomas conveyed their respective one undivided fourth interests in the farm to Patrick. In 1856, the complainant, Dickinson, also conveyed his part to Patrick. The deed conveyed the land from Dickinson to Patrick, with this stipulation: "Provided, nevertheless, and upon the following conditions: That if the said grantor, Dickinson Woodruff shall survive the said grantee, Houstoun Woodruff, he, the said grantor, shall have the right, at any time within eighteen months after the death of said grantee, to purchase back again all the right, title, and interest in said farm "Oaklands," hereby conveyed, at a valuation to be then made by two disinterested persons, one of whom shall be selected by said grantor, and in case of disagreement the persons so selected may choose a third person." Patrick Woodruff died in 1886, leaving a daughter, Louisa, his only child.

The court held that the deed was a covenant, not a condition. Thus Dickinson Woodruff could demand a division for his one-fourth.

The decision was based on the interpretation of the intent.[2]

Case 3.—In West Virginia, A. P. Hodges obtained from F. P. Marshall, an illiterate farmer, a lease of fifty acres for oil and gas.

Subsequently Marshall leased the identical premises to J. J. and J. B. Huggins. Efforts were made later by a Mr. Daley to restrain Huggins and his associates from developing the leasehold for oil and to cancel the lease as a cloud upon the title of Hodges.

The contract, made on March 12, 1897, set forth the terms and conditions of the case, with the following proviso:

"Provided, however, that a well shall be commenced upon the above-described premises within 30, and completed within 90, days from the date thereof; and, in case of failure to commence and complete said well as aforesaid, the lessee shall pay to the lessor a forfeiture of $50."

The lease was not recorded until April 8, 1898. At the same time was recorded an assignment of a half interest in it by Hodges to Daley. The lease from Marshall to J. J. and J. B. Huggins had been executed on November 6, 1897, and recorded on January 31, 1898. Huggins had also leased the adjoining lands and had struck oil. Then Daley filed his bill for injunction on April 15, 1898.

Hodges did nothing towards boring the well. The question was whether the proviso in the Hodges lease constituted a condition precedent and whether the failure of Hodges to do anything towards the boring of the well did not prevent the vesting of any rights under that lease.

The court ordered that the leased premises be restored to Huggins *et al.* and that Daley be directed to turn over to Huggins any moneys in his hands as the result of his operations, after deducting whatever sum might have been actually and necessarily expended upon him in the development and that the bill be dismissed, with costs.

The court considered the common meaning of *provided*: "on condition."[3]

Case 4.—In South Dakota, on July 3, 1885, Mary Simons procured through the American Investment Company, a loan, for which she executed a bond for $1,000 to F. A. Huggins, and at the same time, to secure the payment of the bond, executed a trust deed to E. S. Ormsby, one of the plaintiffs, upon a quarter section of land in Aurora County. To further secure the $1,000 loan, Mrs. Simons procured from the defendant an insurance policy, issued to herself, upon the building on the premises mortgaged; the loss, if any, to be paid to the trustee or holder of the bond. The policy contained a mortgage clause setting forth the duties and rights of the contracting parties and ending with this proviso: "Provided, that in case the mortgagor or owner neglects or refuses to pay any premium due under this policy, then, on demand, the mortgagee or trustee shall pay the same: provided, also, that the mortgagee or trustee shall notify this company of any change of ownership or increase of hazard which shall come to his or her knowledge, and shall have permission for such change of ownership or increase of hazard duly indorsed on this policy; and provided, further, that every increase of hazard not permitted by the policy to the mortgagor or owner shall be paid for by the mortgagee or trustee, on reasonable demand, and after demand made by this company upon, and refused by, the mortgagor or owner to pay according to the established schedule of rates."

The judge said that the term *provided*, as used in the clause, would have to be construed as a condition, according to dictionaries; Webster defining it as: "On condition; by stipulation"; Bouvier in his Law Dictionary saying: "A proviso always implies a condition, unless subsequent words change it into a covenant"; and Anderson in his Dictionary of Law stating: "No word better expresses a condition, and it is always so taken, unless the context shows that the intent was to create a covenant."

There had been a change of ownership of the property insured prior to the loss. E. S. Ormsby, President of the American Investment Company, had knowledge of the change, but he did not notify the insurance company, according to the mortgage clause agreement.

The mortgage clause agreement was thus broken. Therefore the court decided in favor of the Phenix Insurance Company, holding them no longer responsible.

The decision was based on the dictionary meaning of *provided*: "on condition" or "by stipulation."[4]

Case 5.—In North Carolina, in 1879, Burgwyn brought action to recover a hog which had entered Whitfield's property. Whitfield refused to deliver the hog and claimed the right to hold it under the provisions of the Acts of 1876–77, which established the "no-fence law," until double damages were paid him for the injury committed by the hog upon his growing crop. The plaintiff refused to pay the damages and insisted that the act was unconstitutional and that he came within the second proviso of Section 6, which was as follows: "This act shall not apply to stock kept east of Wheeler's swamp, provided a gate is kept up at Bull Hill mill house, so as to prevent stock from passing over the bridge across the run of said swamp."

The jury found that the hog had been kept east of Wheeler's swamp, and that no gate had been kept up at the said mill house.

According to the context of the law, the court decided that *provided* meant "unless." Thus judgment was rendered in favor of the plaintiff, and the hog was delivered to him. The defendant appealed, but the judgment was affirmed.

In this case *provided* has the meaning of "unless"; the meaning being determined from the context.[5]

The word *provided* usually carries with it a condition. At times, however, it takes on a definiteness as is shown in a covenant. The illustrative cases given here fall under the linguistic classifications: (*a*) *Provided* denoting a condition; (*b*) *Provided* denoting a covenant. Cases (1), (3), (4), and (5) belong to classification (*a*); case (2) belongs to classification (b).

(*a*) In case (1), *provided* introduces the condition of the daughter and son-in-law taking care of the daughter's parents. Since they did not look after the mother as long as she lived, the mortgage had to be paid. The mortgage was to be considered paid on condition that the parents were taken care of until death.

In case (3), Hodges' lease was forfeited, for he did not carry out the condition of boring the well. The condition was introduced by *provided.*

In cases (4) and (5), we also find *provided* meaning "on condition." This use of the word is common in everyday speech. If Mr. Brown says, "I shall go, provided Mr. Jones will stay here," he means he will go, on condition that Mr. Jones will stay.

(*b*) Case (2) shows *provided* introducing a covenant. The provision gives Dickinson Woodruff the privilege of repurchasing the land he had sold to Patrick Woodruff, if Patrick dies first. This use of the word is not common and has to be determined by the words that follow the proviso.

So

The word *so* is defined according to: (1) Common meaning.

Case 1.—In Indiana, in 1870, Nancy Clem was indicted jointly with Silas Hartmen and W. J. Abrams for murder in the first degree. The jury found Nancy Clem guilty of murder in the second degree, and the court sentenced her to be imprisoned in the state prison during life. She moved for a new trial.

The fifteenth instruction to the jury had been: "If all the circumstances of a criminative character which have been proved are subject to explanation upon any reasonable hypothesis consistent with the innocence of the prisoner, she is entitled to the benefit of such explanation. So, if it should be that you should have no reasonable doubt from the evidence that Silas Hartman, either by himself or in connection with others, not including the prisoner, perpetrated the murder, and should have a reasonable doubt whether the only connection the prisoner had with the transaction was to harbor, conceal, or assist Silas Hartman, her brother, after the perpetration of the deed, with the intent that he should escape detection of punishment, she would not be guilty of any crime under the law. But if she was present at the time and place of the murder, in any way assisting, aiding, encouraging, or contributing towards the murder, she would be guilty as a principal in the crime. *So if the murder was perpetrated with her knowledge and consent or connivance, she is a principal.*"

The meaning of the last clause of the instruction was to be determined.

The court held that *so* meant "hence" and "therefore," when used to connect that which is an illustration of or conclusion from what has gone before.

The case was thus reversed and remained for a new trial.

The decision was based on the common meaning of *so*: "therefore."[1]

The illustrative case turning on *so* falls under the linguistic classification: (*a*) *So* used as a word of deduction. The word *so* takes on the meaning of "therefore," giving the reason for thinking that Nancy Clem was a principal in the crime. This use of the word is common. If a professor of mathematics states to his class, "So, if you take the data I have given you and apply the methods I suggested you will get a definite result," he means "therefore," summing up what he has said previously.

THAT

The word *that* is defined according to: (1) Interpretation based on intent.

Case 1.—In Virginia, in 1896, Ann Eliza Berry and others filed their bill in the circuit court, alleging that they, the children of Michael and Elizabeth Fackler, should have their share of the property conveyed to F. P. Fackler, one son, in fee simple, by his mother, Elizabeth Fackler. Before Michael Fackler died, he conveyed a tract of land "to J. B. Watts, trustee, to hold as the absolute property of his wife, Elizabeth Fackler, by whom he derived the premises, that she may have a permanent home for her life, and his children by her a pittance after her death." Elizabeth Fackler conveyed the land, in 1888, to her son, F. P. Fackler. Then the other children brought suit. Judgment was rendered in their favor, whereupon F. P. Fackler appealed.

The court held that since Michael Fackler conveyed the property as absolute, it had to be considered as "unrestricted," according to definition, and that the word *that* was equivalent to "in order that." In accordance with this definition the court interpreted the phrasing of the document to mean that the widow was to have a home for life. The court further held that the word *that* was never used to vest any interest or estate in the testator's children by her.

The judgment therefore was reversed.

The decision was based on the interpretation of the intent of the word *that*. The testator conveyed to his wife the land for the purpose of giving her a home. It was his intent to provide for her. Since he secured the land through her, he would naturally think it should go back to her, to be used as she wished.[1]

The illustrative case turning on the conjunction *that* has the meaning of "in order that," or "for the purpose of." This meaning of the word is common. If Mr. Smith says, "I gave John the knife that he might sharpen his pencil," he means that he gave John the knife "for the purpose of" sharpening his pencil.

Then

The word *then* is defined according to: (1) Interpretation based on intent; (2) Dictionary meaning; (3) Circumstances; (4) Context.

Case 1.—In Missouri, Isaac McHose died, in 1852, leaving a wife and five children of ages varying from seven to nineteen years. His will said: "First, after all my debts are paid and discharged, the residue of my estate, real, personal and mixed, I give and bequeath and dispose of as follows, to-wit, viz.: All my estate, real, personal and mixed, I give to my beloved wife Mary Ann, and all money that may be in possession or at interest, or in any situation whatsoever at the period of my demise, including any and all dues to me then owing, shall to the said wife, Mary Ann, be to her as my last will and testament, reserving to her the right of disposal in the manner following, to-wit, viz.: Provided, however, that if my aforesaid wife Mary Ann shall of her own will and free accord unite herself in the bonds of matrimony to another person, then the full meaning of this will, as above devised, shall be transferred to the surviving children of the testator according to law, reserving to the said Mary Ann her right of dower according to said law. And further, that if my wife, the said Mary Ann, shall remain single during the minority of our children, then she shall at their maturity give to the said children, who may then be living, their right, title and interest to, and in, for any property belonging to my estate, real, personal and mixed, reserving to herself the right of dower hereinbefore stated. And further, that the division of the said property then existing shall be made equal among my children, share and share to each alike, without distinction, preferment or feeling. And further, that in order to secure to my said wife Mary Ann the furtherance of my will and testament, and to my children their right, title and interest hereby bequeathed to them out of my property, I hereby appoint and constitute as the executors of this, my last will and testament," etc.

In 1858, the eldest child, Mrs. Margaret Rose, and her husband filed a petition for the distribution to them of one-sixth of the estate of the decedent.

The court held that according to the intent of the testator (whose will declared that if his wife remained single during the minority of his children then she should at their maturity give the children their shares), the word *then* should be understood, not as indicating the point of time when the payment was to be made, for the time was fixed—"at their maturity"—but as simply equivalent to "in that event."

The court further held that the widow did not become invested, by virtue of the will, with the power to dispose at pleasure of the property bequeathed; that those portions thereof to which the children would become ultimately entitled she held as trustee for them; that, although she might, entirely in accordance with the directions of the will and in conformity to the trust confided in her, pay over to each child, on its arriving at majority, its share of the property bequeathed, yet she could not, under all circumstances, be *compelled* so to pay over; that such payment, if it could be enforced at all, must be enforced through the intervention of a court of general equity jurisdiction.

The decision was based on the interpretation of the intent of the will.[1]

Case 2.—In New York, in 1857, a case arose concerning the construction of the will of Elizabeth Ash, who devised certain real and leasehold property to the two children of her nephew Thomas Ash: namely, Mary E. and Thomas F. Ash, their heirs and assigns; "to have and to hold the same unto the said Mary E. and Thomas F. their heirs and assigns forever, to be equally divided between them, share and share alike, and in case of the death of either of them, then to the survivor of them and his or her heirs and assigns. And *in case* of the death of both of them before they should arrive at lawful age, to her nephew, the said Thomas Ash, his heirs and assigns forever." The devisees survived the testatrix, both attaining the age of twenty-one. Mary E. Ash died on December 14, 1843, and Thomas F. Ash on February 12, 1847.

Eliza Ash, the plaintiff, claimed one-half of the premises, under a title derived from Mary E. Ash, and the defendant, Frederick Coleman, claimed the entirety under a title derived from Thomas F. Ash after he became the survivor of the two devisees.

The main question turned on the clause "then she gives the property to the survivor." The court held that the word *then* evidently referred to the event itself and not to the time of its occurrence, for it was almost certain that one would die before the other in which event one would receive only a life estate. He found in Worcester's Dictionary that one of the interpretations of ***then*** was "in that case."

The court further held that the intention of the testatrix was that the secondary devise should take effect, if at all, upon the termination of life at some referable, determinate period; namely, before her own decease, or under lawful age, and not indefinitely. It further held that both devisees having survived the testatrix and having attained the age of twenty-one, each was entitled to an equal moiety of the estate devised, and that upon the death of the shortest liver the whole estate would not go to the survivor. The plaintiff therefore was entitled to the equal undivided half of the premises in dispute.

The decision was based on the dictionary definition of ***then***, meaning "in that case."[2]

Case 3.—In Pennsylvania, in 1889, John Fitzpatrick died, leaving his sister, Catharine Eckert, and a nephew and two nieces, the children of a sister who died before him. His will created a trust for the benefit of his sister for life, and provided that the principal at her death should be given "to her children in equal shares." In the event that no children survived her, he said, "then I give and bequeath the same to my legal heirs." On the death of the sister, who left no children, the question arose as to who were his legal heirs.

The court held that the word ***then*** indicated the event and did not point to the time—that is, it referred to the event upon the occurrence of which the legal heirs took the inheritance, and not to the time when they had a right to claim the inheritance, as was the general rule.

The court further held that the heirs living at the time of the testator's death were entitled to the principal of the fund at the death of his sister.

The decision was based on circumstances. The testator said that if his sister had no children the money was to go to his legal heirs at her death. As there were no children at her death, the living legal heirs received what she had. Thus ***then*** took on the meaning of "in that case."[3]

Case 4.—In New York, in 1899, Connelly, grandson of James

Higgins, who had died seised of certain property in 1855, brought action for a partition of it. Higgins had left a will in which he said: "I give all my estate, real and personal, after the payment of my debts, to my wife, Rose, during her life, and then to such of my children as may then be alive, share and share alike." The wife, died in 1879, and of the six children, Margaret married James Connelly in 1873, and died in 1874, intestate, leaving the plaintiff her only son and heir. The defendant, O'Brien, acquired the premises under the devisees named in the will, who survived their mother, Rose Higgins.

The court held that the words "and then" preceding the gift of the remainder, simply served to indicate the order of the two gifts, as "First, I give . . . to my wife, Rose, during her life, and then (that is, second) I give the remainder," etc. It further held that if the second *then* had been omitted the plaintiff would have been correct, but the will read, "To such of my children as shall then be alive."

Judgment was rendered in favor of the defendant.

Thus *then* was used to denote sequence, its meaning having been derived from the context of the will, especially by the use of the second *then*.[4]

On hearing the word *then*, one immediately thinks of time. As a conjunction it usually takes on a different signification—one of consequence or reason. The illustrative cases given here fall under the following linguistic classifications: (*a*) *Then* denoting consequence; (*b*) *Then* denoting sequence. Cases (1), (2), and (3) belong to classification (*a*); case (4) belongs to classification (*b*).

(*a*) In case (1), *then* means "in the event." The mother "in the event" that she remained single was to give to the children at their maturity their shares. In case (2), the provision was that in case of the death of one of the two children, the other child was to receive the whole estate. Here *then* also means "in that case." The same meaning is found in case (3). This signification given to *then* is common. If Mr. Brown says, "If the letter does not come, then report to Mr. Porter," he means "in case" the letter does not come, report to Mr. Porter.

(*b*) Case (4) shows *then* signifying the order of succession, or sequence. The testator tells what he wants done with his property in the first place and also in the second place. After his wife dies, he bequeaths it to others. This use of *then* is also common. If a professor says, "First I assign the next lesson, and then I begin discussing the problems," he is giving the order in which he conducts a recitation—the sequence.

Till

The word *till* is defined according to: (1) Interpretation based on intent; (2) Common meaning.

Case 1.—In Missouri, Richard Barrett executed the following promissory note, to-wit:

"1,833 33/100. Montgomery Co., Mo., Sept. 1855. On or before the first day of September, 1858, I promise to pay Robert Pitzer $1833.33, with interest thereon till paid, for value received. Richard Barrett."

The legal interest was 10 per cent. The question in the case was whether the note bore interest from the date of execution or from maturity.

The court held that it bore interest from the date of execution.

The decision was based on the interpretation of the intent of the parties. They intended that interest should be paid from the date of execution of the note *till* its maturity.[1]

Case 2.—In South Carolina, in 1913, G. D. Matheson brought action against the Marion County Lumber Company. On December 12, 1898, A. J. Matheson had conveyed to the Cape Fear Lumber Company the timber on certain lands. The deed of conveyance contained the following provision: "The Cape Fear Lumber Company shall have ten years from the 30th of September, A.D., 1898, to cut and remove said timber, and if at the end of that they have not removed said timber, then by payment of 6 per cent per annum upon the said purchase price, within the next ten years or till said timber has been removed, they can have any and may take ten years longer to remove said timber."

On August 24, 1922, G. D. Matheson, successor in title of A. J. Matheson, had brought action against the Marion County

Lumber Company, successor in title of the Cape Fear Lumber Company for the removal of a cloud upon the title, alleging: "that neither the Cape Fear Lumber Company nor its successors and assigns nor the defendant exercised the rights under said deed to cut and remove said timber, or any of the other rights granted therein, upon the tracts owned by the plaintiff, or upon the other tracts mentioned in said deed during the time limited." The company had failed to pay the interest after the expiration of the first ten years. The question the court was called upon to decide was when the interest money should have been paid according to the deed. G. D. Matheson claimed that it should have been paid yearly; the Marion County Lumber Company claimed that it had ten years after the expiration of the original term in which to pay the interest; that it could pay interest a the rate of 6 per cent per annum at any time within ten years from the date of the expiration of its original term.

The court, however, held that *till* carried with it the idea of continued action, so that, if the removal was within the ten years, there must have been continuous payments of interest or the right to revive was gone, and that the only way to keep the second term alive was by the payment of 6 per cent per annum, according to the contract.

Judgment was therefore rendered in favor of the plaintiff.

The decision was based on the common, ordinary meaning of *till*.[2]

The two illustrative cases turning on *till* fall under the linguistic classification: (*a*) Limited meaning of *till*.

In case (1), *till* has definite limits. The interest began at the making of the note and continued from that date up to the time of maturity. This use of *till* is common in connection with notes. If Mr. Brown says, "I will pay 6 per cent interest on the note till paid," every one understands that the note begins bearing interest when made and continues to bear interest to the time of maturity.

Case (2) also shows *till* with a limited meaning. Interest of 6 per cent per annum was to be paid up to the time that the timber was removed. The limit was the time of removal. This employment of the word is frequent. If Mr. Brown says, "John, continue writing till you have finished," Mr. Brown has set a limit, the time of finishing. (See *until*.)

Unless

The word *unless* is defined according to: (1) Interpretation based on intent; (2) Common meaning; (3) Specialized meaning; (4) Dictionary meaning.

Case 1.—In Alabama, in 1912, Georgia Finch, as administratrix of Aletha Allen, intestate, sued the Central of Georgia Railway Company for causing her death. At the trial the jury rendered a verdict for the defendant, finding that Aletha Allen, a deaf woman, more than eighty years old, had been guilty of contributory negligence of the most unequivocal sort in going upon the track at train time after having been warned. A new trial was granted because of faulty instructions given the jury. The railway company appealed from the order granting a new trial.

The charge to the jury had been that unless the jurors believed from the evidence that the engineer did not discover the peril of the woman in time to avoid the injury, they must decide in favor of the defendant.

The higher court held that *unless* meant "if not," the use of the double negative having the effect of making the charge predicate the defendant's right to an acquaintance upon the fact that its engineer did see the dangerous position of Aletha Allen in time to prevent the injury.

The jury overlooked the grammatical inaccuracy, as the court did, and interpreted the charge as a correct proposition of the law.

Thus the court ordered that the original verdict be adhered to.

The decision was based on the interpretation of the intent. The court did not intend to use a double negative; the jury, not realizing that a double negative was used, gave their verdict accordingly. Thus the intent of the charge was considered.[1]

Case 2.—In Massachusetts, in 1871, a petition for the partition of the real estate of William Ramsdill, deceased, was brought into court by his children. Ramsdill devised all his property to his wife, without naming his children or intimating that his omission to provide for them was intentional. The General Statutes provided that "when a testator omits to provide for any of his children, or for the issue of a deceased child, they shall take the same share of his estate, both real and personal, that they should have been entitled to if he had died intestate, unless they shall have been provided for by the testator in his lifetime, or unless it appears that such omission was intentional, and not occasioned by accident or mistake." The respondents, Mary Wentworth and others, asked the court to rule that the petitioners should be compelled to produce the will and show that the omission to provide for the children was occasioned by accident or mistake, and was not intentional. The court declined to make the ruling and they excepted.

The court held that the refusal was correct; for the language of the statute, "unless it appears," implied that the burden of proof was upon those who would make the intention appear, and that unless there was evidence of its existence, it would not appear.

The exceptions were overruled.

The decision was based on the common meaning of *unless*: "if not."[2]

Case 3.—In Ohio, on September 15, 1896, Luceba Kelly leased land for oil. She required certain wells to be completed within stated times. She also included this stipulation: "In case no well is completed within thirty days from this date, then this grant shall become null and void, unless second party shall pay the first party thirty dollars each and every month in advance while such completion is delayed." Two wells were completed within the time specified, but the third was not. In 1902, Luceba Kelly brought an action for judgment against Van Etten *et al.* for $390, together with interest thereon. She obtained a judgment for that sum. The defendants appealed.

Luceba Kelly claimed that in the words "unless second party shall pay to said first party thirty dollars each and every month in advance while such completion is delayed" there was a promise to pay thirty dollars a month for such delay.

The court held that the full force and effect of the *unless* clause, taken by itself was to give the lessee the option, by making such payment, to continue the lease in force to the end of the term without completing the first, or, upon failure to make such payment, to allow the lease to become null and void at the end of thirty days after the date of the lease. He also said that there was no promise or obligation in the lease to pay rent to the lessor for failing to complete the first well, but only a privilege to pay such rent, at the option of the lessee, to prevent the lease from becoming null and void.

The court further held that this did not constitute a promise or obligation to pay rent, and further, that the lessee had the option to complete wells or pay rent to keep the lease alive, and that upon breach of the agreement to complete wells no action would lie for the recovery of rent.

The decision was based on the specialized meaning of *unless* as used in leases.[3]

Case 4.—In North Carolina, suit was brought by Hickory to enjoin the Southern Railway Company from enlarging its depot building on a square to which the city held title by virtue of a deed which recited that the conveyance was "for the purpose of a public square around the depot for the free and common use of both railroad and the town of Hickory; not to be built up or exclusively occupied by any one to the exclusion of the public as a free common. To have and to hold the aforesaid tract or lot of land, and all privileges and appurtenances thereto belonging, to the said Western N. C. R. R. Company in trust as aforesaid, for the public uses and purposes aforesaid."

The North Carolina Laws of 1854–55 gave a railroad power to purchase lands necessary for its purposes. Section 29 provided that on failure to agree for a purchase it should have power to condemn land, and to hold in fee simple lands belonging to the state over which the road should pass to an extent not exceeding 100 feet, and that, in the absence of any contract as to lands, it should be presumed that the land over which the road was constructed, together with 100 feet on each side, had been granted to the railroad unless the owner should apply for an assessment of the value of the land within two years after the location of the road.

The original deed to the disputed land was dated May 26, 1859, and the road and depot were constructed in the same year. The deed was thus executed within two years after the building of the road and the statute did not apply.

The court held that, according to Webster's Dictionary, *unless* meant "upon any less condition than (the fact or thing stated in the sentence or clause which follows); if not supposing that not; if it be not; were it not that" and, according to the Century Dictionary, "if it be not that; if it be not the case that," etc., which indicated a negative condition precedent.

According to the plain wording of the statute and the deed, the court then held that the statute did not give to the railroad any land not belonging to the state, and did not prescribe any fixed width for the right of way, which might vary in different localities, but intended that land in excess of 100 feet on either side of the road belonging to the state, and all land belonging to private owners not freely given, should be paid for in full.

There was no presumption, for the defendant acquired the land by a deed. The claim under the deed was ruled inconsistent with the claim under the statute.

The injunction was granted in accordance with the petition of the plaintiff.

The decision was based on the dictionary meaning of *unless*.[4]

The word *unless* usually introduces a negative condition. Occasionally, however, it introduces an option. The illustrative cases given here fall under the linguistic classifications: (*a*) *Unless* denoting a negative condition; (*b*) *Unless* suggesting an alternative condition. Cases (1), (2), and (4) belong to classification (*a*); case (3) belongs to classification (*b*).

(*a*) In case (1), *unless* has the usual meaning of "if not." It is the wrong word to be employed here, however, for "not," another negative, is also used. For the word *unless* to have been used correctly the "not" should have been omitted. In case (2), we have the correct use of *unless*, meaning "if not." This employment of the word is common. If Mary says, "Agnes, unless you are going, I am not," she means that if Agnes is not going, she is not. The same signification is found in case (4).

(*b*) In case (3), *unless* introduces an alternative condition in the statement "unless second party shall pay to said first party thirty dollars each and every month in advance while such completion is delayed." The lessee had the option of making such payment to continue the lease in force. If he chose not to pay, then the lease ended. This use of *unless* is heard in everyday speech in similar cases. If Mr. Brown says, "Unless I pay the premium on my insurance each year in advance, I shall lose what I have put in," he means that he has the option of continuing the policy until maturity by paying his premium each year, but that if he fails to pay the premium, he will lose what he has put in.

Until

The word *until* is defined according to: (1) Literal interpretation; (2) Interpretation based on intent; (3) Common meaning (4) Technical meaning.

Case 1.—Oliver Davis of Missouri owned a tract of land in Kansas, on which there was a saw-mill. He asked one Johnston for a loan of $2,200. Johnston refused to lend the money as he was unwilling to rely for security on the land and mill, which was old. Davis said that he wanted to build a new mill. Johnston then agreed to lend the money when the new mill was completed. For the money Davis and his wife executed to the plaintiff a mortgage, which contained the following stipulation: "This instrument is to be a mortgage and lien on all buildings, mill, and machinery in said mill, until said notes are paid, and to this end this instrument is to be and remain, also, a chattel mortgage on the mill and all machinery therein, until said notes are fully paid."

Both prior and subsequent to the date of the mortgage, Davis added new machinery to the mill, and also put new machinery in the place of old machinery that was inconvenient, out of repair, or worn out. Davis informed Johnston that he could not pay off the debt and that he had done all he could to save the mill, which was about to be washed away by the Missouri River, and requested Johnston to take the mill and machinery and save what he could. Johnston then removed the mill and machinery to a place of safety at his own expense, from which place Davis, without the knowledge or consent of Johnston, took and carried away a portion of the machinery and delivered it to Morrow. Johnston brought suit to recover it.

The machinery delivered to Morrow had been put in the mill by Davis after the execution of the mortgage.

The only question was whether the machinery acquired afterward was subject to the lien of the mortgage.

After considering the exact wording of the mortgage, the court decided in favor of Johnston. It held that the mortgage embraced machinery placed in the building after the mortgage was given and before the notes were satisfied. The decision was based on the literal interpretation of ***until:*** "to the time specified."[1]

Case 2.—In Alabama, Alonzo Hasty was elected probate judge of Marenzo County on November 8, 1904, but Samuel Prowell refused to turn over the office to him. Prowell said he had been elected to the post on the first Monday in August, 1898, for a term of six years and until his successor was elected and qualified and that since six full years had not elapsed prior to November 8, 1904, Hasty could not be called his duly elected and qualified successor until November 3, 1905. Hasty filed a quo warranto petition, challenging Prowell's right to continue in office.

The Alabama Constitution of 1901 provided that probate judges should hold office for six years and until their successors were elected and qualified. The Code of 1896 provided that probate judges should hold office for six years, "from the 3d day of November next after their election and until their successors were elected and qualified."

The court held that the intent of the words "until his successor is elected and qualified," as used in the constitution and statutes relative to the term of officers, was not to prolong the term of office beyond such reasonable time after the election as would enable the newly elected officer to qualify. After the expiration of such reasonable time, if the newly elected officer failed to qualify, the office, the court held, became vacant, for the effect of the phrasing under discussion was to postpone the time of the relator's election, and consequently to postpone his induction into office for a few days until he could qualify.

The result was a judgment ousting Prowell.

The decision was based on the interpretation of the intent of the word ***until***.[2]

Case 3.—In New Jersey, in 1894, a bill was brought by William Skinner, executor of the estate of A. S. Boyd, who died in October, 1890, against Mary Christie and her husband to foreclose a mortgage.

Prior thereto in Hackensack, New Jersey, in 1890, the following agreement was entered into between Boyd and G. R. Christie: "In consideration of $100 in hand paid to me by Gamaliel R. Christie, I hereby agree to convey all that house and three lots of ground situated on the northwest corner of Palisade Ave. and Lake St., West Hoboken, Hudson County, New Jersey, to Mary R. Christie, wife of said Gamaliel R. Christie, on or before the first day of May, 1890, at which time the said Gamaliel R. Christie and wife agree to pay to me the sum of $5,500, to run for five years, with the privilege of paying $1,000 or more each year during the said period, or the whole amount."

Mrs. Christie paid not only the interest regularly for one year, but also the taxes for 1890. In the fall of 1891, the town authorities demanded of Mrs. Christie payment of the arrears of taxes. This demand was the first notice the Christies had of their existence. The Christies called on Skinner to adjust the matter and objected to paying further interest on their mortgage until the taxes were paid.

Mr. Boyd, who sold the land, was a practicing lawyer in New Jersey. He pretended to be a friend of the father of Christie. Christie thus had full confidence in him and did not look into the matter of the deed to find if there were any encumbrances.

The judge said the mere fact that Boyd gave such a deed to the defendants, who were ignorant of the varying qualities of deeds of conveyance, and were acting entirely without counsel and in reliance upon him, indicated that he had a sinister motive in so doing.

The tax had to be paid according to the Act of 1863, entitled "An Act to reorganize the local government of the township of West Hoboken," the thirty-fourth section of which declared "that all taxes and all assessments which shall hereafter be levied, assessed or made upon any lands, tenements or real estate situate in the said township of West Hoboken shall be and remain a lien thereon until paid, notwithstanding any devise, descent, alienation, mortgage or other encumbrance thereof, and if the full amount of any such tax or assessment shall not be paid and satisfied with the time limited and appointed for the payment thereof, it shall and may be lawful for the township committee to cause such lands," etc., "to be sold," etc.

The complainant argued that the substitution of the words "until paid" for "for two years" in the act of 1863 was not sufficient as a definite time was not designated. The judge said that the clause "until the tax is paid" denoted a period of time.

The court held that the defendant was entitled to credit for the taxes against the unpaid purchase price.

The decision was based on the common meaning of *until:* "to the time that."[3]

Case 4.—In Montana, in 1869, R. B. Field gave to C. T. Collier two promissory notes in which he agreed to pay interest on a loan at 3 per cent a month "until paid." The date of payment was June 1, 1870. In 1872, Collier brought an action to foreclose the mortgage upon certain mining property, given by Field as security.

The question then arose as to the amount of interest Collier should collect. Should it be 3 per cent a month until the note was paid or only until the date of maturity?

The court held that the words "until paid," as used in a note in which the maker agrees to pay a sum "on or before a special day, with interest at the rate of 3 per cent until paid," did not extend the contract beyond the specified date, any more than the words "per annum" or "per month"; and that therefore the holder could collect the statutory interest at the rate of 10 per cent per annum after the note had become due and remained unpaid.

The decision was based on the technical meaning of *until* as used in notes in the expression "until paid."[4]

The words *until* and "till" are used synonymously. The four illustrative cases turning on the conjunction *until* fall under the linguistic classification: (*a*) Limited meaning.

In case (1), ***until*** in the statement, "until said notes are fully paid" has the limit, the paying of the notes. The period extends up to that time. Case (2) gives as a limit of holding office for the probate judge the time of electing and qualifying of their succes sors. In case (3), all taxes and all assessments levied on real estate were to be a lien on the property until paid. The time of paying was the limit fixed. Case (4) fixes the date of maturity as the limit of the time, a rule that is customary in relation to notes. This use of ***until*** in its limited sense is common. If Mr. Brown says, "Wait until the mail comes," he fixes a time limit—the arrival of the mail. (See *till*.)

When

The word *when* is defined according to: (1) Interpretation based on intent; (2) Dictionary meaning; (3) Context.

Case 1.—In New York, in 1906, a case arose concerning the construction of the will of George Egleston, who died in England in 1904 and left a will in which he appointed the Central Trust Company of New York City to be his trustee and administrators. The part that gave trouble was the following:

"At the age of twenty-five years when each child shall reach that age, not before, or when the three children are twenty-five or the youngest twenty-five years old—I donate and give to the three sons Thomas, Harold, and Vivian seventy-five per centum of the net income being held and invested, until each child has arrived at the age of thirty years of age when I bequeath to them after all deductions ninety-eight per cent. of the net income—the balance of two per cent. keeping the estate in heart and to be invested. My son Vivian Hector MacLean to attain the age of twenty-five, and thirty years, before the divisions, making my two eldest boys several years older."

The court held that the testator intended that the sons should have 98 per cent of the income from the time of their arrival at the age of thirty years; the word *when* being equivalent to "thereafter."

The decision was based on the interpretation of the intent of *when* as used in the will.[1]

Case 2.—In 1894, in Indiana, a jury found that one Burton's view and hearing of an approaching train were cut off 375 feet before reaching the tracks; that he proceeded slowly until his horses passed to the end of a stationary box car, when he checked them; that he looked north 100 feet, which was as far as he could see, without seeing or hearing the approaching train, then started forward. The jury further found that when he had passed the west side of the box car, he looked north, and saw the train approaching at forty-five or fifty miles an hour and instantly endeavored to stop his horses, then ten feet from the Pittsburg, C. C. and St. L. Ry. Company's main tracks. The railway company contended that the finding showed contributary negligence on the part of Burton.

The court held that, according to the definitions of the word *when* as given by the Century Dictionary and sustained by Webster's International Dictionary (Edition 1893), the language of the finding was not *when* he had passed the car and his horses had gone to within ten feet of the main track, he looked, and then pulled upon his lines, but that the sense of the language of the finding was that "as soon as" he had passed he looked, or "just after the moment" of passing he looked, or he passed the car, "at which time" he looked.

The Railway's Company's contention was overruled and the judgment was affirmed.

The decision was based on the dictionary meaning of *when:* "as soon as."[2]

Case 3.—In 1807, an action of debt was brought for the state of Pennsylvania in the District Court of the United States for the penalty of a bond dated November 16, 1802, conditioned to pay to the collector of the customs "$7,720.41, or the amount of the duties to be ascertained as due and arising on certain goods," etc., "entered by the above bounden Willings and Francis, as imported in the ship *Missouri*, from Canton, as per entry dated Nov. 16, 1802."

The question was whether the *Missouri* at the time of her arrival from Canton was entitled to the privileges of a registered ship of the United States; for if she was, the sum mentioned in the condition of the bond (which had been calculated as if she were a foreign bottom) was $702.05 too much.

The *Missouri*, when she sailed from Philadelphia for Canton, was under United States registry, owned wholly by Willings and Francis, citizens of the United States. While at sea, and while the register of the ship was on board in the possession of the master, she was in part sold by Willings and Francis, in Philadelphia, to J. G. Koch and others, citizens of the United States, on February 12, 1801, but was not then registered anew by her former name, nor was there any instrument in writing, such as a bill of sale, detailing the certificate of registry. On November 15, 1802, after the arrival of the ship at Philadelphia, and before any report of entry, Koch and others, the vendees, made a parol resale of their part of the ship to Willings and Francis, whereby the whole was revested in them. Afterwards the register was delivered by the master of the ship to the collector of the port of Philadelphia, and the vessel duly reported and entered. T. W. Francis offered to make oath that no foreigner had had any share or interest in the ship.

The Act of Congress of December 31, 1792, read:

"That *when* any ship or vessel which shall have been registered pursuant to this act, or the act hereby in part repealed, *shall* in whole or in part be sold or transferred to a citizen, or citizens of the United States, or shall be altered in form or burthen," etc., "*in every such case* the said ship or vessel *shall* be registered anew, by her former name according to the directions hereinbefore contained, (otherwise she shall cease to be deemed a ship or vessel of the United States), and *her former certificate of registry shall be delivered up* to the collector, to whom *application* for such new registry shall be made, at *the time that the same shall be made*."

The United States District Attorney claimed that *when* meant "at that time," thus designating the precise time when a particular act must be performed in order to save a forfeiture. He based the whole argument upon a particular construction or meaning, applied to the word *when* in the beginning of the statute quoted above.

The judge said that the word was often used for "if," or "in case" and that it was so used in that passage, a meaning explained by the expression "in every such case." He said that the words were not "*when* any ship shall be sold . . . she shall be registered anew"; but, "when any ship shall be sold . . . in every such case . . . she shall be registered anew," thereby excluding the idea that the registering anew was to be at the moment of sale, and negativing the construction which might otherwise be raised upon the equivocal meaning of *when*.

The question was whether an American registered vessel, in part transferred by parol while at sea to an American citizen and resold to the original owners on her return into port before her entry, did by that operation lose her privileges as an American bottom, and become subject to foreign duties.

The judge said that the register was always in the present tense, giving the present owners, and that in the case under discussion the owners possessing the ship when she returned owned the ship at her departure.

Judgment was therefore rendered in favor of the defendants.

The decision was based on the context, *when* taking on the meaning of "if."[3]

We usually think of *when* as meaning "the time at which," but the illustrative cases given here fall under the linguistic classifications: (*a*) *When* denoting future time; (*b*) *When* denoting past time; (*c*) *When* denoting a condition. Case (1) belongs to classification (*a*); case (2) to classification (*b*); case (3) to classification (*c*).

(*a*) In case (1), *when* takes on the meaning of "thereafter" denoting future time. Each year, after they have reached the age of thirty, the children are to get 98 per cent of the net income. To take an example from everyday speech, if a teacher says, "I teach English classes from noon until three o'clock, when I devote my time to music," she means that all the time after three o'clock she devotes to music.

Case (2) shows *when* referring to past time and meaning "as soon as." "As soon as he had passed the car" means "after he had passed the car." This meaning is also common. If Mr. Brown says, "When I had eaten the apple, I left the room," he means that after he had eaten the apple, he left the room.

In case (3), we find *when* introducing a condition, instead of referring to time. It takes on the meaning of "if," as is often heard in common parlance. If John says, "How can he buy it, when he has no money?" the independent clause is conditional and means if he has no money.

Whenever

The word *whenever* is defined according to: (1) Interpretation based on intent; (2) Dictionary meaning; (3) Context; (4) Circumstances.

Case 1.—In California, Melone was secretary of state for the term of four years, ending December 1875. It was his duty to collect and pay over to the state monthly the fees received by him. On July 1, 1886, Dunn, as comptroller, demanded that he account for and pay into the state treasury $11,109.50 (the amount alleged to have been received by Melone while in office, and for which he had failed to account), or make settlement with the comptroller, as required by law. The secretary of state took no notice of the demand and the comptroller proceeded to state an account under the statute which provided: "Whenever any person has received moneys belonging to, or held in trust for, the state, and fails to render an account thereof, and to make settlement with the comptroller within the time prescribed by law . . . or who fails to pay into the state treasury any money belonging to the state, upon being required so to do by the comptroller, within 20 days after such requisition, the comptroller must state an account with such person, charging 25 per cent damages, and interest . . . from the time of failure."

Melone claimed that the statute of limitations did not apply and that the cause of action did not accrue until the account was stated, and demand was made as provided in that section. This claim depended principally upon the use of the word *whenever*.

The judge said that the word simply meant "if"; that is, in those cases in which parties receiving money do not account, etc., instead of "at whatever time moneys have been received" as contended by counsel for Melone.

The court held that the word *whenever*, beginning the statute, when applied to an action brought by the comptroller against an ex-secretary of state for fees received and not paid into the treasury, should not be interpreted to mean "at whatever time moneys have been received," so that no limitation would apply to the action authorized by the statute. The court also held that the liability of the secretary accrued at the time he was in default, and not when the comptroller made demand for the deficit and stated an account; and that the statute of limitations began to run from the former period.

The decision was based on the interpretation of intent of *whenever* as used in the statute. In this case it means "if."[1]

Case 2.—In Georgia, in 1921, M. Griffin and another applied for remission of the penalty incurred by forfeiture of a criminal recognizance.

The principal, S. B. Smith, made bond and forfeited it; the forfeiture being afterwards relieved. He then made the bond involved in this case, and forfeited, so far as appears, willfully. The sureties, on learning of the default, at their own expense, recaptured their principal and delivered him to the deputy marshal, who took him before a United States commissioner, by whom he was again admitted to bail with another as surety. The third bond of Smith was also forfeited.

Griffin made the application under the statute which read as follows:

"When any recognizance in a criminal cause, taken for, or in, or returnable to, any court of the United States, is forfeited by a breach of the condition thereof, such court may, in its discretion, remit the whole or a part of the penalty, whenever it appears to the court that there has been no willful default of the party, and that a trial can, notwithstanding, be had in the cause, and that public justice does not otherwise require the same penalty to be enforced."

The judge said that there was no question concerning the power to set aside the judgment after the term, for the time was covered by the broad expression, "Whenever it appears to the court," the natural meaning of *whenever* and the only one given by Webster's International Dictionary being "at whatever time."

The court held that in cases in which the sureties on a criminal recognizance, after their principal's default, recaptured him and delivered him to the deputy marshal, and he was again admitted to bail, with another surety, and the new bond was also forfeited, and the sureties had not been diligent in applying for a remission of the penalty incurred by the forfeiture of the first recognizance, the penalty should be remitted, except to the extent of $100, on the payment of that amount with costs.

The judge said that if they had applied for relief, it would undoubtedly have been given to them, but that a lapse of time often made difficulties in proof.

The decision was based on an appeal to the dictionary.[2]

Case 3.—In Rhode Island, in 1882, trustees of the will of Rufus Greene filed a bill against the beneficiaries, to obtain the instructions of the court in administering the trusts. The testator had left his estate in trust:

First, to pay from the income of the personalty all repairs and charges on the realty.

Second, to pay the gross rents of certain specified realty and personalty to five daughters, or, in case of the death of any of them to their children or grandchildren.

Third, to pay the rents and profits of the residue to the widow and other children, including children born afterward, until the youngest child of the youngest son attained majority.

And provided:

"Whenever the youngest child of any daughter, in being at my decease, shall have reached the age of twenty-one years, then my said trustees are to divide, distribute, and convey the said property, out of which my daughters' shares are to be derived, especially among said daughters, and the children or grandchildren of deceased daughters, share and share alike, descendants of daughters taking their proportionate share of the father's and mother's estate."

The youngest living child of a daughter, at the time of the testator's death, died in boyhood, but would have attained majority on August 9, 1891, had he lived. The youngest child of the testator's second daughter attained majority on August 2, 1882, and was the first child of any of the daughters to come of age.

The widow and the sons, whose portions, under the will, were subject to the onerous charges in the will, contended that the time had come for the termination of the trust in favor of the daughters, under the clause recited above, a settlement that would relieve them of the burden. The daughters contended that the time had not come for such a settlement, and would not come until the youngest of all the children of the daughters, whether born or to be born, had reached the age of twenty-one years.

The judge pointed out that *whenever* often is equivalent to "as soon as," but that it is also used frequently where the time intended by it is and will be until its arrival (or for some uncertain period at least), indeterminate. After considering the will as a whole, he said the purpose of the trust was to tie up the property for the beneficiaries, giving them the rents and profits and putting the principal beyond their control.

The court held that the time for a division had not come and, further, that it would not then decide whether the words, "in being at my decease," in the cited clause above applied to "youngest child" or to "any daughter."

The decision was based on the context of the whole will.[3]

Case 4.—In New York, in 1913, Frank Williams applied to the board of local inspectors of steam vessels at Oswego for an examination for a license as pilot on steam vessels under 100 tons, running from Ogdensburg to Detroit on the St. Lawrence River, Lake Ontario, Niagara River, Lake Erie, and the Detroit River. The application on its face showed that the applicant had not had three years' experience in the deck department of a steam vessel, motor vessel, said vessel, or barge consort, as required by the board of supervising inspectors. Chestnut and another supervising inspector refused to give Williams an examination. He then brought suit for a decree compelling them to do so. The Circuit Court held that according to the rules of the department the applicant had not had the necessary experience. He then appealed and the decision was reversed. The examination was given in July, 1912, by the supervision inspector at Cleveland, but it was decided that Williams did not possess the experience and qualifications which fitted him for the duties of a pilot. Thus he was denied a license.

In October, 1912, Williams applied to the local board of inspectors at Buffalo for an examination for a first-class pilot's license. The board had been notified of the previous examination. There was a regulation which provided: "Any applicant for license who has been duly examined and refused may come before any local board for examination after one year has expired." Thus the examination was refused. The plaintiff alleged that Inspectors Potter, Chestnut, and Nelson were in league against him and that the regulation which denied him the right to a second examination before the expiration of twelve months was invalid.

The plaintiff quoted the statute which provided:

"Whenever any person claiming to be a skillful pilot of steam vessels offers himself for a license, the inspectors shall make diligent inquiry as to his character and merits, and if satisfied, from personal examination of the applicant, with the proof that he possesses the requisite knowledge and skill, and is trustworthy and faithful, they shall grant him a license for the term of one year to pilot any such vessel within the limits prescribed in the license."

The judge said that if the section meant that every person claiming to be a skillful pilot of steam vessels might offer himself for examination as often as he pleased and that the board of inspectors were bound to give him one, such a person might present himself for examination every week and keep the board in constant session. He also said that *whenever* strictly construed meant "at whatever time, at what time soever," but that if it were construed in that sense, the applicant would be entitled to repeated examinations night or day so often as he should apply—an unreasonable construction to be put upon the word.

The court did not hold that the applicant for a pilot's license on being examined and rejected was entitled to a new examination as often and whenever he saw fit to apply to the same or to another board in the same jurisdiction. It was decreed therefore to dismiss the complaint.

The decision was based on circumstances. The applicant had been examined once and rejected twice. Furthermore, he had not had three years' experience, a necessary requirement.[4]

The illustrative cases turning upon *whenever* fall under the following linguistic classifications: (*a*) *Whenever* denoting a condition; (*b*) *Whenever* denoting time. Case (1) belongs to classification (*a*); cases (2), (3), and (4) belong to classification (*b*).

(*a*) In case (1), *whenever* takes on the meaning of "if," a signification that is heard in everyday speech. A school principal might say, "Whenever any student takes a book without reporting to the teacher that he has the book, he will be made to keep the book and pay for it," meaning "If any student takes a book, etc." Here *whenever* introduces a condition.

(*b*) More often *whenever* denotes time rather than a condition. In case (2), we find the usual signification—"at whatever time" implying future time. The clause "Whenever it appears to the court" signifies at whatever time in the future it appears to the court. This use of *whenever* is common. In the sentence, "Whenever you go down town be sure to look at the dresses on Fifth Avenue," *whenever* refers to any time in the future.

Case (3) shows *whenever* denoting future time with a definite limit. "Whenever the youngest child of any daughter shall have reached the age of twenty-one," points out a definite time. The division of property is not to take place until that particular time. Similar statements are heard in everyday speech in referring to a definite future time.

Case (4) shows another variation of the meaning of *whenever* in referring to future time. The future time has limitations. "Whenever any person claiming to be a skillful pilot of steam vessels offers himself for a license, the inspectors shall make diligent inquiry as to his character and merits . . . and if satisfied, they shall grant him a license" means, of course, at whatever time in the future any person claiming to be a skillful pilot, etc., but it does not mean that that same person can present himself for examination as often as he pleases. If he should be rejected he will have to let a reasonable amount of time elapse in order to gain more experience and become more skillful before he takes the next examination. Therefore *whenever* refers to future time, but future time with limitations. The same meaning is employed in everyday speech. If a teacher says, "Whenever a student presents himself for a re-examination I shall give one," he does not mean that he will give a re-examination at any hour and as often as the student wants one.

Where

The word *where* is defined according to: (1) Interpretation based on intent.

Case 1.—In South Carolina, in 1922, A. K. Graham brought action on an automobile insurance policy against the Standard Fire Insurance Company. The automobile had burned and the company refused to pay. There were three provisions in the policy for forfeiture:

(*a*) The insured must be sole and unconditional owner.

(*b*) The property insured must not be under mortgage.

(*c*) The property insured must not be used in public service.

Evidence of the fact that there was a mortgage on the machine was indisputable. Evidence was also manifested that the agent of the defendant knew it was under mortgage. The car had been used as a public service car, but had been withdrawn from public service before the fire. The agent who wrote the policy also knew that fact. As the company knew that Graham was using his car in a manner not permitted by the terms of the policy and said nothing about it, judgment was rendered in Graham's favor. The company then appealed. One of the chief assignments of error was that the judge charged on the facts when he said: "Where they knew the plaintiff was using his car in a manner not permitted by the terms of the policy, it wouldn't do for them to keep quiet, say nothing, keep the plaintiff's money, and not let him know they would forfeit his policy."

The court said that the preceding statement was not a charge on the facts, for the word *where* was used in the sense of "if"; that is, where they know, or in a case where they know.

Judgment was therefore affirmed.

The decision was based on the interpretation of the intent of the charge, *where* taking on the meaning of "if."[1]

The illustrative case turning on the word *where* falls under the linguistic classification: (*a*) *Where* denoting a condition. In this case *where* takes on the meaning of "if." The clause "Where they knew the plaintiff was using his car in a manner not permitted by the terms of the policy . . ." is equivalent to "If they knew the plaintiff . . . ." *Where* in this sense is heard frequently. If Mr. Smith says, "Where a boy has no pen, how can he write in ink?" he means "If a boy has no pen, how can he write in ink?" A condition is introduced.

Whereas

The word *whereas* is defined according to: (1) Dictionary meaning; (2) Circumstances.

Case 1.—In California, in 1902, Arthur Ennis was convicted of perjury. He appealed, claiming that by the indictment he did not know the charge against him. The language objected to was "whereas, in truth and in fact . . . he, the said Ennis, was down to Sargent's corrall," etc. Ennis claimed that since *whereas* was used, the words were a mere recital and not a positive averment, and that the charge was, therefore, insufficient.

The judge said that it was better, no doubt, to avoid the use of the word *whereas* in a pleading; but that whatever was in itself a positive averment was not turned into recital by the mere fact that somewhere preceding the averment the word *whereas* was used, for according to the dictionaries it was synonymous with "when in fact," "the fact is," and when used in that sense, as was shown by the context, what followed might be a positive averment, and not a recital.

Judgment was therefore affirmed.

The decision was based on an appeal to the dictionary. It was found that *whereas* meant "the fact is" and that the use of it preceding the statement in the case did not change the meaning. *Whereas* was a superfluous word, which made the statement read: "the fact is, in truth and in fact. . . ."[1]

Case 2.—In Connecticut, in 1920, George Hill, Jr., brought action against Janette Smith, administratrix of the estate of Edwin Smith, to recover taxes paid to the city of Norwalk, on land purchased by Hill from Smith, who died intestate. Judgment was rendered for defendant. Plaintiff appealed.

On November 13, 1917, a contract of sale had been made by the two parties. The following statement was included: "Any charges, taxes, interest, water rent, assessments or any other liabilities against the property which have accrued to the date of the transfer of the property to me to be paid by you or satisfactory guarantee given me that they will be paid when due George Hill, Jr."

On November 30, 1917, Smith executed and delivered to Hill a warranty deed of the premises. Upon the same day the two men entered into the following agreement in relation to the apportionment of taxes:

"The parties hereto agree as follows: That whereas Dr. Smith has placed in the hands of the Fidelity Title and Trust Company the sum of $700 to answer for the payment of all taxes which may be a lien on the premises situated in Norwalk, Connecticut, this dav conveyed to Mr. Hill, up to December 1, 1917:

"Now therefore, we, Dr. Smith and George Hill, Jr., agree that Dr. Smith shall pay all taxes after December 1, 1917, on premises this day conveyed to said Hill." This agreement was signed by both men.

The fiscal year in Norwalk ended on August 31. At the time of the conveyance to the plaintiff on November 30, 1917, the taxes on the premises for the fiscal year ending on August 31, 1917, had been paid.

The taxes for the fiscal year ending August 31, 1918, on the property were $534.70, and were payable on January 1, 1918. This tax was laid on the list of 1916 and became a lien on the property on October 1, 1916, under the terms of the charter of Norwalk. Also, the annual taxes for the fiscal year ending August 31, 1919, were laid on the list of 1917 on July 2, 1927, and became a lien upon the property on October 1, 1917.

Under the charter of Norwalk "any lien for taxes annually laid" should date from the first day of the preceding October. A custom had grown up in Norwalk of laying the annual tax for a fiscal year before the fiscal year began, and of laying it upon the assessment list of the calendar year preceding that in which the tax was laid. For example, on July 2, 1918, an annual tax was laid on the assessment list of 1917 for the fiscal year ending August 31, 1919. The tax was payable December 1, 1918, but under the charter of the city became a lien on the land October 1, 1917.

Thus among buyers and sellers of real estate in Norwalk there was much confusion concerning the taxes. The second contract was made under these circumstances.

Smith knew when he executed the second contract that he had paid the annual taxes on the property for the fiscal year ending on August 31, 1917. Hill and Smith both knew that the annual taxes for the fiscal year ending on August 31, 1918, had not been paid.

The judge said that in the light of the surrounding circumstances it was clearly the intent of the parties to dispose definitely and equitably of all questions as to the payment of the annual taxes on the property and that they had met this requirement by agreeing that Smith should pay such proportion of the current annual taxes as the time from the beginning of the current fiscal year to December 1, 1917, bore to the entire year, and that the remaining portions of the current annual tax and all future annual taxes should be borne by Hill.

Hill urged that the clause beginning with *whereas* indicated that the second clause reading, "Now, therefore, we, Dr. Smith and George Hill, Jr., agree that Dr. Smith shall pay all taxes up to December 1, 1917, and Mr. Hill agrees to pay all taxes after December 1, 1917, on premises this day conveyed to said Hill," should be construed as if the word "taxes" therein read tax liens.

The judge said that if the contention above were true the agreement was an idle ceremony and that *whereas* had rather the meaning of "although" than "since," for it was the intention of the parties that the vendor should pay the taxes for the fiscal year ending August 31, 1917, and his proportionate share of the taxes for the following year.

It was therefore decided that the trial court correctly rendered judgment for the defendant.

The decision was based on the circumstances surrounding taxes and tax liens in Norwalk, Connecticut.[2]

The two illustrative cases turning on *whereas* fall under the linguistic classification: (*a*) *Whereas*, with a positive meaning.

In case (1), the expression "Whereas, in truth and in fact" has the meaning of "the fact is, in truth and in fact," *whereas* implying a recognition of facts—the facts that are to follow. In this statement, however, *whereas* is redundant, for "in truth and in fact" conveys practically the same idea. In everyday English this use of *whereas* is common. Mr. Brown may say, "Whereas we're happy here, why think of moving?" meaning "The fact is, we're happy here, etc." The *whereas* only asserts the existence of a certain fact or situation. The same idea is presented in case (2), in which *whereas* has the meaning of "since," a signification implying also a recognition of facts. The statement, "Since a certain thing is true," is a positive assertion that the fact is true. In this case, Dr. Smith had given the Fidelity Title and Trust Company $700. The *whereas* clause merely showed that he had done so.

Wherever

The word *wherever* is defined according to: (1) Interpretation based on intent.

Case 1.—In New Jersey, in September, 1913, Charles Moore applied for a mandamus against Enoch Johnson for compensation on the basis of a salary of $4,000 per annum as prosecutor of the pleas since March, 1913.

In 1908, an amendment had been passed giving an increased compensation to prosecutors of the pleas in counties bordering on the Atlantic Ocean, fixing such compensation at $4,000 wherever the population of any such county by the latest census was more than 50,000 and not more than 65,000.

In 1910, as shown by the federal census, the population of Atlantic County had risen to 71,894. This circumstance led Johnson to refuse to pay the relator's salary under the Acts of 1908 upon the ground that those acts on their face no longer applied to the prosecutor of Atlantic County, whose compensation, it was contended, must then be regulated by the General Act of 1906 (*i.e.*, must fall from $4,000 to $3,000 because of the increase of population).

The judge said that it was absurd to think that the Legislature enacted that $4,000 should be paid for the work entailed by a seaside population barely exceeding 50,000 and that when such work should be increased nearly 50 per cent the proper compensation should be $3,000. He added that the use of the particle *wherever* was equivalent to "as long as."

The court held that, upon a proper construction of the acts, the prosecutor of the pleas in the county of Atlantic was entitled to the salary he demanded, even though the population of that county in the last census exceeded 65,000.

The decision was based on the interpretation of the intent of the amendment.[1]

The illustrative case turning on *wherever* falls under the linguistic classification: (*a*) *Wherever* denoting length of time. In this case it takes on the meaning of "as long as." $4,000 is to be paid as long as the population is from 50,000 to 65,000. This use of *wherever* is frequent in conversation. If Mr. Brown says, "Wherever you find Joe cultivates three acres, always pay him ten dollars a day," he means *as long as* Joe cultivates three acres a day, etc.

Wherefore

The word *wherefore* is defined according to: (1) Dictionary meaning.

Case 1.—In Vermont, in 1883, the Lycoming Fire Insurance Company brought action in general and special assumpsit against Wright and Son to recover assessments on premiums due on promissory notes. The defendants in their answer said that the contract was void, because they had been induced to make it by the fraudulent representations made as to the financial condition of the company. The fire insurance company in reply contended that the answer of the defendants was argumentative; namely, "Wherefore the said defendants say that said premium was and is void."

The court said that the answer was not made argumentative by the use of the word *wherefore*, which was defined as meaning "for which reason"; thus the averment would read "for which reason the defendants say that the premium note described in the declaration was and is void in law."

The court decided that the answer of Wright and Son was sufficient.

The decision was based on an appeal to the dictionary.[1]

The illustrative case turning on *wherefore* falls under the linguistic classification: (*a*) *Wherefore* as a word of deduction. In this case, *wherefore* takes on the meaning of "for this reason." It was for the reason stated that the defendants said that the premium was void. This use of the word is common in everyday speech. If Mr. Brown says, "John stayed away from school; wherefore he was able to make a cabinet," he gives the reason for John's being able to make a cabinet.

Whereupon

The word *whereupon* is defined according to: (1) Context; (2) Circumstances.

Case 1.—A case arose in New Jersey, in 1834, concerning a writ of certiorari. A motion was made to dismiss the writ of certiorari because it appeared from the transcript of the justice, that the plaintiff who brought the writ was present at the rendition of the judgment. According to the Revised Laws, his only recourse would be by appeal and not by writ of certiorari. The transcript stated in part: "I took one week, until the 30th day of May, at four o'clock in the afternoon of that day, to make up my judgment, and gave notice to the parties. May 30th, the plaintiff appeared according to notice *and the defendant did not appear until after 4 o'clock. Whereupon*, I gave judgment in favor of the plaintiff, and against the defendant, for fifty-three dollars, etc."

The court said that the justice gave judgment after the defendant appeared, for the justice first recorded the appearance of the defendant, and then said *whereupon*, meaning upon the defendant's appearance, he gave judgment, etc.

The writ of certiorari was therefore dismissed.

The decision was based on the context, for it was evident that the judgment was actually given after the plaintiff appeared and in the presence of the justice.[1]

Case 2.—In 1885, John Van Ells was justice of peace at Lake,

Wisconsin. August Meyer and Martin Ackermann brought a case against Lyman Green before Van Ells. Green asked for a mandamus to compel Van Ells to enter in his docket an adjournment of the suit. The mandamus was granted and Van Ells appealed. Van Ells denied that any such adjournment as Green claimed was made. Green claimed that the jury brought in the verdict at 7:50 p.m. on June 24 and that Van Ells did not forthwith pronounce or render judgment on said verdict as required by law, but did orally and publicly announce an adjournment of said cause for the rendition of judgment on the verdict until June 25, 1885, at ten o'clock in the forenoon, at his office. The docket entry was: "The jury returned a verdict as follows: 'We, the jury, find for the plaintiffs.' Whereupon the court rendered judgment against the defendant; and it is hereby adjudged that the plaintiffs do recover from the defendant the sum of $8.85," etc. Van Ells claimed that the fair inference from the docket entries was that the justice rendered judgment upon the verdict without any adjournment.

The court said that the word *whereupon* was not definite as to time; but, that taken in connection with the statement of the justice, the conclusive presumption was that judgment was rendered on the verdict without an adjournment and that the entries of the docket imported verity.

The order of the circuit court was reversed and the proceedings were dismissed.

The decision was based on circumstances—the lack of record of an adjournment on the docket entry and the supposition that docket entries are true.[2]

The two illustrative cases given here fall under the linguistic classification: (*a*) *Whereupon* denoting time immediately following. In case (1), the defendant appeared after four o'clock and judgment was rendered immediately before the justice. Therefore *whereupon* introducing the statement took on the import of "immediately after." The judgment was given upon his arrival. The same meaning is heard often in daily speech. If Mr. Brown says, "I received the letter; whereupon I set out to town," he means that he set out immediately after the letter came. The same meaning is given to *whereupon* in case (2).

Whether

The word *whether* is defined according to: (1) Literal interpretation; (2) Common meaning.

Case 1.—In Pennsylvania, in 1845, Nicholas Voegtly brought action against the school directors of the Third Ward of Alleghany. Voegtly had sold a tract to Warner and Painter in 1835, by article of agreement, in which they covenanted to pay $100,000 within twenty years, with interest for the first ten years at 5 per cent per annum, and for the last ten years at 6 per cent etc.—interest payable in advance. In 1845, the principal, $78,328, was still due and the purchasers were paying interest on it.

The point to be determined was whether the defendant was liable for a school tax on the sum above.

By an act of June 13, 1834, the school directors were given authority to assess a tax on certain personal property described as "all ground rents," "moneys at interest," and "all debts due from solvent debtors, whether by promissory notes (except bank notes) penal or single bill, bond, judgment, mortgage stocks," etc.

Voegtly contended that the money due the defendants was not comprehended within any of the descriptions of personal property enumerated in the act; that articles of agreement were not mentioned and therefore were not intended to be included.

The judge said even if *whether* did have the effect of a *videlicet*, which it never had either in common parlance or legal phraseology, and even if the money were not a debt due from solvent debtors by bond, it certainly was money at interest. Voegtly objected to paying the tax twice, but the judge said that if all the money had been paid to him and he had lent it to others on interest it would be liable to taxation. He also said that any man with plain common sense would call that money at interest and if it were not money at interest, it would be hard to tell what was.

Judgment was rendered in favor of the defendants.

The decision was based on the literal interpretation of the law. The conjunctions used were the correlative conjunctions: *whether* . . . *or*, used to indicate alternatives.[1]

Case 2.—In Texas, in 1903, Bud Wade was convicted of selling intoxicating liquor in violation of the local option law. He appealed, objecting to the order submitting the question of prohibition to the vote of the people of Montague County. He contended that the order was defective, because, instead of submitting the issue as "whether or not" a sale of intoxicating liquors should be prohibited, the order used only the word *whether*, omitting the words "or not."

The court said that the objection was untenable.

Judgment was therefore affirmed.

The decision was based on the common meaning of *whether*. In ordinary speech the words "or not" are often left out, but are always understood as accompanying *whether*.[2]

The word *whether* is a correlative conjunction used with "or." The two illustrative cases given here fall under the linguistic classification: (*a*) *Whether* indicating a choice. In case (1), *whether* introduces a series, any one of which may be a cause for taxation. The correlative "or" is implied in the *whether* at the beginning of the statement. It is understood that taxation will apply to all debts due from solvent debtors, whether by promissory notes, or penal or single bills, or bond, or judgment, etc. This use of *whether* is common. If Mr. Brown says, "The monument will be seen whether John goes by train, by car, by bicycle," he means that the monument will be seen regardless of the method of traveling John chooses.

Case (2) presents a slightly different situation. An alternative, which is the negative of the first statement introduced by *whether*, is implied. "Whether such sale should be prohibited" meant "whether or not such sale should be prohibited." The "or not" was understood. This use of *whether* is also common in daily speech. If Mr. Smith says, "Whether you are allowed to go doesn't concern me," he means "whether or not."

While

The word *while* is defined according to: (1) Interpretation based on intent; (2) Dictionary meaning.

Case 1.—In New York, in 1875, a policy was issued by the Oswego and Onondaga Insurance Company upon Urbane Langworthy's "hop-house, while drying hops," from August 15 to October 15. The hop-house was destroyed by a fire which occurred within the time specified, but after the plaintiff had ceased drying hops.

The court held that the defendant was not liable. The decision was based on an interpretation based on intent. Langworthy insured his barn for a certain length of time, not knowing the exact date when the drying of hops would cease. He, of course, extended the time to be sure to cover the most dangerous time. His intention was to protect himself against fire. The fact that a fire occurred after he had finished drying his hops, but before the policy had expired, should not have kept him from recovering for his barn, although the court held that it should.[1]

Case 2.—In Kansas, in 1896, quo warranto proceedings were brought to determine the right of J. H. Leidigh, as against G. H. Lawrence, to be county clerk of Ford County. They had been opposing candidates at the general election in 1895. Leidigh received a majority of the votes, and thereafter qualified and entered upon the duties of the position. But, except for the ballots cast by certain inmates of the State Soldiers' Home, located in the county, Lawrence received a majority of the votes. The right of the inmates of the home to participate in the election was the sole question for decision.

The constitution read: "Every male person of twenty-one years and upwards who shall have resided in Kansas six months and in the township or ward in which he offers to vote thirty days next preceding any election, shall be deemed a qualified elector; but for the purpose of voting no person shall be deemed to have gained or lost a residence while kept at any almshouse or other asylum at public expense."

The judge said that the definition of *while* as a conjunction in the Standard Dictionary of Funk and Wagnalls was "during the time that; as long as" and that therefore no residence was gained, or could be gained, during the time that, or as long as, the person was kept at an asylum.

Therefore the court decided that the inmates of the State Soldiers' Home, located in Ford County, who had removed there from other parts of the state, were disqualified from participating in the election held in that county. Judgment was therefore rendered in favor of the plaintiff.

The decision was based on an appeal to the dictionary.[2]

The two illustrative cases turning on the conjunction *while* fall under the linguistic classification: (*a*) *While* denoting duration of time. In case (1), the expression "while drying hops" means during the period of drying hops. This use is common in everyday speech. If Mary says, "I shall write, while Jane sleeps," she means she will write during the time that Jane sleeps. We find the same use of the word in case (2). The clause "while kept at any almshouse" means during the time one is kept at any almshouse.

Whilst

The word *whilst* is defined according to: (1) Interpretation based on intent.

Case 1.—In England, in 1795, Bullard, after a demise of certain premises, with a portion of an adjoining yard for a term of twenty-one years, covenanted that Rhodes, the lessee, should have "the use of the pump in the yard jointly with himself, *whilst the same should remain there*, paying half the expenses of repair." In 1806, Bullard removed the pump and Rhodes brought action, contending that Bullard unnecessarily and without any reasonable cause, and in order to aggrieve and injure the plaintiff, removed and took away the said pump, contrary to the form and effect of the said indenture.

The court said that if the words "whilst the same should remain there" had not been introduced, he would have thought the lessor had been guilty of a breach of covenant by willfully removing it, but that because the covenant for free ingress and egress through the yard was qualified with the words "whilst, etc," the use of those words must have been to reserve to the lessor the option of removing the pump.

Judgment was therefore rendered in favor of the defendant. The decision was based on an interpretation of intent.[1]

The word *whilst* is just a different form of *while*, and thus the illustrative case turning on the word falls under the same linguistic classification: (*a*) *Whilst* denoting duration of time. The clause "whilst the same should remain there" defines the time the same should remain there. In common conversation, "while" is almost always used instead of *whilst*. (See *while*.)

CONCLUSION

THROUGHOUT the many foregoing pages that have been devoted to an exposition of interpretations placed upon various articles, prepositions, and conjunctions by decisions in the law courts, one aim has been constantly in view; to present these parts of speech in their aspect as form-words, in accordance with the definition and explanation of the term *form-words* in Chapter II. Incidentally, I have sought to bring out the fact that in many instances the signification attached to these words in legal parlance is identical with, or similar to, that of ordinary, everyday speech.

Linguistics has always been important in the formulation of judicial decisions and meticulous accuracy in definition has always been a goal toward which legal phraseology strives. The very redundancy, triteness, and verbosity of such phraseology is but a proof of the efforts made to achieve a completeness of meaning that cannot be misunderstood. It is no fault of the courts or of the legislatures that ambiguity is forever creeping in. Such uncertainty can be charged only against the amazing flexibility of our language.

If the citation at length of the many law cases quoted above has done nothing else, I trust that it has furnished a convincing demonstration of the importance of form-words, particularly in legal terminology, and, perhaps, to some extent also, in ordinary conversation and writing.

BIBLIOGRAPHY OF BOOKS ON LANGUAGE

Bloomfield, Leonard, *An Introduction to the Study of Language*. New York: H. Holt & Co., 1914.

Bradley, Henry, *The Making of English*. New York: The Macmillan Co., 1904.

Brunot, Ferdinand, *La Pensée et la Langue*. Paris: Masson, 1922.

Dwight, B. W., *Modern Philology: Its Discoveries, History, and Influence*. First Series. New York: Scribner, Armstrong & Co., 1877.

Jespersen, Otto, *A Modern English Grammar*. Heidelberg: Carl Winters, 1909–1927, 3 vols.

Jespersen, Otto, *The Philosophy of Grammar*. New York: Henry Holt & Co., 1924.

Jespersen, Otto, *Progress in Language*. London: Swan Sonnenschein & Co., New York: Macmillan & Co., 1894.

Kruisinger, E., *A Grammar of Modern Dutch*. London: George Allen and Unwin Ltd., 1924.

Marsh, G. P., *Origin and History of the English Language*. New York: Charles Scribner & Co., 1872.

Poutsma, H., *A Grammar of Late Modern English*. Groningen: P. Noordhoff, Part I, 1904; Part II, 1916.

Skeat, W. W., *Principles of English Etymology*. Oxford: Clarendon Press, 1887–1891, 2 vols.

Strong, H. A., *Paul's Principles of Language*. London: Swan Sonnenschein & Co., 1890.

Strong, H. A., W. S. Logeman, and B. I. Wheeler, *History of Languages*. New York: Longmans, Green & Co., 1891.

Sweet, Henry, *History of English Sounds*. Oxford: Clarendon Press, 1888.

Sweet, Henry, *History of Language*. New York: The Macmillan Co., 1900.

Sweet, Henry, *A New English Grammar*. Oxford: Clarendon Press, Part I, 1892; Part II, 1898.

Trench, R. C., *English, Past and Present*. London: Macmillan & Co., 1870.

Tucker, T. G., *Natural History of Language*. London: Blackie & Son Ltd., 1908.

Tucker, T. G., and R. S. Wallace, *English Grammar*. Cambridge: The University Press, 1917.

Whitney, W. D., *Language and the Study of Language*. New York: Charles Scribner & Co., 1867.

Whitney, W. D., *Life and Growth of Language*. New York: D. Appleton & Co., 1880.

Wyld, H. C., *The Growth of English*. London: John Murray, 1920.

NOTES

Chapter II

1. *John Horne Tooke*, p. 128.
2. *Diversions of Purley*, Part I, p. 329.

Chapter III

THE

1. *Words and Phrases; Second Series;* Succession of Dupre, 41 South. 324, 326.
2. *Ibid.;* Sanderlin v. State, 21 Tenn. (2 Humph.) 315, 317.
3. *Ibid.; Second Series;* Amundsen v Standard Printing Co., 105 N. W. 424, 426.
4. *Ibid.;* Wetzell v. Dinsmore, 54 N. Y. 496, 498.
5. *Ibid.;* Noyes v. Children's Aid Soc. (N. Y.), 3 Abb. N. C. 36, 40.
6. *Ibid.;* Born v. Home Ins. Co. of New York, 81 N. W. 676, 678.

A

1. *Words and Phrases; Second Series;* Moynahan v. City of New York, 98 N. E. 482, 484.
2. *Ibid.; Second Series,* United States v. Perry, 133 Fed. 841.
3. *Ibid.;* State v. Martin, 30 S. W. 422, 423.
4. *Ibid.;* Hurley v. Brown, 98 Mass. 545, 547.
5. *Ibid.; In re* Sanders, 54 Law J. Q. B. 331, 332.

AN

1. *Words and Phrases;* Plastic Fireproof Const. Co. v. City and County of San Francisco (U. S.), 97 Fed. 620, 623.
2. *Ibid.;* People v. Ogden, 40 N. Y. Supp. 827, 828.

Chapter IV

ABOUT

1. *Words and Phrases;* Lake v. Sewell, 43 Law J. Ch. 378.
2. *Ibid.;* Powell v. State, 63 Ala. 177.
3. *Ibid.;* Diffey v. State, 5 South. 576.
4. *Ibid.;* Thompson v. Banks, 43 N. H. 540.
5. *Ibid.; Second Series;* Peterson v. Chaix, 90 Pac. 948, 951.
6. *Ibid.; Second Series;* Co-operative Bldg. Bank v. Hawkins, 73 Atl. 617, 622.

7. *Ibid.;* Wompelmeir and Co. v. Levi Moses, 63 Tenn. (3 Baxt.) 467, 476.
8. *Ibid.; Third Series;* United Eastern Mining Co. v. Hoffman, 230 Pac. 1099, 1102.
9. *Ibid.*, Bennett v. Lingham (U. S.), 31 Fed. 85.

ABOVE

1. *Words and Phrases;* Williams v. McKay, 46 N. J. Eq. 25, 75.
2. *Ibid.;* McLeod v. Burroughs, 9 Ga. 213.
3. *Ibid.; Third Series;* Landau Grocery Co. v. Hart (Mo.), 223 S. W. 793, 794.

ACROSS

1. *Words and Phrases; Second Series;* Crowley v. Chicago St. P. M. & O. Ry. Co., 99 N. W. 1016, 1017.
2. *Ibid.; Second Series;* Texas and P. Ry. Co. v. Felker, 90 S. W. 530, 531.
3. *Ibid.;* Hannibal and St. J. Ry. Co. v. Missouri River Packett Co., 125 U. S. 260.
4. *Ibid.;* Evans v. Pratt, 3 Man. and G. 759, 763.

AFTER

1. *Words and Phrases;* Menges v. Frick, 73 Pa. (23 P. F. Smith) 137, 140.
2. *Ibid.;* Atwell's Ex'rs. v. Barney (Ga.), Dud. 207, 208.
3. *Ibid.;* King v. King, 14 R. I. 143, 146.
4. *Ibid.;* Sands v. Lyon, 18 Conn. 18, 27.

AGAINST

1. *Words and Phrases; Third Series;* Hawkins v. First Nat. Bank (Tex.), 175 S. W. 163, 164.
2. *Ibid.; Second Series;* Lobsitz v. Leffler, Thiele & Co., 124 N. Y. Supp. 533, 534.
3. *Ibid.;* State v. Prather; 54 Ind. 63, 64.
4. *Ibid.;* Malone v. Commonwealth, 15 S. W. 856.
5. *Ibid.;* Hogan v. Curtin, 88 N. Y. 162, 169.

ALONG

1. *Ibid.;* Quigley v. Clough, 53 N. E. 884.
2. *Ibid.;* Burt v. Lima and H. F. R. Co., 21 N. Y. Supp. 482, 483.

3. *Ibid.;* Martin v. Grand Trunk Railway of Canada, 32 Atl. 976, 977.
4. *Ibid.; Third Series;* State v. Downes, 112 Atl. 246.
5. *Ibid.*, Salter v. Jonas, 39 N. J. Law (10 Vroom) 469–470.
6. *Ibid.;* Postal Telegraph Co. v. Norfolk & W. R. Co., 14 S. E. 803, 805.
7. *Ibid.;* Pratt v. Atlantic and St. L. R. Co., 42 Mo. 579, 585.
8. *Ibid.;* Church v. Meeker, 34 Conn. 421, 425.
9. *Ibid.;* Stahr v. Carter, 90 N. W. 64, 65.

ALONGSIDE

1. *Words and Phrases; Third Series;* Board of County Com'rs. of Mitchel County v. City of Beloit, 220 Pac. 1020.

AMONG

1. *Words and Phrases; Third Series;* Dwight Mfg. Co. v. Word, 75 South, 979, 983.
2. *Ibid.; In re* Holder, 41 Atl. 576.

AROUND

1. *Words and Phrases; Third series;* Hawkins v. First Nat. Bank (Tex.), 175 S. W. 163, 164.

AT

1. *Words and Phrases;* Vaux v. Vollans, 4 Barn. and Adol. 525.
2. *Ibid.;* Stewart v. Patrick, 68 N. Y. 450, 454.
3. *Ibid.;* Mason v. Brooklyn City and N. R. Co. (N. Y.), 35 Barbour, 373, 377.
4. *Ibid.;* Graham v. State, 1 Ark. (1 Pike) 171, 181.
5 *Ibid.; Third Series;* People v. Washington, 154 N. E. 435, 436.
6. *Ibid.;* Christian v. State (Ala.), 11 South. 338.
7. *Ibid.;* O'Conner v. Nadel, 117 Ala. 595.
8. *Ibid.;* Lee v. Lee (N. Y.), 27 Hun, 1, 4.
9. *Ibid.;* Knoxville, C. G. and L. Ry. Co. v. Beeler, 90 Tenn. (6 Pickle) 548.

BEFORE

1. *Words and Phrases; Second Series;* Quereau v. Computing Scale Co. of Ohio, 133 N. Y. Supp. 501, 503.
2. *Ibid.; Second Series;* Potter v. Village of Hammondsport, 98 N. Y. Supp. 186, 187.

3. *Ibid.;* Baum v. Rainbow Smelting Co., 42 Oregon, 453.
4. *Ibid.;* Everett v. Chicago, R. I. and P. Ry. Co., 28 N. W. 410, 411.

BEHIND

1. *Words and Phrases;* Porter v. Bradley, 3 Term R. 143, 146.

BELOW

1. *Words and Phrases;* Donnell v. Joy, 26 Atl. 1017, 1018.
2. *Ibid.;* Lee v. Stahl, 22 Pac. 436, 438.

BENEATH

1. *Words and Phrases;* Truman v. Deere Implement Co. (U. S.), 80 Fed. 109, 116.

BESIDES

1. *Words and Phrases; In re* Beckett's Will, 8 N. E. 506, 508.

BETWEEN

1. *Words and Phrases;* Richardson v. Ford, 14 Ill. 332, 333.
2. *Ibid.; Third Series;* Rogers v. Smith, 88 S. E. 963, 964.
3. *Ibid.; In re* Morrison's Estate (Stettinius v. Wann *et al.*), 71 Pac. 453.
4. *Ibid.;* Records v. Fields, 55 S. W. 1021, 1022.
5. *Ibid.;* Edwards v. Kelly, 35 South, 418, 420.

BEYOND

1. *Words and Phrases;* Williams v. City of New York, 11 N. E. 829, 832.
2. *Ibid.;* Hadden v. Barney, 72 U. S. (5 Wall.) 107, 113.
3. *Ibid.; Second Series;* Amer. Bridge Co. of New York v. Glenmore Distilleries Co. (Ky.), 107 S. W. 279, 283.
4. *Ibid.;* Murray v. Baker, 16 U. S. (3 Wheat.) 541.

BY

1. *Words and Phrases;* Jones v. Cowman, 4 N. Y. Super. Ct. (2 Sandf.) 234, 237.
2. *Ibid.;* Blass v. The Robert Campbell, 16 Mo. 266, 267.
3. *Ibid.;* Commonwealth v. Griffin, 105 Mass. 175, 176.
4. *Ibid.;* Ruprecht v. Delachamp *et al.*, 165 Fed. 381, 382.
5. *Ibid.;* Fraser, v. Ott, 30 Pac. 793, 794.

6. *Ibid.;* Elizabeth City Cotton Mills v. Dunstan, 27 S. E. 1001.
7. *Ibid.;* Sibley v. Holden, 27 Mass. (10 Pick.) 249.

CONCERNING

1. *Ibid.;* Commerford v. Thompson (U. S.), 1 Fed. 417, 420.
2. *Ibid.;* United States v. Fulkerson (U. S.), 74 Fed. 631, 632.

DOWN

1. *Words and Phrases; Second Series;* Carter v. Elk Coal Co., 191 S. W. 294, 298.
2. *Ibid.;* Brown v. Huger, 62 U. S. (21 How.) 305, 320.
3. *Ibid.;* French v. Bankhead (Va.), 11 Grat. 136, 155.

EXCEPT

1. *Words and Phrases;* Austin v. Willis, 8 South. 94.

FOR

1. *Words and Phrases;* State v. Cherry County, 79 N. W. 825, 826.
2. *Ibid.;* Commonwealth v. Jennings (Va.), 3 Grat. 624, 627.
3. *Ibid.;* Sawyer v. Chicago N. W. Ry. Co., 22 Wis. 403, 409.
4. *Ibid.;* Emerson v. Providence Hat Mfg. Co., 12 Mass. 237, 240.
5. *Ibid.; Second Series;* McGannon v. State *ex rel.* Trapp, 124 Pac. 1063, 1067.
6. *Ibid.;* State *ex rel.* Weber v. Tucker, 32 Mo. App. 620, 631.
7. *Ibid.;* Ready v. Sommer, 37 Wis. 265, 268.

FROM

1. *Words and Phrases;* People v. Louisville and N. R. Co. (Ill.), 5 N. E. 379.
2. *Ibid.;* Salisbury Com'rs. v. Powe, 51 N. C. 134, 136.
3. *Ibid.;* Sindall v. City of Baltimore, 49 Atl. 645, 647.
4. *Ibid.;* State v. Shuler, 19 S. C. 140, 141.
5. *Ibid.;* Chicago Title and Trust Co. v. Smith, 62 N. W. 792, 793.
6. *Ibid.;* Sefton v. Prentice *et al.*, 37 Pac. 641, 642.

IN

1. *Ibid.;* Van Bokkelen v. Travelers' Ins. Co., 54 N. Y. Supp. 307, 311.
2. *Ibid.;* Savary v. Goe (U. S.), 21 Fed. Cas. 549, 550.
3. *Ibid.;* Old Ladies' Home of Muscatine v. Hoffman, 89 N. W. 1066, 1067.

4. *Ibid.;* Uhl v. Ohio River R. Co., 41 S. E. 340, 341.
5. *Ibid.;* Feree v. Moquin-Offerman-Hessenbuttel Coal Co., 61 N. Y. Supp. 120, 121.
6. *Ibid.; Second Series;* Depue v. Travelers' Inc. Co., 166 Fed. 183, 184.

LIKE

1. *Words and Phrases; Third Series;* Vinegar Bend Lumber Co. v. Soule Steam Feed Works, 62 South, 279, 282.

NEAR

1. *Words and Phrases;* Kellogg v. Inhabitants of Northampton, 70 Mass. (4 Gray) 65.
2. *Ibid.;* Manis v. State, 50 Tenn. (3 Heisk.) 315, 316.
3. *Ibid.;* Fassett v. Town of Roxbury, 55 Vt. 552, 554.
4. *Ibid.;* Griffen v. House (N. Y.), 18 Johns, 397, 398.
5. *Ibid.; Second Series;* Haughawont v. Percival, 119 Pac. 649, 650.
6. *Ibid., Second Series;* Western Union Telegraph Co. v. Klitzke, 89 N. E. 405, 406.

OF

1. *Words and Phrases;* Commonwealth v. Delaware Division Canal Co., 16 Atl. 584, 585.
2. *Ibid.;* Rocha v. State, 63 S. W. 1018.
3. *Ibid.;* Jordan v. State, 41 N. E. 817, 818.
4. *Ibid.;* State v. King, 51 Atl. 1102, 1103.
5. *Ibid.;* Hannum v. Kingsley, 107 Mass. 355, 361.

OFF

1. *Words and Phrases; Second Series;* American Fisheries Co. v. Linnen, 118 Fed. 869, 874.

ON

1. *Words and Phrases; Second Series;* Hutchinson v. State, 70 S. E. 63, 65.
2. *Ibid.;* Hoskins v. Iowa Land Co., 96 N. W. 977, 978.
3. *Ibid.;* Hempstead v. City of Des Moines, 3 N. W. 123, 126.
4. *Ibid.;* Connell v. Richmond, 11 Atl. 852, 853.
5. *Ibid.;* London Assur. Corp. v. Thompson, 62 N. E. 1066, 1068.
6. *Ibid.;* Niblett v. City of Nashville, 59 Tenn. (12 Heisk.) 684, 686.
7. *Ibid.;* Smith v. Slocomb, 75 Mass. (9 Gray) 36, 37.

OVER

1. *Words and Phrases;* Commonwealth v. Warwick, 40 Atl. 93, 94.
2. *Ibid.;* Boston and Maine R. v. City of Lawrence, 84 Mass. (2 Allen) 107, 109.
3. *Ibid.; Second Series;* Milling v. State (Tex.), 150 S. W. 434, 436.
4. *Ibid.;* Newburyport Turnpike Corp. v. Eastern R. R. Co., 40 Mass. (23 Pick.) 326, 328.
5. *Ibid.;* Ill. Cent. R. Co. v. City of Chicago, 30 N. E. 1044, 1046.

THROUGH

1. *Words and Phrases;* Fiske v. Wetmore, 10 Atl. 627, 628.
2. *Ibid.; Second Series;* Berry v. Powell, 105 S. W. 345, 348.
3. *Ibid.;* Provident Life and Trust Co. of Phila. v. Mercer County, 170 U. S. 593.
4. *Ibid.; Second Series;* Flint's Adm'r. v. Central Vermont R. Co., 73 Atl. 590, 591.

THROUGHOUT

1. *Ibid.;* Inhabitants of the Town of Quincy v. City of Boston, 19 N. E. 519, 521.
2. *Ibid.;* Thomas v. Austin, 30 S. E. 627, 628.

TILL

1. *Words and Phrases;* De Haven v. De Haven, 46 Ind. 296, 298.
2. *Ibid., Second Series;* Oberhaus v. State *ex rel.* McNamara, 55 South. 898, 902.
3. *Ibid.; Third Series;* Lancaster Farmers' State Bank v. Buckner, 198 N. W. 1016.

TO

1. *Words and Phrases;* Heeley v. Boston and M. R. Co., 67 Me. 163, 165.
2. *Ibid.;* Scales v. Masonic Protective Ass'n., 48 Atl. 1084, 1085.
3. *Ibid.;* City of Garden City v. Merchants' and Farmers' Nat. Bk., 60 Pac. 823, 824.
4. *Ibid.;* Oxton v. Groves, 68 Me. 371, 372.
5. *Ibid.;* Littleton Bridge Co. v. Pike, 47 Atl. 108.

UNDER

1. *Words and Phrases; Second Series;* Ruckert v. Grand Ave. Ry. Co., 63 S. W. 814, 818.

2. *Ibid.;* Bates v. Riverside Independent School Dist. (U. S.), 25 Fed. 192, 194.
3. *Ibid.;* Newburyport Turnpike Corp. v. Eastern R. Co., 40 Mass. (23 Pick.) 326, 328.
4. *Ibid.; Second Series;* Hewey v. Metropolitan Life Ins. Co., 62 Atl. 600, 602.
5. *Ibid.;* Bassett v. Mills (Tex.), 34 S. W. 93, 94.
6. *Ibid.; Second Series;* Osborne v. Kanawha County Court, 69 S. E. 470, 471.

UNTIL

1. *Words and Phrases; Second Series;* Davis v. State, 70 S. E. 148, 149.
2. *Ibid.; Second Series;* Robinson v. Bonaparte, 61 Atl. 212, 216.
3. *Ibid.;* People v. Hornbeck, 61 N. Y. Supp. 978.
4. *Ibid.;* Croco V. Hille, 72 Pac. 208.
5. *Ibid.; Second Series;* Fulton v. Woodward, 24 Atl. 402.
6. *Ibid.;* Houghwont v. Boisaubin, 18 N. J. Eq. (3 C. E. Green) 315, 318.

UNTO

1. *Words and Phrases; Second Series;* People v. Rathbun, 63 N. W. 973.

UP

1. *Words and Phrases;* Wharton v. Brick and others, 8 Atl. 529, 530.
2. *Ibid.;* Murphy v. Copland 1 N. W. 691, 692.
3. *Ibid.;* Buckley's Lessee v. Blackwell's Heirs, 10 Ohio, 508, 510.
4. *Ibid.;* Jackson v. Louw (N. Y.), 12 Johns. 252, 255.

WITH

1. *Words and Phrases;* Leeke v. Bennett, 1 Atl. 470.
2. *Ibid.;* Kimball v. Woodruff, 55 Vt. 229, 231.
3. *Ibid.;* State v. Freeman (S. C.), 1 Speers, 57, 61, 65.
4. *Ibid.;* State v. La Bounty, 21 Atl. 730, 731.
5. *Ibid.;* Eckhardt v. People, 83 N. Y. 462, 464.
6. *Ibid.; Second Series;* State v. Pemberton, 104 Pac. 556, 557.
7. *Ibid.;* Brooks v. Ratcliff, 33 N. C. 321, 326.
8. *Ibid.;* Town of Southold v. Parks, 84 N. Y. Supp. 1078, 1079.

WITHIN

1. *Words and Phrases;* Daggett v. State, 4 Conn. 60, 64.
2. *Ibid.;* Harrison v. Reeves, 28 Atl. 653, 654.
3. *Ibid.;* Baddeley v. Tingell, 1 Exch. 319, 334.
4. *Ibid.;* Hakes v. Peck, 40 N. Y. (1 Keyes) 505, 508.
5. *Ibid.; Second Series;* Preston v. Ætna Ins. Co., 85 N. E. 1006, 1008.
6. *Ibid.;* Robinson v. Longley, 18 Nev. 71, 73.
7. *Ibid.;* Levert v. Read, 54 Ala. 529, 531.
8. *Ibid.;* City of St. Louis v. Wiggins Ferry Co., 78 U. S. (11 Wall.) 423, 431.

WITHOUT

1. *Words and Phrases;* Wood v. Boyle, 35 Atl. 853, 854.
2. *Ibid.;* Carpenter v. Hopkinton School Trustees, 12 R. I. 574, 576.
3. *Ibid.;* Antole v. Gill and Fisher (U. S.), 5 Fed. 128, 129.
4. *Ibid.;* Sage v. Hawley, 16 Conn. 106, 118.
5. *Ibid.; Second Series;* Evans v. McFarland, 85 S. W. 873, 879.

Chapter V

AFTER

1. *Words and Phrases;* Judd v. Fulton, (N. Y.), 10 Barbour 117, 118.
2. *Ibid.;* Smith v. Coup (N. Y.), 6 Dem. Sur. 45, 48.
3. *Ibid.; Third Series;* Wetzel v. Hecht, 220 S. W. 888, 889.
4. *Ibid.; Second Series;* Conklin v. Clarke, 96 N. Y. Supp. 914, 915.

ALSO

1. *Words and Phrases;* Williamson v. Williamson, 57 N. C. 281, 286.
2. *Ibid.;* Loring v. Hayes, 29 Atl. 1093, 1094.
3. *Ibid.;* Mace v. Mace, 49 Atl. 1038, 1039.
4. *Ibid.;* van Dusen v. Fridley, 43 N. W. 703, 704.
5. *Ibid.;* Morgan v. Morgan, 3 Atl. 63, 64.
6. *Ibid.;* Sherrill v. Echard, 29 N. C. 161, 164.

ALTHOUGH

1. *Words and Phrases;* Hogan v. State, 36 Wis. 226, 244.

AND

1. *Words and Phrases;* Davis v. Boardman, 12 Mass. 80, 83.
2. *Ibid.;* Smith v. City of Madison, 7 Ind. 86, 90.
3. *Ibid.;* City of La Salle v. Kostka, 60 N. E. 72, 74.

4. *Ibid.; Third Series;* Baker v. State (Okl.), 254 Pac. 512, 513.
5. *Ibid.;* Tipton v. People, 40 N. E. 838, 839.

AS

1. *Words and Phrases;* McQuery v. State, 51 S. W. 247, 248.
2. *Ibid.;* Colt v. Hubbard, 33 Conn. 281, 286.
3. *Ibid.;* Roberts v. Wills, 20 N. J. Law (Spencer) 591, 598.
4. *Ibid.;* Hooper v. Wells, Fargo and Co., 27 Cal. 11, 30.

BUT

1. *Words and Phrases;* Chesapeake and O. R. Co. v. Miller, 19 W. Va. 408, 436.
2. *Ibid.; In re* Cox's Estate, 36 Atl. 564, 565.
3. *Ibid.;* First Nat'l Bank v. Foster, 61 Pac. 466, 467.
4. *Ibid.; Second Series;* Winter v. Dibble, 95 N. E. 1093, 1099.

BUT ALSO

1. *Words and Phrases; Second Series;* Julian v. Kansas City Star Co., 107 S. W. 496, 504.

EITHER

1. *Words and Phrases; Second Series;* Jones v. Sabin, 107 N. Y. Supp. 508, 510.
2. *Ibid.; Second Series;* Detroit Electric Light and Power Co. v. Applebaum, 94 N. W. 12, 13.
3. *Ibid.; Third Series;* Lankford v. First Nat. Bank, 183 Pac. 56, 57.
4. *Ibid.; Second Series;* Aldrich v. Bay State Const. Co., 72 N. E. 53, 54.

IF

1. *Words and Phrases;* Baum v. Rainbow Mining, Milling, and Smelting Co., 71 Pac. 538, 541.
2. *Ibid.;* Firemen's Insurance Co. v Congregation Rodelph Sholom, 80 Ill. 558, 559.
3. *Ibid.;* Barney v. Cunyes, 33 Atl. 897, 898.
4. *Ibid.; In re* Alexander's Estate, 85 Pac. 308, 309.

LIKEWISE

1. *Words and Phrases;* King v. Sharp, 25 Tenn. (6 Humph.) 55, 57.

2. *Ibid.; Third Series;* Doyle v. Maryland Casualty Co., 102 S. W. 946, 947.
3. *Ibid.;* State Bank v. Ewing, 17 Ind. 68, 74.

MOREOVER

1. *Words and Phrases;* Dermott v. Wallach, 68 U. S. (1 Wall.) 61, 65.
2. *Ibid.; Third Series;* Aldersley v. McLeod, 168 Pac. 153, 155.
3. *Ibid.; Third Series;* Pagano v. Cerri, 112 N. E. 1037, 1040.

NEVERTHELESS

1. *Words and Phrases;* Commonwealth v. Rowe, 66 S. W. 29, 32.

NOR

1. *Words and Phrases; Second Series;* Reed v. Longstreet (N. J.), 63 Atl. 500, 501.

OR

1. *Words and Phrases;* Dumont v. U. S., 98 U. S. 142, 143.
2. *Ibid.;* Warren County v. Booth, 32 South. 1,000, 1,001.
3. *Ibid.;* Kuehner v. City of Freeport, 32 N. E. 372, 374.
4. *Ibid.;* Arthur v. Cumming, 91 U. S. 362.
5. *Ibid.;* Austin v. Oakes, 1 N. Y. Supp. 307, 310.
6. *Ibid.;* Kennedy v. Haskell, 73 Pac. 913, 914.

PROVIDED

1. *Words and Phrases;* Stoel v. Flanders, 32 N. W. 114, 117.
2. *Ibid.;* Woodruff v. Woodruff, 16 Atl. 4, 6.
3. *Ibid.;* Huggins v. Daley (U. S.), 99 Fed. 606, 610.
4. *Ibid.;* Ormsby v. Phenix Ins. Co., 58 N. W. 301, 303.
5. *Ibid.;* Burgwyn v. Whitfield, 81 N. C. 261, 263.

SO

1. *Words and Phrases;* Clem v. State, 33 Ind. 418, 433.

THAT

1. *Words and Phrases;* Fackler v. Berry, 25 S. E. 887, 888.

THEN

1. *Words and Phrases;* Rose v. McHose's Ex'rs., 26 Mo. 590, 596.
2. *Ibid.;* Ash v. Coleman (N. Y.), 24 Barbour 645, 647.

3. *Ibid.; Second Series; In re* Fitzpatrick's Estate, 81 Atl. 815, 816.
4. *Ibid.;* Connelly v. O'Brien, 58 N. Y. Supp. 45, 46.

TILL

1. *Words and Phrases;* Pittman v. Barret, 34 Mo. 84, 85.
2. *Ibid.; Third Series;* Matheson v. Marion County Lumber Co., 78 S. E. 970, 971.

UNLESS

1. *Words and Phrases; Second Series;* Central of Georgia Ry. Co. v. Finch (Ala.), 59 South. 619, 620.
2. *Ibid.;* Ramsdill v. Wentworth, 106 Mass. 320.
3. *Ibid.;* Van Etten *et al.* v. Kelly, 64 N. E. 560, 562.
4. *Ibid.; Second Series;* City of Hickory v. Southern Ry. Co., 49 S. E. 202, 205.

UNTIL

1. *Words and Phrases;* Johnston v. Morrow, 60 Mo. 339, 341.
2. *Ibid.; Second Series;* Prowell v. State, 39 South. 164, 167.
3. *Ibid.;* Skinner v. Christie, 29 Atl. 772, 777.
4. *Ibid.;* Collier v. Field, 1 Mont. 612, 626.

WHEN

1. *Words and Phrases; Second Series;* Central Trust Co. of N. Y. v. Egleston, 77 N. E. 989.
2. *Ibid.;* Pittsburgh, C. C. & St. L. Ry. Co. v. Burton, 38 N. E. 594.
3. *Ibid.;* The U. S. v. Willings and Francis, 8 U. S. (4 Cranch), 48, 54.

WHENEVER

1. *Words and Phrases;* People v. Melone, 15 Pac. 294, 296.
2. *Ibid.; Third Series;* Griffin v. U. S. (D. C. Ga.), 270 Fed. 263, 264.
3. *Ibid.;* Robinson v. Greene, 14 R. I. 181, 188.
4. *Ibid.; Third Series;* Williams v. Potter (D. C. N. Y.), 210 Fed. 318, 325.

WHERE

1. *Words and Phrases; Third Series;* Graham v. Standard Fire Ins. Co., 112 S. E. 88, 89.

WHEREAS

1. *Words and Phrases;* People v. Ennis, 70 Pac. 84, 86.
2. *Ibid.; Third Series;* Hill v. Smtih, III Atl. 840, 842.

WHEREVER

1. *Words and Phrases; Third Series;* Moore v. Johnson, 88 Atl. 699, 701.

WHEREFORE

1. *Words and Phrases;* Lycoming Fire Insurance Co. v. Wright, 55 Vt. 526, 531.

WHEREUPON

1. *Words and Phrases;* Bartow v. Smyth, 14 N. J. Law (2 J. S. Green) 286, 288.
2. *Ibid.;* State v. Van Ells, 32 N. W. 32, 33.

WHETHER

1. *Words and Phrases;* Voegtly v. Third Ward School Directors, 1 Pa. (1 Barr) 330, 332.
2. *Ibid.; Second Series;* Wade v. State, 109 S. W. 191, 192.

WHILE

1. *Words and Phrases;* Langworthy v. Oswego and Onondaga Insurance Co., 85 N. Y. 632, 633.
2. *Ibid.;* Lawrence v. Leidigh, 50 Pac. 600, 602.

WHILST

1. *Words and Phrases*; Rhodes v. Bullard, 7 East. 116, 119.

INDEX

A, 36–41
About, 44–53
Above, 53–57
Across, 57–62
Adjectives, as form-words, 11
Adverbs, as form-words, 13–16
After, 62–65, 202–5
Against, 65–72
Along, 72–79
Alongside, 80
Also, 205–11
Although, 211–12
Among, 80–82
An, 41–43
And, 212–16
Around, 82–83
Articles, as form-words, 12–13
As, 217–20
At, 83–91

Before, 91–95
Behind, 95–96
Below, 96–99
Beneath, 99–105
Beyond, 105–9
But, 220–24
But also, 224–25
By, 109–14

Concerning, 114–16
Conjunctions, as form-words, 15–21

Diversions of Purley, The, 7
Down, 116–18

Either, 225–30
Except, 118–19

For, 119–25
Form-words, 4–25
From, 125–30

Hazlitt, William, 7

If, 230–33
In, 130–35

Like, 135–36
Likewise, 233–36

Moreover, 236–41

Near, 136–40
Nevertheless, 241–43
Nor, 243–44
Nouns, as form-words, 8–9

Of, 140–44
Off, 144–45
On, 145–50
Or, 244–51
Over, 150–54

Prepositions, as form-words, 21–22
Pronouns, as form-words, 9–11
Provided, 251–55

So, 255–56
Spirit of the Age, The, 7

That, 256–57
The, 29–35
Then, 257–62
Through, 154–58
Throughout, 158–60
Till, 160–63, 262–64
To, 163–68
Tooke, John Horne, 7
Tucker, T. G., 17

Under, 168–73
Unless, 264–68
Until, 173–79, 268–72
Unto, 179–80
Up, 180–83

Verbs, as form-words, 22

Wallace, R. S., 17
When, 272–75
Whenever, 276–82
Where, 282–83
Whereas, 283–86
Wherefore, 287–88
Whereupon, 288–90
Wherever, 286–87
Whether, 290–93
While, 291–93
Whilst, 293–94
With, 183–90
Within, 190–97
Without, 197–201
Words and Phrases, 3

Yarborough, M. C., 7

COLUMBIA UNIVERSITY PRESS
Columbia University
New York

FOREIGN AGENT
OXFORD UNIVERSITY PRESS
Humphrey Milford
Amen House, London, E.C.

Bei Fragen zur Produktsicherheit wenden Sie sich bitte an:
If you have any questions regarding product safety,
please contact:

Walter de Gruyter GmbH
Genthiner Straße 13
10785 Berlin
productsafety@degruyterbrill.com